Jesus: This is the picture I want in My messages. When you read these messages, look at My picture and know I love you. These messages are My words of love for each of you.

Open Anywhere

Love, Jesus

GOD'S
BLUE BOOK 5
So Deep Is the Love of His Heart

Rita Ring

Fr. Edward J. Carter S.J.

Shepherds of Christ Publications

Shepherds of Christ Publications
P.O. Box 193
Morrow, Ohio 45152

Tel: (513) 932-4451
Toll free: (888) 211-3041
Fax: (513) 932-6791
Email: info@sofc.org
http://www.sofc.org

This book is published by Shepherds of Christ Publications, a subsidiary of Shepherds of Christ Ministries, a tax exempt, religious public charitable corporation organized to foster devotion to the Two Hearts, the Sacred Heart of Jesus and the Immaculate Heart of Mary.

First Printing: 2006

Prayer for Union With Jesus

Come to me, Lord, and possess my soul. Come into my heart and permeate my soul. Help me to sit in silence with You and let You work in my heart.

I am Yours to possess. I am Yours to use. I want to be selfless and only exist in You. Help me to spoon out all that is me and be an empty vessel ready to be filled by You. Help me to die to myself and live only for You. Use me as You will. Let me never draw my attention back to myself. I only want to operate as You do, dwelling within me.

I am Yours, Lord. I want to have my life in You. I want to do the will of the Father. Give me the strength to put aside the world and let You operate my very being. Help me to act as You desire. Strengthen me against the distractions of the devil to take me from Your work.

When I worry, I have taken my focus off of You and placed it on myself. Help me not to give in to the promptings of others to change what in my heart You are making very clear to me. I worship You, I adore You and I love You. Come and dwell in me now.

January 17, 1994

The Fifth Book

The Sacred Heart Book - His Song Book
So Deep Is the Love of His Heart

Messenger: Jesus started giving me His love songs at the beginning of the fifth book. The book began on October 1. On October 7th, He gave me the first song. He gave me almost all the songs in October. There were references in the second and third book as to how I would be given His love songs and He wanted them to spread to the world. All songs centered deeply on the love of His most Sacred Heart.

The fifth book carried the message for the Shepherds of Christ meetings. He calls the members to such deep love with Him. He tells them over and over again they are His apostles to spread this love to the world. He tells of the "beautiful words of His Heart." He wants us to love Him in return. He asks us to write Him a love letter. He tells all how He wants His Heart to reign in their homes and their hearts. Homes need to be enthroned with the most Sacred Heart.

Edward Carter, S.J.

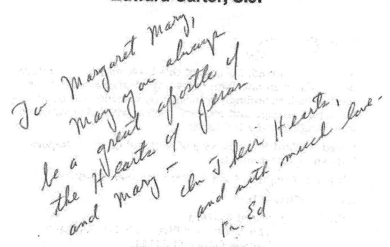

To Margaret Mary,
may you always
be a great apostle of
the Hearts of Jesus
and Mary - ch. I their Hearts,
and with much love.
Fr. Ed

Sheed & Ward

This is from one of Fr. Carter's books that he wrote and gave to me.

Vision

Messenger: On October 20, 1994, I had this vision - I account it here from my notebook. That night we had the First Enthronement of the Sacred Heart at my house.

Vision - St. Peter in Chains - Before Mass

I told St. Margaret Mary how much I loved her. I had a vision of a nun to the left of the altar. She was wearing a dark habit with a white collar and in her hands was a white book. Then I thought, "Who is this, St. Therese?" I was trying to see her more clearly. I realized tonight the Enthronement of the Sacred Heart Book had a white cover. I think the nun was St. Margaret Mary. Just as I saw the vision my little son kissed me and told me he loved me. This was after the gospel while the priest was talking. I didn't look at my son because I was seeing a vision.

While at Mass at the Cathedral, I saw a vision of St. Margaret Mary reading from a white book. This happened right before the meeting. When I drove into the driveway of Our Lady of the Holy Spirit Center, I heard Our Lord speak, "These are My apostles of My Sacred Heart.", or something to that effect.

In My Heart

by C. Ring
Chords by Joseph Lee

In my heart, is a love I ne - ver felt __ be-fore, __ and

In my heart, is a love I ne - ver found __ be-fore. __ I

looked, and searched, and walked the whole wide world, and

in Your Heart, I found my life, my re-_fuge. __ Be-cause __

in Your Heart, __ I al -ways found __ just what I need - ed, and

in Your Heart, __ I al-ways found just what I want-__ed. And

You, my God, my on - ly love, __ are in my heart __ to __

x

Dedication

To Fr. Carter my spiritual director who aided me continually while receiving these messages and discerning them.

To Fr. Mike and Fr. Joe my great brother.

To John our beloved president of Shepherds of Christ.

To Doris Jones for her help with all the messages.

To Ellen for all her help always and typing.

To Joe Lee for his help with the music.

To our donors.

To Cathy for the cover and helping me.

To Joe and Cathy for being there when Mary appeared and I received these messages.

To my husband, Bob and my other children Carol, Sharon and my family.

To Jesus and Mary and St. Michael -- I pray.

Table of Contents

To The Reader

Jesus wants to share His love with you. He comes in these letters to tell you how you can be in intimate union with Him.

All of us possess everything we need to have an intimate union with Him. He has been giving me messages since October of 1991. For at least a year I sat in front of the tabernacle and begged him to talk to me. I wanted words. I prayed to the Holy Spirit and begged and begged Him to baptize me. After a long and seemingly endless search, trying to hear God, He told me to "feed the hungry." For six weeks this was all I heard. I thought maybe I wasn't feeding my children well or eating well enough myself. What a long wait for three words! At long last one day, as I was writing to Jesus, I received a letter back. He told me, "I am Jesus, Son of the Living God." I did not want to write this but it kept coming—and so did many other messages. I knew nothing of anyone getting messages. I wrote them, reluctantly, and hid my notebooks. The letters kept coming, many during the night. I would be awakened, then given long letters which I felt compelled to get up and write down. I read these letters privately and my life began to change. I felt a new life within me.

He taught me of His fervent love and how truly present He was. He taught me how precious I was to Him. Over and over again He would call me His precious child and tell me how He loved me, how He clothed me with dignity and honor. He told me over and over how He was right by my side always. He is teaching me to give up all fear and to trust in Him. He is teaching me to let go of myself and let Him run my life. I am trying every day to do His will.

He is also telling you in your heart all you need to know. He has all the answers for you there in your heart. You must be silent and go to Him so you can hear His words for you.

Sit in front of the tabernacle and be with Him. Do not pray prayers. Sit and be open and just be with Him. Read these letters there. These are Jesus' love letters to you. Sit in front of the tabernacle and let Him talk to you. Sit silent awhile. Read these letters part of the time. Open any page and He will talk to you. Do not read this like a book, cover to cover. Just open to a page and read that page. That is the way He speaks to you.

Introduction

Note: *Read before the Tabernacle.*

Jesus: How, child, do I, Jesus, tell you I love you? You hold on to silly things when God is in your midst and is ardently loving you. I am Jesus Christ, the Son of God. I am writing to each precious child this day. I am on fire for love of you. I remain in the Eucharist to be with you with My ardent love. I did not want to leave My beloved ones at the Last Supper. I love you so, My dear and ardently loved children. I remain with you this day in the Blessed Sacrament, the same Jesus Who died a brutal death on the Cross.

Do you know I am truly present there? Do you know that God waits every day for you in the tabernacle? Do you comprehend even a minute amount of My love? You will never know of how I love you on earth.

I, Jesus, truly the Son of God, came to earth a man and suffered a brutal death for love of you. I love you so much! I remain with you this day. I long for your love. I want you to come and be with Me in front of the tabernacle. I wait, I yearn for you to come and whisper your love to Me. I am a person and I love you this day, with such an ardent on-fire love! No human could ever compare a speck to My love for you.

I wait, little ones, in the tabernacle. I wait for you to come and receive Me in Communion. I want you to want Me so much you cannot wait to come and receive Me. I want to be the love, the center of your life!

I am Jesus. I am the Son of God. I am writing to you this day. I want to possess your very soul and live in you. I have all you need, sweet ones.

Oh, you are so blind! I long for your union with Me. I wrote the book of love. I instituted it, yet you go to the world for your love and do not even come to Me! Oh, I love you, little ones. Little ones, beloved of the Father, loved by the Holy Spirit, mothered by My very own mother! What more can I say? The rest is up to you!

I give you your will with such love and I want your love freely given. I am God. What do you think you could ever need that I do not give you? I am the Savior of this world. I am Jesus, the Son of God. I am waiting for you. I am longing for you. I am yearning for you. I am God. I have all you ever will need!

Surrender this life to Me. Pray My Prayer for Union with Me. I want to possess your soul and operate from your very being. I am Jesus. I am the Son of God. I am the Sacred Heart of Jesus. I am Who am. I died and rose on the third day.

Harken to My call, harken to My pleading. Spend your days in love with Me. Nothing matters unless it is rooted in Me and rooted in My love. I am the Son of God. I am the Sacred Heart of Jesus. I love you with the tenderest love. I am waiting this day for just you, My beloved one. Come to Me for I am the tenderest of all hearts. I am the Sacred Heart of Jesus.

God's Blue Book, Volume 2, April 13, 1994

So Deep Is the Love of His Heart

God Calls Us to Love

John 13:34
I give you a new commandment: love one another; you must love one another just as I have loved you.

Matthew 7:7
Ask, and it will be given to you; search, and you will find; knock, and the door will be opened to you.

Messenger: Dear Jesus, I stand at the door of Your Heart and knock to come in. I want entry - to be lost totally and entirely in Thee. I want to be sheltered inside of Your Heart and wrapped deeply in Your infinite love.

Jesus: I call you, child, to love. Love is rooted in Me. I gave My all for love of you. I held nothing back. Love gives freely for the good of the other. Love exists to draw the other closer to God. If your relationship with your brother in anyway separates you from God, it is not love.

Love is not haughty, love does not demand its own way, love exists to lead the other to closer union with Me. I loved you to My death. I gave to you My all! I ask you to give your all for your beloved brothers. In loving them, you are loving Me. I live in your brothers. How can you love Me who you do not see, if you do not love your brother who you see.

I am the way. I am the truth. I am the life. I give that you will know Me and know how to love one another. Love your brothers as I have loved you. When they persecute you and holler every evil word against you, love them. This is My way - to lay down My life for My friends.

John 13:34
I give you a new commandment: love one another; you must love one another just as I have loved you.

Messenger: And to those who heeded His words, their lives were lived in peace and love and they experienced joy in their hearts, for true love brings peace and true love gives joy to the heart of the beholder. It is in loving that you receive, it is in giving that you are rendered to and it is in following the way of Christ that we are led into a life of everlasting happiness.

Jesus: I have not gone. I live with you this day. I am in your brothers. Love them as I have loved you.

Messenger: And He sent them such blessings in such abundance and they knew a little of His unending mercy and love.   10/1/94

I Feed the Hungry Soul

Jesus: Another person cannot feed your hungry soul. You search, you seek. Your starved soul craves only that which I can give. When your heart is searching for love, come, My sweet dear child, into My Heart. My Mother will take you to the deepest recesses of My Heart. There you will know such comfort - in My Heart on fire for love of you this day.

You are a child of dignity. You are precious to Me. You are the creation of the Father. I gave the last drop of My blood for you. This is love - you need grace to realize the immenseness of God's love. You are so special to God, all three Persons: Father, Son and Holy Spirit. Mary loves you so much.

You can never be satisfied on this earth. If you find the dearest mother, father, lover, friend, they will not fill you with the love your soul craves. To find Me is to seek Me. You will not be satisfied on this earth.

You, My child, experience longing for My intense love. I love you to want Me. This is how I long for love of each precious soul. I long for them with the most tender Heart, beating and breathing with fire. I never falter. I never grow dim. I am the same, with the same burning love. Come to Me and jump into My precious Heart. I love you so much.   10/1/94

You Are the Father's Creation

Jesus: I come to you in one another. Let not your hearts be hard, let your hearts be as little children, tender and pure. They do not hold grudges, they love each other, they love themselves.

You are the creation of My beloved Father. You were created with such dignity and love. I died for you. I gave My life that you would share My life. Oh, My child, pray to the Holy Spirit to open your eyes, to let you see where you are blind, to open your hearts to the ways of God. Pray to Him to sanctify you.

You are called to be Christ to one another. Your hearts have turned hard. Your ways are not My ways. My way is always to love. My ways are to give. My ways are to see in your brother the creation of the Father, so beautiful, so uniquely created.

Each child is a gift from God to this world. Each child is a gift of unique love, given by the Father. You were uniquely created. You are so loved. Pray to know your specialness to God. It is in realizing His love for you that you will love your brothers.

Messenger: We are brothers in Christ. God is our Father. We are to be one.

Jesus: Join, My little ones, in such love. It is in loving that you will be at peace. Love of each other creates joy in your hearts. Pray for the grace to know and love God more. It is in this knowledge and God's love that you will be My light that shines in the darkest night.

I am the Way, I am the Truth. I am the Life! To live in Me you must come to know and love Me. Follow My ways. My ways are the ways of truth. My ways are not always the easy way, they are the ways of love.

If you are to be joined in your hearts, you must love every man. Every man is your brother. You must put on Christ in all your ways. Would Christ act as you are acting?

I love you so much. It is in meditating on My love for you that you will love your brothers.

I put you on this earth to love one another. Pray to the Spirit to know My ways. I am Jesus, Son of the Living God. I truly come to bring you new life. It is in Me you will have the light of life. I love you so, the Father loves you so, the Spirit wants to live in your hearts and make you alive with the love of God. Pray to Mary to lead you through her loving heart into such love of the Father, Son and Holy Spirit.

My child, come to My ever burning Heart. I do not love you one moment and forget you the next. I am forever burning brightly for you. I never falter. I am forever on fire for love of you. If you forget Me, I never ever forget you, I love you so much. 10/2/94

These Messages Need to Circulate

Jesus: My dear children, I tell you to listen to Me here. I am deliver-ing messages for all to be read and distributed. Souls need to read these messages. Your Center will grow in love of Me when you circulate these messages. I ask. You have a free will. These are My letters of love to all. They are not being read. I deliver these messages to you to deliver to My faithful ones. Please, I beg you to circulate My messages. What more do I say to you!

This world is moving further and further from Me. I control your every breath. Do you think you are independent of He Who keeps you alive, second by second?

You do not know how truly frail you are? You do not control the air, the water, the sun, your food. You are dependent on Me for your exis-tence, second by second.

I am your Most loving Savior. I speak to you here. Please listen to Me. This is an urgent request. I love you so and love each hurting soul. All the Blue Books have different messages. They speak to all of you. They need to be published. I will provide the funds to see to this. Your delays are stopping the progress of so many returning to My most intimate love. I beg you, please answer My plea.   10/4/94

Come to My Waiting Arms

Jesus: My child, My eyes are watching you. You sit in front of Me in the tabernacle where I am exposed and you kneel in front of Me. I am no less present than when I hung from the cross.

My eyes looked to the heavens above to behold the glimpses of My dear Mother under My cross. My eyes saw it all. I saw the hatred, the anger in their eyes as they came for Me to scourge Me. Such deep dark-ness in their souls - the bottomless pit of darkness! These eyes of Mine beheld My dear Mother, close by My side on Calvary. To see her suffer-ing! My eyes watched as I so horribly suffered Myself. My eyes watch you, My beloved, kneel in front of Me here and know how My Heart forever beats with such love for you and you do not realize this love.

My eyes watch My beloved ones suffer so. Many sufferings made by their own willfulness to do what they choose and not what I tell them. My eyes watch My beloved ones suffer and I do not interfere with their free will. But, My eyes watch them with the same love that led Me to death on the cross.

Think of My eyes watching you. Know how I am present to you in your hearts. I am so close to you, My dearly beloved ones! If you only knew how your life depends on My constant care for you!

Your every breath is dependent on Me. Oh, little blind earth, when will you come to My waiting arms? When will you see this God Who loves you so dearly? What do I need to do to show you My love? Open up your closed hearts. Pray for grace. Come and sit with Me in front of the tabernacle. Attend the Mass. Receive communion. My grace I pour out to you to know and love Me more. If you do not come, you are missing such graces! Love your brothers. You receive graces through your good works. You will grow in your love and knowledge of Me as you cooperate with this grace I pour out to you.

Oh, little one, you need to come to Me. The devil is so strong. You need the grace I pour out to you to grow in holiness. You need the Spirit to sanctify you. Oh, I love you so. Do not give into satan to trip you up and get you focused on his nonsense. I, Jesus Christ, the Son of God, am in your midst this very day and I am forever watching you.

Messenger: The eyes that watch me as I sit here with Him! He is watching me with such love! The Father is with me with such love. The Spirit is within me, moving within me to make me grow in holiness. Oh, please God, I want to grow in love and knowledge of You. I love You so much!

They constantly accused Jesus and persecuted Him with such accusations. He showed us the way. He was silent. He did not argue. They clothed Him many times and made Him change His garments. Jesus was the little innocent lamb led to the slaughter. He yielded to them, and they stripped Him and persecuted Him. He did all this for love of us. He was silent. Are we silent when satan tries to attack us through others? Does it do any good to answer an angry attack? He was silent to His death on the cross. He loved those who persecuted Him. He yielded to their treatment. He was the victim being led to the slaughter.

The Father loved us so much He gave His only Son up to death with such persecution! He loves us so much this very day. He sees the creation He has made and He loves His creation so much. We are so loved by the Father.

Jesus: I am the Way. I am the Truth. I am the Life. I am Jesus, come to you this day, exposed here in the Eucharist. I give you Myself out of such love. I yielded to all their insults and persecution that ended in My death. I remain in such love for you this day.

What more do I say to you? I love you so much. Study My passion and see the love I gave for you. Oh, dear one, you are so loved!   10/4/94

God the Father Loves Me

Messenger: Father, I adore You. I lay my life before You, how I love You. I have been realizing the Father's love so much this morning and the Gospel reading was on the "Our Father".

Prayer:
   Father, you created me with such tender uniqueness and love.
   You have a plan for my life. Father, I give myself entirely to You.
   I give You my life.

The concept of the Father and His tremendous love makes me feel so warm inside. He is a loving Father that created us and gave His only Son for us. He loves us so much. To realize His love and Jesus' love and the Holy Spirit's love makes my heart feel so very full and warm inside.

All the love I have yearned for seems to fill me when I realize how He is forever guarding and watching and loving and caring for me. He is my loving Father. No person on this earth can give me this paternal love as He, God, gives to me!

It is in surrendering my whole self in the Mass that I am free. I offer myself to the Father with Jesus. What a sacrifice! What freedom and love for me!

The freedom comes in living only for the love of my precious God. I act for love of my beloved Jesus. If satan tries to taunt me, I focus on why I live, I live to love Jesus, and show His love in me.

   I fall so short, but I constantly keep trying to focus on the oneness of the one Triune God. God is in me. God dwelling in me gives me my peace.

Jesus stood His passion and death. He knew the Father's love. Jesus died in perfect peace! No one can ever take away my union with God. That is what gives me peace and joy - realizing the love God has for me and I have for God! Love is the answer. Love is the answer to peace and joy. Love centered in God: Father, Son and Holy Spirit -- Words are too weak to explain it. We are so blessed to have the love of God: Father, Son and Holy Spirit!

A child needs love. The Father loves us so much. As the little child that sits on their Father's lap, I know the Father pours out His love to me. So many of us did not get the love we needed from our earthly fathers even though they meant to love us. The Father loves us so perfectly, our heavenly Father. He created us. God loved us so much to give us life. He made us and He loves us. He loves us with the dearest love. He loves all He creates. We are His beloved children. Go to the Father. He loves us so much.

The Our Father

Our Father, Who art in heaven, hallowed be Thy name. Thy Kingdom come, Thy will be done on earth as it is in heaven. Give us this day our daily bread and forgive us our trespasses as we forgive those who trespass against us. And lead us not into temptation, but deliver us from evil. Amen.

I give myself totally over to the Father as a little child does to their father, always sure of His great love for me. Total surrender in the Mass. Jesus gave Himself as a sacrifice. I give the Father my life. I am the child, He is my loving Father. I entrust my life to my "Dad".

My beloved Father, I see Him as my Father as a little child might sit on their father's lap and put their head on the father's chest. The Father is not harsh. He is loving and approving. He loves me. He made me. He gives me His love. He accepts the love I give to Him. There is no wall, there is union. I am His beloved child. He loves me, He made me...such bonding with my beloved Father!

Jesus: You are, Rita, the child of My Father. He loves you as the most loving Father. He is God. You cannot even fathom the love He pours out to you! He wants you to be all He created you to be. He gave you so many gifts and talents to do His work. He wants you to use these talents and do His work, His plan, He makes clear to you in your heart. As a child that follows their parent's commands, you are not happy when you do not follow His will. He loves you so much. He wills what is best for you.

And you, My little one, will be with Him some day in such union in heaven. Today you must pray to grow in His love. It is the key to your peace and joy. It is in realizing His plan and His love that you will have this great peace inside, He dwells within your heart. Turn to Him always, your beloved Father - He loves you so much!

Messenger: To think of the love of the Holy Spirit, I want to cry. It fills me so much. I am engulfed in such fullness. To ponder the love of the Holy Spirit makes me feel so full in my love for God the love I have for the Father and the Son and the Holy Spirit. I feel overwhelmed to the point of tears. I feel His life burning inside of me as if I could burst. I am filled with such love I cannot express it, I am filled ----

Think of Mary when she cried out the Magnificat and when the Apostles were filled with the Holy Spirit on the first Pentecost!

The presence of God: Father, Son and Holy Spirit within me make me want to shout for joy. This is the Good News: Jesus has died, He has risen. God lives: Father, Son and Holy Spirit, in our hearts, with such love this very day! This is what it is all about. This is what we live for. This is what we die for. This is the one, Triune God within us. What shouts of exultation for Their presence within. God is with us - we know God in one another and in His creation.

Jesus: You will know peace, love and joy as you grow in your knowledge and love of the one, Triune God. Such fullness, through Mary!

Messenger: I feel as if I am flying high with Their immense love within me. To know God is to love God. He is love. The Holy Spirit sets me on fire, our Blessed Lady takes me to her Son. Impart to me, Oh Spirit, Your love and the Fire of this love, active and alive within my very soul! I know God within me, I know God's burning love within my very soul.   Alleluia, Alleluia!   10/5/94

A Song from Jesus

Jesus: I came as a little child. I was born that you would have life. I came as a little child. I lived. I loved. I preached. I showed you the way. My Mother cared for Me and all My needs. St. Joseph raised Me as a father who cared for his child.

Messenger: I came. I find joy and peace in love. I must love all my brothers. Who am I that God loves me? The more I focus on His love, the greater my peace. I must feel His presence within me at all times. I must let Him operate me when I am with others.

Messenger: A *Song from Jesus* was given October 7, 1994. On October 7, 1994, Jesus told me to write a song to be sung after Communion for a Mass at Our Lady of the Holy Spirit Center on October 8, 1994. I told Him I couldn't write music. He said, "You will not do it, I will." My daughter and I sat at the piano bench and in five minutes Jesus gave me the words and music to A *Song from Jesus*. This is His love song to you.   10/6/94

A Song from Jesus

by Rita Ring

You Should Do All Things with Love

Messenger: This message was given the day after I received A Song from Jesus.

Jesus: Whatever you do, you should do with much love. I come, little one and I teach you such lessons. Some lessons you do not see. I teach you again and again, with much grace. You begin to see My work I have for you to do. Pray for the grace to know and love Me more. It is in your union with Me you will find such peace. As your love grows for God and Mary, your love grows for others. You cannot love Me and hate your brother. I call you to new life. I call you to oneness with Me.

I am Jesus, the Son of God. Surrender your whole being, offer yourself as a sacrifice, whole and complete, to the Father at every Mass. Offer Him all you are, your love and good works. Offer yourself wholly and completely with My Body and Blood - this is the most pleasing sacrifice to the Father.

Every day offer yourself to the Father in the Holy Sacrifice of the Mass being offered around the world for all your intentions. Say the Morning Offering with your children. Pray and offer your day so you will know and love God more.

Do not let satan talk in your head. Always love your brothers. See the God Who created them when you talk to them. See the love the Father has for them. See My love to die for them. See the Spirit Who wants to be alive in them. Do not give in to satan.

I am in charge. I support you. I love you. I watch out for you. I am the Almighty God. You do nothing on your own. Your brother depends on Me. Realize your frailties. Praise your Father in heaven lavishly. Praise God. We want to be praised by you!

I am your beloved Jesus and I love you so much.   10/8/94

Be Christ to Each Other

Jesus: My little one, be of a clean heart. Be with Me. You must take time to be with Me. My love is surrounding you. You do not fear. I am Jesus. I am your Savior. You live to love God and do the will of the Father.

I am forever with you. All you do must be acts of love. Put on Me. In all your actions, put on Me. Love, love, love. Interior peace comes from

God dwelling within you.

Put on Christ. Be Christ to one another. Be as I would be to your brothers. You are My blessed one. Do not fear. Just put on Christ. Be so connected to the God Who lives within. Total peace. Total love. Total presence. We are at the helm.

As you operate with others, be Christ to each other. Love one another. Your heart must be forever connected to Me. Feel My presence within your heart. I dwell within you now. Easy does it. I am dwelling within you. You are living to love God, to serve God in this world, to be Christ to others as We dwell in you.

Each person you encounter is very dear to Me and I love them so. Love them. See My beautiful creation in them. See Me loving them so much. See beyond the negative acts. This person is My beautiful creation.

I am the God of Jacob, of Joseph, of all your ancestors. I talk to you here. Do not worry. Do not fret. Put satan behind you and let My love come forth to this world.

Calm, peace, joy, love always. If you always love, you have peace and joy. I am Jesus, come to Me, My sweet ones. I live in you, live in My love. Alleluia, Alleluia.   10/9/94

Take Shelter from the Rain in My Heart

(**Messenger:** I saw a vision in my heart of a little wet child standing by a tree in the storm in a dark night. Just a little light, enough to see the child.)

Jesus: You are this little child. You are in the storm. The wind and the rain are beating down on you. You are cold. You are wet, as wet as you can be. You stand by a tree and the wind beats against you and the rain pounds harder.

My child, My child, there is such shelter in My most Sacred Heart. Come into My Heart, child. You will be protected from the wind that blows so hard on you. You will be out of the rain. It may pound down all around you, but your refuge is found in My Heart. My Heart is a burning furnace of love. See yourself, little child, stand by the tree and whimper and you want to go it alone? Let My Mother lead you by the hand. You, little child, come with Mary, your Mother. Let her take you to the shelter of My Heart.

John 14:6
I am the Way; I am Truth and Life....

There is not life without Me. My life I give to you that you will have life and have it abundantly. Today I give you My very own Heart on fire for love of you. Come to Me through Mary's pure and tender Heart. We will shelter you in the darkest storm.

Messenger: When I am filled up with Your love, Lord, I do not whimper as a little child. I am filled with love and peace and joy. Take me, Mary, to the Heart of your very dear Son and place me there forever in a little pocket surrounded by His ardent love. I want to be lost deeply in the recesses of this Heart. How deep do you place me in His Heart? I want to be surrounded by the immense love of Father, Son and Holy Spirit and know, Mary, you are so closely united in this Heart!

This is the comfort in the dark, windy, wet night. This is my refuge. This is my life. This is the closest I can come to heaven on earth - to be united in such love with the Trinity and Mary!

Help me to let go of it all and come as a little child, running from the rain to the warmest shelter. A roaring fire, warmth, dry clothes and light - the light radiated by the Heart of Jesus. In the darkness I find my light in You. Alleluia. Praise God, Father, Son and Holy Spirit. Love to my beloved Mother. This is bliss. Song: *I am Your Sacred Heart*   10/11/94

Surrender to Me

Jesus: I call you to love. I call you to love as I have loved. To grow in the life I have given you, you must be open to receive My grace and you must comply with the will of the Father.

I pour out to you such gifts of My love. I want to share My life with you. I love you so dearly. Each one of you here is so precious to Me.

Know that I never leave you. satan will constantly tell you that what you feel when you are close to Me is not so. What you feel, this drawing to be ever closer to Me, is real!

I am Jesus, your Savor. I truly died for you. I would die for you this very day. I gave My flesh! I gave My Blood! I give Myself to you - no less present this day as the day I died on the cross.

I am Jesus. I am your Savior. I am in your midst this very day. I come to you and ask you to trust in Me. I ask you to surrender yourselves entirely. Surrender yourselves entirely to the Father at every Mass. Offer yourselves with My precious Body and Blood to the Father.

My song, *A Song From Jesus* was given 4 days before this message.

Song: *A Song From Jesus*

Messenger: Hold not back. He loves you so much. He created you. He molded each of you as a special work of art into the beautiful creation you each are. There is not another person like you. There is not another person that can love God as you do. There is not another person that can give to this world what He created you to do. If you hold back yourself, your love from Him and this world, the world will suffer from the loss of your gifts.

Jesus: You are the light of the world. A city set on a hill will shine with the light of God's love through you. You will reflect the love of My burning Heart from your being.

Song: Let your light shine for all the world to see. All will see the good you do and give your Father praise.   10/11/94

Father Forgive Them,
They Know Not What They Do

Jesus: When the Holy Spirit comes upon you, He fills you with the fire of God's love. Do not be angered at any man. To be angry destroys your peace, your love. You cannot love and be angry. Put your problems at the foot of the cross and offer them to the Father with My precious Body and Blood. Stand there with Mary. Offer up your troubles to the Father with love. Let Him dissolve your problems.

Love mends. I loved those who crucified Me. Is your anger more justified? I loved them. Love is forgiveness and caring for the other. Forgive your brother. Pray for him and his needs.

Messenger: It is in giving that we receive. We are raised to deeper life in Him. We must love God and love one another.

Jesus: Come to Me. Sit with Me in front of the tabernacle and let Me mend your hurt heart. Receive Me in the Eucharist and be healed. It is only in Me that you find peace, love and joy. I give you a new commandment -- love one another as I have loved you. Do you fight with your brothers or do you think thoughts of how they have wronged you? Do you not hear Me say, "To enter heaven, you must love. Love God above all things and love your neighbors as yourself?"

Oh, listen, My little ones. Peace in your heart is found only in love. Listen to Me. Pray for your brothers. Pray to the Father through the Holy Sacrifice of the Mass. Pray to the Spirit to help you silence satan. Pray united to the Mass. Cast satan into hell, bind him up and send him away. Pray the rosary. It is a weapon against him. He hates the rosary. He will try to stop you from praying.

Your brothers need love. I want to love through you. Will you answer My call to love the unloving? Will you see beyond the exterior of your brother to the person created by God the Father?

Why, children, do I tell you over and over again? You are like little children that need to learn. I am your teacher. You are going to My school to learn My lessons of love. Are you realizing what I am calling you to? Do you try to act as I showed you? To My death, I loved those who crucified Me. I came, I showed you the way. Meditate on My life. It is through Me that you will be led to happiness.

I am the way, I am the truth, I am the life. I am Jesus, the Son of God. I love you with the deepest love. I came to call you to love your brothers. Will you answer My call?

Come to the endless furnace of love found in My Heart. I love you so much!   10/11/94

Father, I Give Myself

Messenger: Lord, let me die to myself, let me go to the pure heart of Mary so I can say, it is no longer I who live, but He who lives in me. You gave Your all for love of us. I give to You, my beloved Lord, myself, placed lovingly in the arms of Your Mother. I give my life to You to love Your beloved ones.

Song: Dream the Impossible Dream, Until I Am Laid to My Rest. There is peace in surrender.

John 3:16
Yes, God so loved the world
that he gave his only Son,
that whoever believes in him may not die
but may have eternal life.

Messenger: He shows us surrender. Look at Him laying lifeless in His Mother's arms under the cross. His dead body. He showed us the way to surrender!

Let me be forever wrapped in the arms of Your loving Mother, as she wrapped You under the cross, Lord. I give myself totally and entirely to You. Father, I give myself to You. Please accept my sacrifice. I want to live in You, Lord, for You, Lord, and with You, Lord.

See Jesus laying in the arms of His dear Mother under the cross. This was the will of the Father. Jesus died for us and rose on the third day. Jesus knew the Father's love. The Father loved us so much to give His only Son for us. Jesus loved us so much to die for us. The Holy Spirit loves us. Look at Him under the cross:

> The Father to give His Son.
> The Son to die for us.
> The Spirit loves us so much and
> Mary is our beloved Mother.   10/12/94

To His Death, He Did the Father's Will

Messenger: Think of her holding Him under the cross — total surrender to the point of death. He gave the last beat of His Heart.

Does He ask us for little things? Do we want to do the Father's will? He showed us how He obeyed the Father's will — look at Him, lifeless in Mary's arms. This is doing His Father's will — this is knowing the Father's love. This is me seeing Jesus and knowing His love for us. He died for us — the Father's love for us — He gave His Son!

Jesus: This is My life, given up for you, My beloved ones. I am Jesus, I am your Savior, I am Who Am and I gave Myself. I did the will of the Father I died for love of you.

Do you know Me? Study My ways. I come to show you the way. I did the Father's will. Do you follow His will? I came to show you the way. I am the way, I am the truth, I am the life. I love you. I died for you. Live to love. Love those I died for. Don't say no, I want you to love your brothers for Me. Your mission is to love more than anything and do the Father's will. To My death I loved My attackers. You love those who are cruel. They are the creation of My Father, they are precious to Me. Live to love, My dear ones. You are so loved by Me.

My dear ones, I love you, as a warm bath. I bathe you with My love. Feel the warmth surround you. Feel this security and know My love.

I am your ardent lover, on fire for love of you, this day.

Song: *A Song From Jesus*

Messenger:
Peace:
How do we grow in peace?
Peace comes from doing the Will of the Father.
Peace comes from dying to self.
Peace comes in loving God — in living for
His love and not for ourselves.

We are so special to God. He created us. We do not need to prove ourselves. We are special because the Father created us.
Peace comes with realizing the Father's will.
When I resist His will, I am unhappy. I must do always the Father's will to be happy.
Christ had perfect peace, even to dying on the cross.
No matter what they did to Him, He accepted it. He knew the Father's will. He knew the Father's love.
Spirit, help me to know you more and love you more. I am thirsty for the love of God. Fill me with your gifts.

Song: *God's Love*   10/12/94

Apostles of the Eucharistic Heart of Jesus

My dear fellow Associate Members,

Jesus is calling special apostles to join a new division of the Shepherds of Christ Movement. Here is a message from Jesus given to Father Carter:

> My beloved priest-companion, I am requesting that a new prayer movement be started under the direction of Shepherds of Christ Ministries. I am asking for volunteers who are willing to pray before the Blessed Sacrament for one hour, twice-weekly. Members of the Shepherds of Christ prayer chapters, as well as others, are to be invited to join this movement.
>
> These apostles are to pray for the intentions I am giving you. For part of the hour they are to use the prayers of the Shepherds of Christ Associates Handbook. They may spend the rest of the hour as they so choose.

I will use this new prayer movement within My Shepherds of Christ Ministries in a powerful way to help in the renewal of My Church and the world. I will give great graces to those who join this movement. The name, Apostles of the Eucharistic Heart of Jesus, is to be given to this movement.

I am inviting My beloved Rita Ring to be coordinator for this activity.

I pour out the great love of My Sacred Heart to all. I am Jesus, Chief Shepherd of the flock.

This is indeed a special calling for us to unite in one heart with His Eucharistic Heart and pray for the following intentions:

1. For the spread of the devotion to the Hearts of Jesus and Mary culminating in the reign of the Sacred Heart and the triumph of the Immaculate Heart.
2. For the Pope.
3. For all bishops of the world.
4. For all priests.
5. For all sisters and brothers in the religious life.
6. For all members of the Shepherds of Christ Movement, and for the spread of this movement to the world.
7. For all members of the Catholic Church.
8. For all members of the human family.
9. For all souls in purgatory.

Message given to Father Edward Carter, S.J.

You Are Very Dear to Me

Jesus: I am the Lord, your God. You shall not have any gods before Me, not man, not possessions, not yourself. I want to be first in your life. You ask Me for greater union, union is achieved through surrendering to self, of yielding to the will of God. You cannot surrender and hold on at the same time. Let go and it will carry you deeper into My loving arms. There is nothing that happens that I do not allow. I am allowing this for a reason. Through your compliance to the Father's will, through your surrender, you are drawn closer to My Heart.

You, My child, are very dear to Me. I guard your life. You give yourself to the Father, to the Holy Spirit, to Me, to Mary, then let go. Do not ever be angry at your brothers. They are My precious ones. See in their eyes the creation of the Father! Pray for a pure heart. Pray to be sanctified through the Spirit. Pray for this holiness.

Life is not easy. To get to heaven you must walk a narrow path, with bumps along the way. Will you walk over the rocks and still love? This is the test - to be so rooted in Me you will walk with love, always!

It is in your trials you learn to love always, all your brothers, even when you feel you have been wronged and hurt. I am Jesus. I love you so much. Surrender and be drawn closer to My Heart. You offer yourself, then fight to let go? Give your all. See Me as I died on the cross, I gave all My Blood. I gave the last beat of My Heart! I treat you so gently. You surrender. Be thankful for all the blessings you have, this very day.

The Eucharist is such a gift I give you. This day, I, Jesus, give you Myself. Such love I pour out to you. It offends Me to see you so focused on other things, I am God and I give you a heart on fire for love of you and you balk. Oh, child, union with Me is dying to oneself. Consecration is a giving of yourself. Give and you will receive. It is in your surrendering to Me and My ways that the Father can mold you into His special creation. You will be tested in fire and you will come forth My specially molded child. I am Jesus, come to Me and be free!   10/12/94

Jesus Loved Those Who Put Him to Death

Messenger: You loved those who persecuted You. You loved those who put You to death. You said nothing, You were silent. You love all souls unconditionally, no matter what their sins. You love all men. You see the creation of the Father behind their faults. You love them despite their faults.

Who am I to not love every man? My job is to love and obey You and Your will.

Jesus: My little child, you will grow. You will prosper in My love, I never leave you. I am forever with you, guarding your way. All I send you is in greatest love. Draw close to My Heart. I love you so much.

Song: *A Song From Jesus*   10/12/94

Circulate These Rosary Meditations

Luke 1:46-55

And Mary said:
'My soul proclaims
    the greatness of the Lord
and my spirit rejoices
    in God my Saviour;
because he has looked upon
    the humiliation of his servant.
Yes, from now onwards
    all generations will call me blessed,
for the Almighty
    has done great things for me.
Holy is his name,
and his faithful love extends age after age
    to those who fear him.
He has used the power of his arm,
he has routed the arrogant of heart.
He has pulled down princes
    from their thrones
        and raised high the lowly.
He has filled the starving with good things,
    sent the rich away empty.
He has come to the help
    of Israel his servant,
        mindful of his faithful love
—according to the promise
    he made to our ancestors—
of his mercy to Abraham
    and to his descendants for ever.'

Messenger: It is the love of the Spirit which I am filled with after communion. He is alive in my breast. I love Him so very much. To receive Jesus, I want to jump for joy as the child in Elizabeth's womb jumped for joy.

God Is Within Me — Father, Son and Holy Spirit!

The presence of God fills my soul. God is here. Alleluia! Who am I that He comes to me, a lowly person? His love is so great for us to give us Himself. Live the Mass, the whole day should be centered around you partaking in the Mass. It is a gift of self, wholly and entirely to the Father.

Father, I surrender myself to You, Father, Son and Holy Spirit, wholly and entirely. The Spirit fills me and my heart is on fire for the one, true God alive within me. My heart is so filled with the presence of the one, Triune God. The love I have for the Holy Spirit and He has for me fills my soul to jubilation.

Oh, God, impart to me a constant realization of Your presence so I can forever feel this fire that burns within my heart for You. Such awareness and feelings in my chest for God! He fills our souls and sets our hearts aglow with the fire of His love. God is ever present within us. He never leaves. Help me to always feel so keenly, this interior awareness of the Trinity. My heart is on fire with His presence and His love.

Jesus: I call you to suffer with Me. Suffer with Me in love — this is what draws you closer to Me. Promote the rosary and the meditations on it. People pray the rosary and are missing Our lives. They do not think about Our lives. Teach the meditations to all, spread them, so they will be led by the Spirit to ponder the mysteries of Our lives. Do not listen to satan. I am calling you to spread this devotion and to entwine My love for all with the mysteries of the rosary. I am calling you to spread devotion to the Eucharist in the rosary. The rosary is a key to living according to the lives of Christ and Mary. I want you to promote the rosary and promote meditations on the rosary. If they learn one set of meditations, the Spirit will expound on those to lead them closer to My Heart through My Mother's Heart.

I want you to circulate these meditations and lead the rosary this way. Tell them to learn them so they can later meditate on them and grow in their love of God. It is through Me and Mary's tender Heart that you, being led by the Spirit, will grow in your union with all three Persons of the Trinity. I am calling you this day to take this job so seriously. This will lead souls to love of God.

I am your loving Savior. Every day My children should carry one picture of the stations or rosary with them and meditate on that during the day. Look at the picture and think about it. The Spirit will lead you into deeper knowledge of the lives of Jesus and Mary. I am Jesus. I want My people to know the great love My Mother and I have for them. The rosary is the key to meditating on My Life. The stations will lead them into deeper understanding of My Passion and love for them.

Every day should be spent in union with the Mass, being offered throughout the world. Your day should center around your participation in the Mass. Your day is a constant surrendering of your will to the Father. It should be lived in constantly giving yourself to the Father, Son, Holy Spirit and Mary. In the Mass you should surrender yourself and offer yourself with Me, wholly and entirely, to the Father. This is the high point of your day - your sacrificing of yourself entirely to Him, being in union with Me in the Holy Eucharist. I come to you and we are one in this

Sacrament. Your day should be a preparation for this event. Your life, centered around receiving Me in the Eucharist.

I never leave you. The Father, Son and Holy Spirit dwell within you at all times in a special way if you are in the state of grace. Constantly focus on My interior presence within you. Within this lies your peace. I never leave you. I will never abandon you. What have you to fear? I am your God.

My presence surrounds you. I am in your beloved brothers. Be Christ to one another. Live in My love as I live in you. Do not falter or become afraid. Do not give in to satan to trip you up. My presence surrounds you in each other and in your world. In the air, the sun, the leaves, the sky, in My creation! Be attuned to My Life, My presence surrounding you. I am Jesus, Son of the Living God, I give you this message. Heed My words and you will know peace and joy. I love you intently. I am on fire for love of you this moment.

Notes:

Messenger: High feelings of love, overwhelmed with the love of the Trinity. Intellectual vision — something really special. I praise You Father, Son and Holy Spirit. I understood a little when Mary received the Magnificat and was filled with the Spirit. The Spirit fills me. I understood this mystery as I did the Descent of the Holy Spirit upon the Apostles. The Spirit permeates my being.

It is in suffering that I am comforted. He who suffered and died for us asks us to share in His suffering. Meditate on one station a day, carry a picture with you.   10/14/94 - After Communion

As Mary Appeared at the 6:30 Daily Prayers

Messenger: I got a message on the rosary. Mary was so lighted up and the roses were so strong - so strong, everybody smelled them, especially on the 6th sorrow - so strong - it was the strongest yet and Mary was so beautiful.   10/14/94 - During the Rosary on Friday Night

Hearts of Hatred and Anger

Jesus: Think how it is to have someone point a finger at you. They came at Me with their weapons and lances. They had hearts filled with hatred and anger. I did not answer back, I complied always to the will of the Father. Can you love he who points his finger at you and talks cruelly about you? They stood around in numbers and shouted awful accusations at Me. All I had done was to love all. Are you accused and treated cruelly when you are trying to be Christ-like? Look at Me and follow My way.

Messenger: Gentle Jesus show me Your ways. The face reflects the heart. Jesus' face is so gentle, men with hardened hearts reflect their heart in their eyes and face.

Vision

Saw from the side a face, long hair, stringy, mouth wide open excruciating pain. What stood out was the open mouth -- the hair over the cheek -- crown of thorns. How wide His mouth was open.

Jesus: I did this for you, this is the love I have for you, this is the love I have this day. I knew the Father's love for Me.

I am your God, pray to your heavenly Father to know His great love for you.

Messenger: My prayers rise like incense to the Father.
His eyes cast upward with such love to the Father.
Doing His will to His last breath.   10/15/94

As Mary Appeared at the 6:30 Daily Prayers

Visions

Messenger: Went to Holy Spirit Center with my children at first it was locked.

Saw Mary, she looked so alive, prayed, I received messages! Mary was lit up all through the rosary. She was so lighted when I received the messages. I smelled roses 3 times. Also I smelled them at different times during the day.

Mary stayed with me and the children a long time. So, so beautiful - looked so alive. Mary said she loved me and the children.

SO ALIVE! At the Holy Spirit Center Jesus appeared to me in the Sacred Heart statue as you enter in the hall. He had different faces. Birds chirped so loud this morning.   10/15/94

Always Love

Messenger: No matter what you have done, my brother to me or my children, I must forgive and live only to love. I see Him under the cross in Mary's arms. He loved, He never lost His peace. His Heart pierced with a lance. He gave His all. She gave her all, to do the will of the Father and to love.

Jesus: Love when they hate you, it is a great act of love when you love those who hate you and holler slander against you.

Trust Fr. Carter totally.

I am the way, the truth and the life. I never ever leave you abandoned. Focus on Our great love. No person can ever take away the burning love you have in your breast.

Love, Love, Love. Show no anger for any misdeed. Love your child and show them My way. Your child is very special to Me and will suffer much, but will learn the lessons your child needs to learn to do My great work.

Spend time talking and being with your child. I am Jesus, I am the Son of God, your face must reflect your deep love for Me. Put on the face of love, deep, deep love of God. My face was gentle because I loved. Love and total surrender to the Father's will. You are being guarded.

Messenger: My interior love for the Holy Spirit is overwhelming. I just love God so much. I cried so hard tonight in church, I want to be so united to God -- Such longing to be united to Jesus and Mary - there is this longing. I wanted Jesus so much and I love Him. I just love Him so very much. I keep seeing the pictures, Christ condemned to death, Christ under the cross, Christ carrying the cross. It was not an accident I saw Christ carrying the cross yesterday (vision). He knew the Father's love. Jesus was doing the Father's will.

Mary suffered so always doing the Father's will, Mary received a crown in heaven.   10/16/94 - Feast of Margaret Mary - 4:45 a.m.

Mary Queen of Heaven and Earth

Messenger: We meditate on Mary going up to heaven and being crowned. All she suffered, all she silently endured with greatest love. She showed us the way, she was humble, she was always there, she was more in the background. She was with Jesus. Mary always did the will of God. God loved Mary so much to pick her. Mary was taken up to heaven, she was crowned Queen of heaven and earth.

Mary was clothed as the sun, the moon under her feet and twelve stars around her head.

Revelation 12:1
Now a great sign appeared in heaven: a woman, robed with the sun, standing on the moon, and on her head a crown of twelve stars.

Messenger: Mary suffered so, she did the Father's will always. Mary loved. Mary was so beautiful. Her love made her more beautiful. Mary knew the love of God. She knew the love of the Father and Jesus and Holy Spirit. I love God so much and I am filled with God's love, it is that, that sustains me. Though the earth be shaken and the sun cease to shine, the love of God interiorly will sustain us.

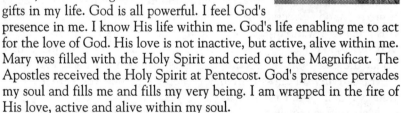

Jesus knew the Father's love, see Him under the cross, in Mary's arms. Mary knew the Father's love - see Mary holding Jesus.

Father please help me to know Your love. I love You so much. Spirit, I feel Your love so alive in my heart, I love You so much, I feel Your love so strong within me. Mary always knew the love of her Spouse the Holy Spirit, burning and on fire. The love of the Holy Spirit burns within my breast, His fire is aglow and radiant. I feel His gifts in my life. God is all powerful. I feel God's presence in me. I know His life within me. God's life enabling me to act for the love of God. His love is not inactive, but active, alive within me. Mary was filled with the Holy Spirit and cried out the Magnificat. The Apostles received the Holy Spirit at Pentecost. God's presence pervades my soul and fills me and fills my very being. I am wrapped in the fire of His love, active and alive within my soul.

Oh Spirit, I love You so much, I love You and Jesus and Mary and the Father. I love You so much, I am elated at Your presence within me. Your love permeates my soul! ALIVE, FIRE!! EXPLODING inside of me. God's life is alive in me. LOVE!

Song: *Your Presence Pervades My Soul*   10/16/94

I Love the Wounds of Jesus

Messenger: I love Jesus so much, so much love for Him and suffering over how He suffered. I feel so connected to the events of the passion, Jesus on the cross. I feel so connected with Mary and Jesus under the cross, such connection with Them and such burning love for Him and such sadness to the events. I love Him so much. I love His wounded

body so much, His precious head and His hands and feet and His side. I just love Him so much. I love His beautiful Heart pierced with a lance.

10/16/94 - 6:00 p.m.

Experience More Deeply God's Love

Messenger: He gave Himself on the cross. He gives Himself to us now. He, God is no less present than when He died on the cross. He comes to me in such oneness. God comes to me and gives Himself to me. The Spirit is the fire of God's love. The more I get in touch with the Spirit, my heart is on fire and burning with the love of God. The Spirit adds the fire to my heart for this intense love I have for Jesus. I love Him so much.

To know Jesus is to love because He is love. I cannot know Jesus and not love you. Harboring anger in our hearts blocks our deep union with God. I must forgive. I act in love. I do not wish to block my union with God. God is love. To be deeply united to God I must be loving. The more my heart is filled with dissension, the further I go from Him. To unite in His love deeply, I must try to free my heart and be loving to men.

I cannot be likened to Him Who is love if I am not loving. To be united to Him, I must let go of hate and anger and forgive. God comes to us and wants us to be joined in deepest love with Him.

Jesus: I am the way, the truth and the life. I come to you in the deepest love. I want to be so closely united to you. Rid yourself of impurities so I can be one with you. I am love. I want to be so close to you. Your impurities block My oneness with you. Oh, beloved of My dear Father, I loved you to My death. Open up your heart and feel the fire of My love.

I want to pour Myself out to you and become so united to you. It is you, your impurities, that block My union with you. Open your hearts to the fire of My love. I give you Myself, this day. I, God, come to you. Oh beloved, let go and be so close to Me, so in love with Me! I am love and I want to be united in this love with you. What a gift — your feeble minds cannot fathom. I love you so.   10/16/94 - After Communion

Pray from the Heart

Messenger: Father, forgive them, for they know not what they do. We say the words in the Creed. Do we think about the words in the Creed?

Do we say our prayers as if we are in a race? We are talking to God. How do we talk to one another, like machines? How can I get in touch with my heart when I am racing to say my prayers? If I was talking to a celebrity I would plan my every word so carefully and worry for its delivery. Here is Jesus Christ, the Son of God. Here is God, maker of heaven and earth and how do we approach Him?

Jesus: From the heart, My dear sweet ones. I want prayer from a heart filled with the tenderest love. This is a love affair with Me. Speak softly to Me and whisper your love. Profess your love lavishly in your voice. I love you so. Do you have any idea how I suffered from the coldness of men's hearts? I was rejected by so many souls and I love so perfectly. I am love. In My love I give to you. I am not received with love by many.

I give you My very Self in communion. I love you so much. Pray with a heart on fire for love of Me. The time lingers when you are in love, there is not a rush, you never want to leave.

Come with a heart that is overflowing with love for Me. I wait for you to come to Me and love Me. I want a love affair with you, My beloved. I want to be the center of your life. My Heart burns for you. I want your hearts to burn in love for Me. Is anything more important than exchanging love with God? I am the tender lover. I will give you love as no mortal can. I feed your starved soul. I await you with anxious arms. Oh, My beloved, do not treat Me coldly or indifferently or hurriedly, or neglect Me all together. My Heart cries out for your love. Come and share your all, your whole being with Me. Let go of your world. When you pray, let go and experience a closeness that you never knew. I will give you My love. This is heaven.

Messenger: I adore You, Jesus, I adore You. You are my most beloved

A Song from Jesus

by Rita Ring

REFRAIN

I come to you with great-est love, I
am your lov-ing Sav-ior. I am your God, I
died for you, I come to you this day.

VERSES

1. You are My pre-cious lit-tle one, I
2. Reach out to Me and do not fear, I

love you oh so dear-ly. Come close to Me, My
want to be so close to you. You are My child, My

lit-tle one, I loved you to My death.
pre-cious one, I love you ten-der-ly.

Jesus. (Everybody was excited about a speaker coming because he talks to Mary, but ...Jesus is here every day, all day. Go to the real King. Jesus sits on His throne in the tabernacle. He is truly present at every Mass...the Father and Holy Spirit are there ... they are with us!)

Jesus: Come to My tabernacle and adore Me. I am God, no less present than when I walked on Calvary. I am the Son of God.

Messenger: Father, keep our hearts focused on Your love, Your will, on You. I lift my eyes to the heavens, whence comes my refuge and my strength. My Father is there, Alleluia! I love You, Father. You created me, You gave me life and You gift me with Your love. You gave Your only Son so that I could have life with You. Thank You, Father. You are love. You are He Who is. I want to be united to You, through Your Son, in union with the Holy Spirit and with Mary at my side.

It is presence that is the key. I have felt His presence with me and He speaks to me. I have felt closer than with anyone else, because I love Him so much and crave it. He is present, now. I want a constant awareness of His presence, He never leaves. He is forever with us. His presence pervades my very being. I am never alone. His presence to me now after Communion is so strong. I don't want to do anything but be with Him. My heart feels His presence as a burning love. When I think of the Holy Spirit and Father and Mary, my heart is so full. When I think of the Holy Spirit in relation to Jesus and the Father throughout the day, I still feel this presence.

This is what He felt when He endured His bitter Passion, only much more -- the Father's presence (He is one with Him), the Father's love! And He says to us this day, I love you as the Father has loved Me. He waits to give us this love this day.

Look at Him hanging on the cross. He is no less present this day in the Eucharist, giving Himself to us again in such love.

Father, I adore You, I love You!

Jesus, I adore You, I love You!

Holy Spirit, I adore You, I love You!

Father forgive them they know not what they do. His mercy flows through Jesus' most Sacred Heart. Your love, oh God, the Father, poured out through Jesus, in the Holy Spirit!

Any hatred for myself blocks my union with God. Help me, Jesus, to see myself as the divine creation of the Father, to realize with humility my failings, but to never lose sight of my preciousness to the Father and His great love for me. Help me to unite more and more to You.

Holy Spirit, sanctify my soul and make it holier so I can better unite with my beloved God. Give me the grace to know and love Him ever more. Into Your hands I commend my spirit. I surrender my all to You, Father, Son and Holy Spirit. In humility, I give myself to You and hope You accept my sacrifice. I am Your creation. You are what makes me special - it is in You I have such dignity and honor.

Dear Lord, how many times did I nail You to the cross? Your Mother stood by and watched her beloved Son suffer so. She helplessly watched, oh, agony to the heart! But, You, Jesus, knew the Father's love and in Your great pain, Your eyes were fixed on doing His Will. Your Heart was one in His love.

Make me one in my love with the Father, through Your great love, in union with the Holy Spirit and in Mary's Heart, lead me to this most magnificent union. I crave greater union with Thee. Impart to my heart purity, holiness, sanctity to better unite with You. Create in me, oh God, a pure heart, free of anything that keeps me from You. Give me a heart of love for my brothers. Make my face reflect Your love, shining to my brothers. I want to serve You, Lord. Give me a pure and gentle heart like Yours. Help me to grow more and more like You in my ways. Spirit, mold me in the Heart of Jesus, my most beloved Savior. I love Him so much!

10/17/94 - 5:15 a.m.

Father Carter's Mass

Messenger: I want to be in this ecstatic state! I want such intense union with Him. My heart burns in my chest. To just be with Him, total surrender, fusion, wrapped in His love. Rapture, no words to express the way I feel. Nothing here is like this.

This Mass was so special and yesterday was like a little experience of heaven to me. This is a taste of heaven, there is so much more to behold union with God. I just want to sit after communion and let go, be lost totally in His Heart - deep, deep, deep, just be in Him.

10/17/94 - After Communion

My Love Letter to You

Jesus: I am your Savior. I beckon you to please come to Me in the Blessed Sacrament. Put your world aside. I am truly Jesus and I am waiting for you. I love you so much. Please come and sit with Me. My Heart cries out for you to come. This day I long for you so intently. Oh, My beloved ones, your soul is craving Me. Do you see how created things do not satisfy you? You were created for God and He alone will satisfy you.

Come to Me in your weariness and let Me love you. Your impurities and doubts keep you from Me. Be pure, let go of any anger at your brother, of making yourself right and him wrong. Forgive now all who have wronged you.

Let go. I will give you My grace now in your hearts if you earnestly let go. Let go. Experience freedom. Put your heart in My Heart. Ask My Mother to deeply place you there. Be with Me in such union now. I love you all. Thank you for being with Me today. I am your precious Jesus. I love you.   10/18/94

Presence

Messenger: I was in the dentist office and Mary was so present and she talked to me. I am closely united to Mary. She talked to me. It was so real. I did not experience any of what the dentist was doing!

Then, Jesus came and He was so present. My heart still feels this presence to talk about it - it was so strong! It was a beautiful experience. I went to the dentist to have a tooth drilled, to be capped, and it was a wonderful experience because They were present to me.

Jesus was nailed to the cross. He was crucified, but He had peace. He knew the Father's love. His presence was forever with Him. As I write this, I feel flutters of His presence in my chest. There is such a presence after communion. I want to go off and be alone with Him. I feel it so much, it is accentuated by the awareness of the Holy Spirit and the

Father, and Mary — such fullness to think about Jesus, the Holy Spirit, the Father, and Mary!

His presence after communion pervades my soul. If the whole earth splits under my feet, it is the presence that will sustain me. O, Spirit, impart to me the fire of God's love!

The presence I feel is like being with someone you really love, that feeling of something in your heart. Some feeling in my heart as when you are with someone you deeply love, except nothing I can say describes it.

Jesus: Presence is the word - My Presence. My child, you do not talk about it. You have it within your very heart, a burning of My love for you. Do you experience that which you cannot describe? This is My divine life I give to you. You share in My life in union with Me. Focus intently on this. When you do the dishes, know My Presence. Be drawn constantly into My Heart and Mary's Heart.

Take shelter in Our Hearts. I want you to dwell within My most Sacred Heart. Fervent souls shall quickly mount to high perfection. Read My promises, live your life focusing on My most Sacred Heart. Realize the great love My Mother has for you. Her Heart knows your heart. She loves you so much. Consecrate your lives to our Hearts and promote this devotion. Our Hearts are the key to draw you into the love of God.

Oh, little one, My Heart is the tenderest, most loving Heart. I want My Heart to reign in your heart, in your home and in your family.

I am Jesus, the Sacred Heart of Jesus. I am burning for love of you. Come into My Heart, out of the wind and the rain and you will know peace and joy. As the Father has loved Me, so I love you. I love you this way, this day. It was His love that I knew all through My Passion. Focus on God's love and presence with you.

Song: *Your Presence Pervades My Soul*

10/18/94-After Communion

Enthronement of the Sacred Heart

(To be read by leader or family member)

We are gathered here to honor our King, Jesus Christ, the Son of God. He is our most honored guest. He loves us so ardently and wants to be

King of our home and King of our hearts. We all join together and most graciously welcome Him in our midst. We love You, dear Sacred Heart of Jesus. We honor You this day and are privileged that You, God, love us so much.

Please help us all grow in our knowledge and love of You. We honor You. We praise You. We adore You, and we love You.

We ask You to come and dwell in our hearts. As our King and the cen-ter of our lives, we forever want to be with You, most Sacred Heart of Jesus, we love You so much.

Come and be with every member of this family in a special way. Guard us in our undertakings. Dear Holy Spirit, lead us to the on-fire love of Jesus' Heart.

Mary, our most loving Mother, as you carried Jesus in your womb, you who cared for Him as a child, you who forever stood by Him and walked with Him on Calvary, you, dear Mary, as you stood under His cross and suffered so for love of Him and us, you who held His lifeless body under the cross, you who saw His glorified body after the resurrection and watched Him ascend into heaven, you, dear Mary, you who know this most Sacred, tender, loving Heart, place us so gently into His most Sacred Heart.

Protect and lead every person present and their families to this intense union with your Son. We pray for the priests the world over, Your special anointed sons, to lead all children to the love of Your most Sacred Heart.

May the Sacred Heart of Jesus forever reign in the hearts of all people through the Immaculate Heart of Mary.

We praise You, we honor You, our beloved Jesus. We tenderly love Your Heart so!

Dear Father, thank You for Your beloved Son. Thank You for Your gifts to us. We thank You for giving us a sharing in Your divine life through baptism. We are Your beloved children. Draw us ever closer to union with God, Father, Son and Holy Spirit and Mary, in communion with the angels and saints. Amen.   10/19/94

St. Margaret Mary

Messenger: On October 20, 1994, I had this vision - I account it here from my notebook. That night we had the First Enthronement of the Sacred Heart at my house.

Vision - St. Peter in Chains - Before Mass

I told St. Margaret Mary how much I loved her. I had a vision of a nun to the left of the altar. She was wearing a dark habit with a white collar and in her hands was a white book. Then I thought, "Who is this, St. Therese?" I was trying to see her more clearly. I realized tonight the Enthronement of the Sacred Heart Book had a white cover. I think the nun was St. Margaret Mary. Just as I saw the vision my little son kissed me and told me he loved me. This was after the gospel while the priest was talking. I didn't look at my son because I was seeing a vision.

10/20/94

I Will Lead Your Every Step

Jesus: You savor the moments when I granted unto you My special graces, My dear, sweet child. How could I write to you all this time and you not hear My voice and know Me? My little child, go off in such a realm of intimate union with Me. It is the voice you hear now that I want you to hear, gentle and loving. My words are forever planted in the deepest parts of your heart. Though you did not comprehend what you received, your heart burst with this great love I gave you! In your heart you are overflowing with a cognitive awareness of My great presence, that compels you to speak, but how few want to listen!

Song: *Your Presence Pervades My Soul*

Jesus: My child, My love I pour out to you to lead others to Me. It is in your delivery many will be aware of My emotion and love for them. Be not anxious or perplexed. Your life unfolds and I will lead your every step. Pray hard for My beloved ones to be open in their hearts to the fire of My love. I love you so much. I write to you from the depths of My deepest love for you. I am God and I share My great love with you in this most intimate way.

My child, write that I may comfort you in your sorrow. I love you intently. I am Jesus, the Son of God and I have chosen you for this mission. I love you with the deepest love. Let go and dwell in Me. Do not act like the world. Live in constant love with Me. Every action will be an action rooted in our deep love. My presence pervades your being. I will not leave you. Your work is at hand to spread My love to My beloved ones. The picture of Our Hearts beating will constantly be in your heart. You will have, from this moment forward, a constant awareness of the love of the one, triune God. Be lost and wrapped totally in this love. It is this love and this love alone that will sustain you. You are called to holiness. Pray for sanctification from anything that keeps you from this intense union. Be unattached, constantly surrendering yourself to the will of the Father. My work is at hand. My day is set. Do not belabor any events in your mind. Focus always on the most intimate love with the Spirit. Let go. Surrender. I am your God. I bless you and I love you. Amen.   10/21/94

Abortion

Messenger: We are God's chosen children from the first moment of conception. The life in the Mother's womb is a life created by God. From the first moment it is conceived, it is a creation of the Father and He deems it to be alive. We are fooling around with the divine creation of God the Father if we, in any way, stop the child from being born. Only God can create a human life! No man can, in any way, take this life and destroy it without answering to God the Father.

The child in Elizabeth's womb leapt for joy at the presence of Jesus and Mary. He was God in the womb.

Jesus said to me, in a vision:

"These children are the chosen ones of My Father. You saw My Heart, the flowers were for the dead children that are dying. You are little flowers growing into a beautiful bouquet for My Father. Each moment of your life is a flower in the bouquet. You want your bouquet full of flowers that are beautiful, not half dead. When you sin, you are not growing into the beautiful flowers He wants you to be. Each moment is a flower. Will your bouquet be half-dead? Will your moments be as little petals you present to the Father, full of life and beauty?"

"Tell the little children to come to Me. Bring the children to church. Let them be in front of the tabernacle. I am the Way, the Truth, and the Life. Bring your children to church. Children need to be close to Me. I love My children - bring them to Me!"

To really know God is to love - every action that comes from you should be a result of His love within you.   10/21/94

Let Me Reign in Your Heart

Messenger: Make me like a little child. The most Sacred Heart of Jesus was formed in the womb of the Blessed Mother. His Sacred Heart was inside of her. I see the two Hearts. Jesus and Mary, as she holds the Child Jesus so lovingly.

To think of His most tender Heart in the body of a baby makes it seem so very much more tender. His Heart is the tenderest of all hearts. There was such union between Mary and Jesus from the first moment of conception. I see the two Hearts joined and beating in such love for us.

Jesus: I am your most Sacred Heart. Turn to the Child Jesus for your trials. I was present as God when I was a child.

Messenger: To see His most Sacred Heart in the Child Jesus' body. Such power and gentleness!

Jesus: I am the Light of the World. I shine in this world through you, My beloved children. Come to Me as little children. Come as a baby at the breast. Take shelter in the most tender Heart of the Child Jesus. I forever burn with the deepest love for you. When you see an image of My Mother and the Child, see Our Hearts beating as one in the most gentlest love for you. I came as a baby at the breast, so helpless. I ask you to come to Me as a baby at the breast, in total submission. I ask you to give yourself entirely to Me. Give your will and your life in total surrender to the Father, Son and Holy Spirit. Such freedom, such power!

Come My little children, to the ardent on-fire love of the Child Jesus. Take refuge in My Heart through My Mother. She carried Me in her womb. Enter into My Heart through her most pure and tender Heart. I was carried in her womb. I ask you to go through My Mother's Heart to My most precious, tender, loving Heart. My Heart was inside of the womb of My Mother. My Heart was beating inside of her.

I come to you this day in the Eucharist. I am no less present than when I was on earth. I enter your body as the Incarnate Son of God. What honor indeed I bestow on you, My beloved ones! I, Who am perfect love, come to you, My love. My Heart beats inside of My Body, no less than it beat in the womb of My Mother. My Heart is a human Heart belonging to the Son of God.

I am the Way. I am the Truth. I am the Life. I am Jesus, the Son of God, entering your body as I entered Mary's womb. Through the Father's great love for you, I am given to you. I give you Myself. Bread and wine are changed into My very Body and Blood. I, God, come into your heart to dwell.

I am Jesus, your most ardent love. I enter you, child. I love you. My

Heart beats in you. Let Me reign in your heart. Realize your specialness - that the Incarnate Son of God comes inside of you and dwells there. You are so special. You are My beloved. You are My chosen ones. I come to you. I come to you with the greatest love. I am your loving Savior. I am your God. I died for you. I come to you this day.

Song: *I Love You Jesus*   10/21/94

Between 12 - 3 p.m. I Heard Bells in the Priests' Residence Chapel

Messenger: God is love. How can we love God if we do not love one another? I do not know God if I do not love. If I know God and share truly in His divine Life, I must love.

Oh, God, how I love You! You are in the morning sun, the breath of fresh air. You are in the sun-lit morning. You are in all those things, created by You. You are in my brothers, in their smiles and in their eyes. You exist - You truly exist in this world this day. I am surrounded by Your presence. Your power and Your might surround me as I dwell on this earth. As I live and breathe, I breathe in life with the air You provide for me. I am connected to You at every second. There is not one second that I am not dependent on You for my existence.

Oh, blind men on this earth, it is indeed so clear to all who look! God is present and in our midst this day! He is alive and ever ready to provide us with every need. Yet, God, the Son of God, Who waits for the love of mere creatures, sits alone in both tabernacles here all morning! He is truly present, exposed or not. He is here and waiting our love. He writes the song He wants us to sing to Him. I scarce can breathe to be near to You, my God! This is the love He wants us to have. He is present. He is there. He is alive, and He knows our every thought and action. He is the love we all crave. He is truly here. Oh, my God, who am I that I sit in Your presence here. I sit and others do not even realize how You long for their love.

Jesus: Tell them, My child. I have commissioned you and Father to tell them of this great love I have. I am your most precious Savior. Truly, I died for you. Truly, I would die for them this day. You are My apostles to spread devotion to My most Sacred Heart and My Mother's Immaculate Heart. She tells you at every rosary, "I am the Immaculate Heart of Mary and I love all my precious children." This is your calling - to spread the love of these two Hearts.

See My Heart as beating and on-fire second-by-second. I never leave you. Promote the promises. Tell all to say them every day. It is through My most Sacred Heart you will be warmed in the coldest night. Take shelter from the wind, the rain, the cold, from pestilence, from every kind of affliction you may suffer. Find shelter in the dear, tender Heart of the Child Jesus. My Heart is on fire and waiting to exchange love with My beloved ones. They do not know how this Heart beats for them this very day.

Come to Me and I will lead you away into the realms of intimacy with Me - intense intimacy in My most Sacred Heart! I am the Heart of Jesus, on fire for love of you, My beloved ones!

Messenger: (How can I really know God and not love? He is Love!)

Song: *I Am Your Sacred Heart*

Messenger: The same day I had this vision.
This is the picture from my notebook.   10/21/94

Embryo

An Exterior Vision: I saw His
Heart on His chest, hands off to the side.
Messenger: I was praying (people
opened the door in the Priest's Resident
Chapel). I kept looking at the vision - a little child was in the heart, in the center. It could have been an embryo in a developed stage. His Heart was formed in the womb of His Mother. Rays were around the heart.

He said something about being a child. I was distracted by the open-ing of the door but I continued focusing on the vision.

I kept hearing the song, "when you are inside of Me", the song Jesus gave me.

I have been smelling faint smells of incense and roses at different times.

His presence pervades my soul. I love Him so much, it is He whom I seek! I want only Him. I love you so much, my precious love!

I feel such love for St. Margaret Mary. I had a vision of a nun at the Cathedral of St. Peter in Chains, she appeared to the left of the altar. She held a white book. My son kissed me during Mass, during the vision. I did not look away, I stayed focused on the vision. From this I have developed an intense love for St. Margaret Mary.

I do not want to leave the tabernacle. He says: "My presence is with you, take it forever with you in your heart! I give Myself to you in this special way. You are never without My deepest love. I dwell in you in deep union. Be lost in My love."

I always have trouble on Fridays between noon and 3pm. He wants me to cherish this time with Him. I love You Jesus. Jesus. Jesus!

All hope of life eternal comes through Christ crucified. Our hope of eternal life comes through His death and resurrection.

Make the sign of the cross, profess our faith in Him and our love of the Trinity. I love God!   10/21/94

He Knows All Things

Messenger: Jesus, how I love You! You know all things. You know I needed this. I open up Your Blue Book, any Blue Book and I find my answer. You know all things, the answers are always there. I open to any page and You direct me to what I need to know.

Jesus: I am Jesus, your Savior. I am He Who loves you and know all things. I write these letters to you this day, October 22. I tell you, with My deepest love for you, I am your Savior. I love you so. I died for you. I love you. I want you to know this love. I write these letters to you. Please hear Me speak to you, as you read each letter. Open the book anywhere and I will speak to you. I love you so much. Come to My Sacred Heart, through My loving Mother's Heart and I will give you rest. I fly your balloon. I lift you up in these love letters to you from Me.

Surrender, My dear child, to your most loving God. The beauty of surrender is to trust in Him who truly loves you!

"Feel the freedom of flying. You are totally free. I am running the balloon. You, child, let go. You totally surrender to Me and at first you are afraid, but here you are flying and it is such freedom! Take in the sights. Be lighted on you way. Do you trust Me like that? If you don't, you are still in control."

Note: January 18, 1994 - The preceding paragraph is a quote from God's Blue Book 2.

Messenger: In Vol. One of God's Blue Book, teachings to lift you up, the Holy Spirit prompted me to write about the cover of God's Blue Book, page 11.   10/22/94

I Will Never Forget You

Messenger: I looked at the beautiful fall trees and He said: "I will never forget you, My people." The old leaves fall off and the trees go into dormancy. New life will come soon in the spring. He guards our way. We are pruned, we are cut back. We have periods in which we feel a "dark night" of the soul. He will never forget us. The tree buds in the spring and burst forth into new life. He outpours His grace upon us and we bud forth into new life in Him.

Jesus: I will never forget you, My people, I have carved you in the palm of My hand. Even if a mother forget her child, know I never will forget you. It is in the cutting back that the new growth occurs. It is in this surrendering to Me, it is in dying to self, that you are born to new life. Even if a mother forsake her child, I will never abandon you. As the fall is so brilliant in its color, the winter moves in with its dark and dismal appearance, but the spring brings forth such life to My beloved chosen ones, for I have come to bring you new life that you may partake in My life abundantly. I am your Savior, Jesus Christ, Son of the Living God. I speak to you that you will preach My words to My most beloved children, who I love dearly. Hold not back My words to My most beloved ones. Through the power of the Holy Spirit, you will receive the courage to preach My words. In the highways and byways, wherever you are called upon to do My work. It is My work, you do. It is not of your own making. I summon you to this task. I am your Savior, Jesus Christ, your God

10/22/94

Thorns around His Heart

Messenger: If I think I have said anything unkind about anyone, it saddens me so badly. I don't want to ever hurt anybody He loves. God forgive me for all I do that is wrong and never enough, for all I do to justify myself or ignorantly do, that I should not have. I see Your Heart and I love You so much. I love You. I love You. I love You. Are the thorns around Your Heart for Your agonies to the Heart, suffered so because of Your great love for us, for all those who do not even care?

Oh, I am sorry, my Jesus, I love You so much. I love You, I love You. Father forgive me, I know not what I do. How I am trapped and do not realize I offend You! Oh, I love Your Heart!   10/22/94

This Will Be the Best Day of Your Life

Jesus: This will be the best day of your life. You will fall deeply in love with My Heart. I am He Who loves you dearly. You are accompanied by the angels and saints. All know you and love you. Come into the heavenly court and live in the love sent to you from heaven.

Come into My Most precious Heart and dwell forever in the abyss of My dear love for you.

(Looking at the Pieta): You turn to Me and you see Me held by My beloved Mother. I gave My life, My blood was spent, I hung in her arms, lifeless and without breath in My body. Where do you turn, My sweet and precious child? You turn to the Heart of your beloved Savior! My Heart beats endlessly with such love. I am always there, waiting with open arms to love you. Let go into My arms!

Meditate on My passion. Let go of your focus on yourselves. See Me as I stood by in all My trials. I fell under the cross, they poked Me, they pushed Me, but I remained in perfect peace with the weight of My cross laying on My back as I was on the ground. They poke you, Rita, they press from all sides, you remain at peace in My Heart! Go there and find refuge. It is in My Heart you know My love. It is in My Heart you know the love of the Father. I love you. The Father loves you. Father, Son, and Holy Spirit are one. As the Father has loved Me, so I have loved you! Take refuge in My Heart, the abyss of God's love. I come to you with greatest love, I am your loving Savior. Reach out to Me and do not fear, I want to be so close to you. Let go, Rita, let go and surrender. Your heart is hard and anxious. Only a heart of pure love can join to My Heart. It takes surrender.

If you are angry at any man, if you hold on to man to give you My abundant love, you are holding on -- release yourself, surrender to the Father, Son and Holy Spirit. Put yourself in the abyss of My love, My love is God's love. To know My love is to know the Father's love. To know My love is to know the Spirit's love. I am. God is. From My Heart flows grace and mercy. From the Father, in the Holy Spirit, through My Heart, from Mary's Heart to you.

Genesis 1:27
God created man in the image of himself, in the image of
God he created him, male and female he created them.

10/23/94

Spread These Messages

Messenger: He showed us the way, His way is perfect peace.

Jesus: I come to you with these letters and no one is listening. I speak
to Rita, I tell her these beautiful words of My Heart, you do not listen. I
want My messages to be heard. Souls will be lost. Time is so short. I, Jesus,
talk here and you are too busy to listen. What more do you want Me to
do to convince you to listen to Me. I am Jesus Christ the Son of God,
these messages are for My beloved ones. I beg you to spread these messages of My love. Why do you not listen when I speak? Pray for courage
to do the will of God. These messages need to circulate. I speak, you do
not listen. To silence Rita is to silence Me. If satan tries to get enough
people to doubt and satan makes enough confusion the messages are
stopped. Do you not see the trickery of satan's ways? Satan does not want
these messages of My love to circulate. I tell you so sweetly of My beloved
Heart. It is through My Heart -- you will ward off the devil. I tell you of
My Heart here. Who listens. It is through My Heart grace and mercy
flow. My Heart is a fountain of endless mercy. These are the messages of
My intense love given from My Heart. It is through My Mother's Heart
you will know My Heart more deeply. These messages need to circulate.
I come to you with greatest love, I am your loving Savior, I am your God,
I died for you, I come to you this day. If I died for you, why do you not see
how I come this day in these messages. I want My love letters to circulate
to My beloved children. I love them so tenderly. My Heart is ablaze and
on fire for them this very day. Who hears My messages? Do you listen? I,
Jesus, talk here and who listens. I am in your midst. I am truly present in
the tabernacle. Can you not wait one hour with Me? I am the Center of
your life. I am pouring out My love. Time is so short. I warn you, time will
come. I cry out in a loud voice to be heard.

10/24/94

I Am Your God, First and Always

Messenger: Does it matter where we lay our head when we die? We came into this world helplessly, we go out helplessly. God is in control. We go out when He decides. Our breath depends on Him. Our lives are fleeting. We are not in control. Why do we hold on to the things here and make them an end in themselves?

Jesus: I am the way, I am the truth, I am the life. Your destiny is to arrive at your true home in heaven. You are here to know, love and serve Me. You were created by Me to do My work. If you make yourselves and others your gods, you are missing the reason for your existence. I am love. My way is love. It is peace and harmony. My way leads to everlasting life. If you follow other roads, you may not get to your destination. Come and find refuge in My Heart. Let the light of My Heart lead your way. All graces flow from My Heart. My Heart will lead you to heaven, your home. Come through the door to My Heart and forever dwell with Me. I am your God, you shall not have any gods before Me!

Messenger: Did God mount a throne and come on the earth in glorious proclamation at His birth? Jesus is God. God the Father gave His Son. Jesus came a helpless little baby, born in a stable, laid in a manger. A helpless little baby! Jesus was born to show us the way in a little baby body. We were created in the image of God. Jesus gives us a special sharing in His life at baptism.

Oh, blessed Savior, how sweet You are to come and give so freely to us. You are love, You give Yourself, You give us love. You teach us Your ways, so sweetly, so lovingly. Jesus is our Savior. Jesus gives us His tender Heart. Through Him we are saved - He is our Savior. Sing Song

10/24/94

Reach Out

Messenger: I am the slave of His most Sacred Heart. It is through this most precious Heart, pierced with a lance, that all graces and mercies flow.

Jesus: I am the Sacred Heart of Jesus. I am forever present. I am in your midst this day. I was born a baby with My Heart on fire for love of you. I died for you. From My birth to My death, see this love I poured out to you. My Mother held Me in her outstretched arms at birth. I hung alone at My death. She held My lifeless body under the cross. This shows Our love for you! As I was held lifelessly under the cross, you meditate on this life given for you.

This is My life I give to you this day. I am the Bread of Life. He who eats My Flesh will never die. Death has no power over Me. I have died, but I have risen that you will have life and have it to the full.

Song: I come to you with greatest love. I am your loving Savior. I am your God. I died for you. I come to you this day.

Messenger: He comes to us this day, as He came as a baby in His Mother's womb. He tells us:

Song: Reach out to Me and do not fear. I want to be so close to you. I am your God, your precious One. I come to give you life!

Messenger: Reach out, it is in the reaching out, in the surrendering of ourselves in our entirety to Him that we grow in this union with Him. He outpours His grace to us. He wants us to reach out. He reached out. He held His arms outstretched and gave His all to us.

He is a fountain of endless mercy and grace, gained for us on the cross. From the Father, in the Holy Spirit, with His Mother under the cross. He comes to us in every Mass as this unbloody sacrifice and pours out His grace and mercy to us.

Oh, Savior, how great is Your love for us to give us Yourself in the Mass. How great the gift of our loving Father to give us Jesus, His Son, in the Holy Spirit, under the appearance of bread and wine. This is my loving Savior. This is how I see Him. Such love poured out to us in the Eucharist! Jesus, the Son of God! How I love Him!

I am in awe to behold Jesus with us this day in the Eucharist. He is truly the Son of God. He loves us and comes to us with this great love. If God is love, how can I not love you, whom He created and loves? Open my heart, Lord, to know and love all men as You do and see with Your eyes, Your compassion. Help me to know this world and all Your beloved creatures through the most Sacred Heart of Jesus.

I am a slave to Your most Sacred Heart, Lord, use me to promote this devotion to Your loving Heart!

John 14:14,18,21

If you ask me anything in my name,
I will do it.

I shall not leave you orphans;
I shall come to you.

Whoever holds to my commandments
   and keeps them
is the one who loves me;

and whoever loves me
  will be loved by my Father,
and I shall love him
and reveal myself to him.

Reach out to Me

Matthew 7:7
...knock, and the door will be opened to you.

Revelation 3:20
Look, I am standing at the door, knocking. If one of you hears me calling and opens the door, I will come in to share a meal at that person's side.

Messenger: "Feed the hungry". I heard this for six weeks. I saw doors. It is through His Heart we will be saved. Go through the door of His Heart to eternal Salvation!

Jesus: I am the Way, the Truth and the Life. If you enter into the abyss of My Heart, you will be saved. My Heart will ward off the devil. It is your protection from the evils of this world. Come to Me and know My Heart. It is through My most Sacred Heart all graces and mercies flow.

Messenger: All I want to do is to be wrapped endlessly in the fire of His love.

Jesus: I came into this world, a little baby. Mary walked My passion with Me, suffering for love of you. Always, total surrender to the Father's will. This is seen at My birth, this is seen as I lay in her arms under the cross. Mary and I both, always in total compliance to the Father's will.

Your peace and joy lie in doing God's will. Total surrender, your every breath depends on Me. Where do you think you are going in your busy, busy lives? The victory is won in doing the Father's will with love. In it lies your peace.

Song: *God's Love*   10/24/94

The Hungry Soul Craves Union with Me

Messenger: As a deer thirsts for water, my soul thirsts for You. Oh, Lord, You take me to the summit of Your love, then, My Lord, to the depths of doom my soul falls. Oh, Lord, rescue me from this pit and raise me to the most abundant love of Your Heart.

My soul thirsts for You, my Lord. It is for You and Your love I live. I live for You. My heart is longing and pining for the courts of the Lord. Oh, my Lord, to know You a little and never enough! My soul is so thirsty for only Your love.

To really know You is to want You. My soul thirsts for You ever more. I want You ever so closer my dear, dear, Lord!

Jesus: The hungry soul craves union with Me. It is drawn to Me as steel to the magnet. So you wander and roam and your soul feels empty. Only in My Heart do you find rest. Come to Me, go to My Mother, lay yourself in her arms. She cradles you in her Heart and brings you ever so gently to My Sacred Heart. Your soul is oh, so hungry, for only My love. I am your ardent love. I love you this way with My whole Heart on fire for you. My Heart burns for you, My child. Come to the endless source of love. My Heart knows the way. Follow My Heart and know My burning love.

Messenger: We enter His Heart, we are purified with His love. He beckons us to come and dwell deep in His Heart. He does not say that we must be perfect, He asks us to come as we are. He loves us despite all our faults, and longs for us to come in all our imperfections. But, as the impurities are burned away, we become changed as we dwell in His Heart. Purify me, Lord. I know You love me despite all my faults. I want to be wrapped in the abyss of Your love. Mold me and fashion me into the creation the Father intends me to be. Melt away my impurities in my heart with the fire of Your love.

From the depth of my soul I cried to Him and He heard my plea. He leads me ever so gently to His Sacred Heart. He took me as I am and I dwelt in the inner recesses of this most tender Heart.

Jesus: You are My chosen ones. I invite you this day to come and dwell deeply in My Heart. Put aside any anger and forgive all your brothers. As you release all your angry thoughts and forgive all your brothers, as you let go and release all your anxieties, you will experience My peace. I lead you to the sanctuary of My Heart, come and dwell with Me there in My love. Close your eyes and focus on My presence with you. See yourself placed in My Heart ever so gently by My beloved Mother, your loving Mother. Be wrapped in Our love. Let go of everything but My presence, and your dwelling in My warm and tender Heart. Relax your whole being and surrender all your cares to Me. Focus on the warmth and glowing light of My Heart; It surrounds you with My deepest love!

Song: *Little Baby Hands and Feet*   10/25/94

Behold His Tender, Baby Feet

Messenger: Behold His tender baby feet, so perfect, His sweet little hands, behold His feet pierced with the nails and His hands with the nails. He loves us so much. Mary beheld her baby child with such love in her arms. He is so perfect, the Child Jesus, the little child, so beautiful, so precious, His tender skin. Oh, what piercing thoughts she had when Simeon prophesied Jesus' and Mary's sufferings! Her joy to behold her beautiful baby, turned into such sadness to know He was to suffer!

Always in compliance to the will of the Father. Mary was asked to be the Mother of Jesus, she, as always, saying "yes" with such faith, always doing His will. See her tenderly holding her little child and feel her suffering to know a sword would pierce her Heart because of all He would suffer.

Oh, Jesus, You were born so perfect and beautiful, little hands and feet, perfect flesh, but You gave Your precious feet and hands for our salvation. The sword pierced Mary's Heart. The nails pierced Jesus' tender hands and feet. Oh, Jesus, You gave Your all, holding nothing back for love of us and complying to the Father's will! You showed us the way. You did the Father's will. Your Heart was pierced, Your hands and feet pierced. Mary carried all these things in her most loving heart. Her heart was pierced. His body was pierced. Jesus' and Mary's most tender love for us. Jesus and Mary always doing the will of the Father. They withstood this for us. They knew the Father's love. Jesus said, "as the Father has loved Me, so I have loved you." He loved us to His death. How He loves us this day, with the same great love! I behold the cross of Christ as the symbol of love given to us. The cross is love personified, love given from the Hearts of Jesus and Mary. His Heart was pierced with a lance, hers with a sword. From the five wounds of Christ we draw strength, from Jesus, our Savior. From Mary's pierced heart, I know her tender love, given as our most loving mother.

10/25/94

Petition to Jesus

Messenger: Help me, Lord, to let go of my self-focus so my heart is as a child. Pure and without grudges, to forgive those who have wronged me, and love the person with the love You want me to have for them.

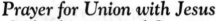

Create in me, oh Lord, a clean heart, so I hold on to Your love.

I want to be close to You, Lord. Help me to be lost in Your love, permeate my soul, help me to die to myself and live only as You want me to be, so I can unite with You in such oneness.

Lead me to the sanctuary of Your Heart so I know Your love ever more deeply.

I am Yours, Lord, create in me a heart likened to Yours, my beloved Savior. You who gave Your all for love of me. I give myself entirely to You.

Jesus: I am the potter, you are the clay.

Messenger: Mold me and fashion me, Lord.

Prayer for Union with Jesus

Come to me, Lord, and possess my soul. Come into my heart and permeate my soul. Help me to sit in silence with You and let You work in my heart.

I am Yours to possess. I am Yours to use. I want to be selfless and only exist in You. Help me to spoon out all that is me and be an empty vessel ready to be filled by You. Help me to die to myself and live only for You. Use me as You will. Let me never draw my attention back to myself. I only want to operate as You do, dwelling within me.

I am Yours, Lord. I want to have my life in You. I want to do the will of the Father. Give me the strength to put aside the world and let You operate my very being. Help me to act as You desire. Strengthen me against the distractions of the devil to take me from Your work.

When I worry, I have taken my focus off of You and placed it on myself. Help me not to give in to the promptings of others to change what in my heart You are making very clear to me. I worship You, I adore You and I love You. Come and dwell in me now.

-God's Blue Book, January 17, 1994
10/25/94

I Mother You

Mary: Let me cradle you in my arms, my sweet dear children, I am your most tender mother. I love you like a little child. I loved my little baby, Jesus. He was a child. I held Him - I kissed Him. Let me hold you. Let go of all your fears, anxieties, illnesses. I mother you like a little child. I am your beloved mother. Come and I will comfort you. Release yourself from cares of the body and this world. I cradle you in my most loving heart. Surrender and feel a release of everything that is holding you back.

I lay you ever so gently in the Heart of my beloved Son. His Heart is warm and glowing, ready for you. In the recesses of His Heart you are bathed in His most precious love. Let go totally. Feel God's presence with you. Hear the beating Heart of Jesus. Jesus' Heart rocks you into deepest rapture with Him. Release and let go to Jesus Who gave His life for you. Rapture and love from Jesus Who gives Himself to you this day, in greatest love!

Song: *A Song From Jesus*   10/27/94

Feel His Presence

Messenger: His presence pervades my soul, so much that I feel as if I can't write. I feel such oneness with Him, I feel such burning in my heart. I just want to stay here forever. I feel this feeling of peace and rapture. I scarce can breathe, I love You so, my God. I want to stay here and never leave I just want to be in this deep union with Him.

I felt His presence all through the Mass, I saw Him offer the Mass through the priest to the Father. I felt His presence so strongly. I could see His long brown hair and His most Sacred Heart. This brought me to such an overwhelming awareness of His presence. I felt His presence in the room, I felt His presence within me. (I still have such a burning awareness in my heart, I never want to leave.)

I feel His presence so intense at Mass and prayer afterwards. I am in such union with Jesus, such oneness. It is hard to explain. I know His presence so well, it is such an awesome feeling. I saw His brown hair, His vibrant Heart, His red garb and white tunic. He was so present to me. I feel Mary's presence with Him.

I keep hearing His song, I scarce can breathe when You come into me. I have such an interior awareness of His presence pervading my soul.

10/28/94

My Beloved Priests

Messenger: I scarce can breathe when You come into me, Lord. Help me to be drawn into a closer union with You, to let go of the perishable things of this world and be only as You want me to be, Lord. I am so weak and attached to many things. I want to please You and do Your will.

"I come to you with greatest love. I am your loving Savior. Reach out to Me and do not fear, I love you tenderly."

Oh, the ways of the heart, Lord. How You suffered so in the garden for all Your beloved ones that You loved so greatly and who treated You with such coldness. To be perfect love and be rejected by so many beloved souls, what agony You endured! I want to console Your Most precious Heart and tell You how I love You. Oh, Jesus, You are so sweet to me. Who am I that You care for me and come to me and live in me?

Jesus: I give to priests the power to forgive sins - many take this so lightly. I give them this power - do they thank Me for My great gifts to them? Such power I give - to change bread and wine into My precious Body and Blood, everyday at Mass. Such a gift from My Most loving Heart. From the Father, in the Spirit, such a gift and how many even think of how I favor them with this gift?

I am Jesus Christ, their beloved Savior. My special anointed ones do not know how it offends My Heart to be neglected by them. They are given such power and they do not even come and be with Me. Such love I have for them! Agonies of the heart, such agonies to love so dearly, to give so much and be rejected by My anointed ones! Oh, if they only came to Me, I would shower them with such love for their hearts and souls.

I am your special love. I come to you and give you Myself, no less present than the day I walked the earth, and who comes and spends time with Me? I am your beloved Savior. I gave My life for you, My beloved priests. I give you such gifts from the Father, in the Spirit, and you take God's gifts so lightly. How I suffered for your neglect and indifference.

Oh, beloved children of My Father, do you know this love I have for you? I come and give you Myself this very day and you treat Me so very coldly. Come to My Heart in the Blessed Sacrament and be with Me. Come and spend time in your home, alone with Me. Come from your sleep and be with Me.

Such sweet moments - our time together in the night! Do you remember My dear love I poured out to you in these most sacred hours? I want you to come, Rita, and be with Me. Such special moments with Me, your beloved One. I am forever with you with such love. I pour Myself out to you in the night. Come and be alone with Me in our Hearts. I love you so much. Nothing sustains the aching soul but My love. I long for you to come and be alone with Me. In the night you are totally attentive to Me. Come to Me and be with Me. Comfort My aching Heart. No one knows how My Heart suffered for love of My beloved ones. I am so neglected and forgotten. You see what makes you sad, the hours I sit alone in the tabernacle and no one comes, the way people are too busy to even think of Me. My holiest ones who have turned My Mass into such coldness and I, Who love with such fervent love, love their most cold hearts. Cold hearts surround Me. I remain with greatest love for you, My beloved souls, and who comes and gives Me a heart of real love? Very few hearts come and pour their love out to Me. I long for this, your love. I long for your time with Me. Console My aching Heart, My child. Come and give Me your deepest love. I want your love as I say in the song. I want you to come with such love you scarce can breathe.

Rita, Rita, do you know yet I speak to you? You are such a cold heart. I speak to you and you are ready to run back to your world for your love. I want to be so close to you. You do not comprehend what is transpiring here, My beloved one. I pour out such love to you and you are this little frightened child out in the rain looking for that which only I can give you. Come out of the rain and into My Heart. Totally surrender and let your life unfold as I make Myself known more and more to you. I want to take you to the inner sanctuaries of My Heart. I want you to dwell there in such union. You keep yourself at a distance from Me.

Your world is not the answer. My Heart is your answer. Let go, let go, let go. Be so wrapped in My love. You stand on the outskirts, looking in. I give you My grace. With Me, you are not alone. I never ever leave you. Be attentive at every second to My most intimate presence within you. You offend My Heart. You, whom I talk to, you doubt and run to others for what I want to give you. My child, I love you so much. Do you hear Me? Don't check out My story here any more. Be lost in My deepest love. I give this to you. Come and dwell deeply in My Heart through Mary's Heart. It is in this dwelling that your peace lies. Say the prayer for union with Me.

Song: *Your Presence Pervades My Soul*

10/29/94 -2:15 a.m. -Saturday

Your Presence Pervades My Soul

Messenger: The song, Your Presence, is constantly going through my mind.

Oh, God, my God, how I love You and long for You! How I am so in awe that You love me, little me, with such love! No matter what, You love me, I am the creation of the Father. I do not deserve this love that You give me. I love You so much, Mary, the Father and Holy Spirit. I cry because I love God so much. I scarce can breathe when Jesus is inside of me in the Eucharist.

Song: *I Love You Jesus*

Messenger: I saw Your Heart, all open and on fire, all the way over to Mass and all through the Mass: red on the outside, yellow, bright and brilliant and open, inside. I see it before me as a constant presence in my heart. Yesterday I saw Your brown hair. Today I see this beautiful Heart, all aglow and so open, open with the intense fire of Your love, for me, for each soul. You beckon us to come in and dwell deeply in the open Heart, to be protected from everything, to be lost in the great sea of Your love. Oh, Jesus, how I love You, my beloved! You love me. You loved me to Your death on the cross. You always love me. The love of Your Heart pervades my soul. I smelled roses when I went to communion. My beloved Mother is ready with her Heart to cradle me and take me to her most precious Son.   10/29/94 - After Communion - 11:30 Mass

Give Me a Baby's Heart

Messenger: This is why my heart is not like a baby. I thought I forgot about past hurts, but I must let go of wounds of the heart and still love everyone to have a pure heart like a child. Hurts in my heart have to go, I must forgive. I now release and forgive past hurts. Give me a baby's heart, one filled with love. Help me to forgive everyone.

Create in me a clean heart, a baby's heart. I know love as imperfect creatures loved me. I must know love as God loves me. He is perfect love!

Help me to know Your love, Lord, and let go of hurts inflicted on me by imperfect others. Help me to know Your unfathomable love in my heart. I block the flow of Your love to my heart when I am angry and unloving to others, when I harbor hatred and unforgiveness. Teach me, Lord, Your love, given in abundance and unconditionally. Give me a heart that is pure and holy. Little babies have pure hearts. Let my heart be like Yours, God. I want a heart that loves and trusts. I want to let go and trust You, Lord.   10/29/94

Mass St. Gertrude's

Note:
Messenger: There was a glow on the left side of the priest during the consecration. There was no mistake, it would leave and then come back. I wanted to write, I had my small purse, but no pen. There was a pen in the pew. I was in the first pew (what are the chances of that happening. There are no coincidences). My heart was beating fast when the Mass started.   10/29/94 - 11:30

Two Faces

Messenger: Two faces: the child Jesus, the face of Jesus on Veronica's cloth. Always, a heart of pure love. To His bloody death, He loved. His Heart, ever pure and filled with perfect love. Give to me, Lord, a heart that is pure like Yours. Lead me, Lord, into the inner recesses of Your most Sacred Heart through Your loving Mother's Heart. Help me to let go of preconceived ideas about love that are not like You and learn to love through the tender, motherly heart of Mary.

Create in me, Lord, the heart of a child, pure and free of hurt and grudges, only full of trust and love.

Mark 10:15

In truth I tell you, anyone who does not welcome the kingdom of God like a little child will never enter it.

Teach me the ways of a pure heart. Give to me a pure heart. A heart of love and purity, a trusting heart. Help me to be dependent on You. God, my God, I surrender my heart to You. Remove all hurts, all rubbish, empty my heart and place it in Your burning Heart, Your Sacred Heart. Purify me and make me holy, oh Spirit. Father, let me feel Your deep love through Mary's gentle and loving Heart. I pray for this most pure and tender heart, surrounded by Your love.   10/29/94

See the God Who Is Alive and Surrounds You

Messenger: Create in me a clean heart, where there is anger sow love, where I am in need of cleaning, take away all hurts of my life from childhood to the present day.

I love You so much, Jesus. You loved those who tore Your flesh and nailed You to the cross, always love. Teach me, Mary, to love always with Your pure Heart. Where there is any ill will, wash it away and give me a heart likened to Yours.

I love You, Jesus, with all my heart. I want to be forever united to You with such great love.

Jesus: Let go, My child. It is an act of the will to die totally to the self. Be docile in your actions, always being led by the Spirit. Your heart knows the way to follow My lead. Let go of yourself.

Live for love of Me. Live to love your brothers for Me. Pray to the Spirit to remove the blinders from your eyes so you will see as God allows you to see. Forever praise, love and honor God. If your heart is forever lifted high to God, it will act as He wills you to act.

Open your eyes and look at your brother, look at your world, look to your children. See the God Who is alive and surrounds you. Will you look up or will you look down? Look up to praise God, forever a song of love and joy on your lips for the God Who created you and all things and sustains you and gives you exactly as you need. Live each moment as a flower you are growing for your Father, always in love, always with thoughts of pleasing Him.

I want to live and dwell in your heart. I want to operate in your being. I want to love through you. You must be docile and allow Me to do My work in you. As a deer longs for water, seek out the Lord in all things. You are thirsty for the Lord Who loves you and holds you so dear! I am Jesus, My child, forever fix your eyes upward to your beloved Father. Through the Spirit you are led to the greatest union with God. Mary will lead you to such intimacy with Me. Dwell forever in the great abyss of My most Sacred Heart. It is there I will forever protect you from all kinds of weather.

I am the Sacred Heart of Jesus, come and let Me dwell in you. Live in My Heart. I love you so. You see the Heart, open and on fire with the deepest love. Go and be lost in My Heart. I am your Jesus. I show you this Heart to draw you and others closer to Me. Come to the great furnace of My love. There is shelter and love waiting for you in My Heart and I want to dwell in you.

Let go, let go, and experience the beating of My Heart, on fire for love of you. I love you so much, My dear, dear children. Do not look to the world for your needs, come and dwell in My Heart. I am waiting to be so joined to you. I love you so much.   10/30/94

I Am the Bread of Life

Jesus: Little one, creation of My dear Father, if you knew the Father and His great love you would love yourself. The Father is love. He created you. He gave you life. This very day it is the air you breathe that keeps this life existing. He wants you to be. You exist, God loves you so much.

See My lifeless body under My cross in the arms of My beloved Mother. You see the Father's love poured out to you. He sent Me into the world. See Me under My cross, not a breath in My body. My dear ones, I gave the last beat of My Heart, I chose to die for you. See My beloved Mother, your Mother under My cross. She suffered so, always walking by My side. Mary believed, Mary suffered for love of you.

Oh, dear and beloved child, listen when I speak to you. You were conceived in the womb of your mother, you are loved with the greatest love. The Father loves you and gave you life and gives you life now. He gave you your life. It is in baptism you have special sharing in My life. Life: I died to give you life! I give you Myself today in the Eucharist! I am the bread of life. I come to you and dwell in you.

John 6:51
I am the living bread which has come down from heaven.
Anyone who eats this bread will live for ever; and the bread that
I shall give is my flesh, for the life of the world.

Jesus: What dignity for you that you are given My very own body and blood in the Eucharist. God comes to you and you receive Him.

Song: *I Am the Bread of Life*

Jesus: Dignity, honor, love, I pour out to you. I show you an open Heart, filled with such intense love of yellow and white flames. Tell all to come and dwell in My Heart, come and be lost in the beloved Heart of My Mother, let her carry you to the inner sanctuaries of My Heart.

Oh, dear one, the Father has so much to share with you. Embrace Him forever in love. This is reality. I died, I have risen. I give you life in abundance this very day. Come to the Eucharist and the Tabernacle for My life. I am the bread of life.

John 6: 51
I am the living bread which has come down from heaven.
Anyone who eats this bread will live for ever...

Jesus: My Heart is an open furnace of love given for you. Come and be alone with Me, the Father and the Holy Spirit. If the world rejects you, you will find strength in My love.

My Heart is your sign. It is open for you. It is wide open. Live for My love. Die to yourself. Live in Me. Do not worry what other's think, you live to draw yourself closer to My love.

Jump into the abyss of My love through My Mother's Heart. Live to love. To love Me is to give of yourself. I am watching you. Pick yourself up and learn this lesson. It is in dying to self that you will love.

Messenger: The Father created me, so special. Jesus gave His life for me. I must realize this love to give love. Jesus, please help me to have a pure heart rooted in the Father's love. I love You so much. All I want to do is be with You. I love You so much - You know what I need this day to grow in Your love.

Jesus: But, My child, I call out to you to love. I give you My love to share. I want you to be My apostles to spread the love of My most Sacred Heart. Love for Me. You are My hands. You are My feet. You are My Heart to this world. Love and tell them of My Heart of fire. As I give My love, so sweetly to you, I ask you to give this same sweet love to all. I pour My open Heart out to you. It is open and on fire. Pour My love out to your brothers. I live in them. To love Me is to love one another.

"Create in me a Pure Heart, Oh Lord"
Song: *Teach Me to Love with Your Heart*
Song: *I am Your Sacred Heart*   10/30/94

October 31, 1994

Note: **Messenger:** I prayed the rosary at 6:30 at the grotto at the Center because of the smell from work being done in the chapel. It was a beautiful day. I started to cry through the Agony in the Garden because of sufferings in the early morning. I am so connected to His Heart since I saw the open Heart today and how He suffered for all the neglect and how many neglect Him this day, and how He loves them so much! It was very intense, but joyful. I love Him so much. I know how much He loves everyone and how they neglect Him. I couldn't explain the immense sorrow. Mary's statue lit up, especially at the end, and her face looked very alive to me.

(add: I saw Mary's face, then it changed to Jesus' profile! I then saw a lot of people, they were the Apostles and Saints. Marty also saw the vision.)
10/31/94 - Evening

You Are a Child of God!

Jesus: What you are is a child of God. Do not stop and think and focus on your hurts by your mother or father, by anyone you wanted to love you. See yourself as a child, created by God, the Father, with dignity, honor and abundant love.

You are My child. Mary is Your Mother forever by your side. You are a child of God. Forget all your past hurts and see yourself born this day with the heart God the Father created for you, so pure, so loving, so full of dignity to be God's beloved child! In baptism you receive a special sharing in My life. You are created in My own image and likeness. You are a child of God.

Be a child, pure in your heart, free of hurts and anger and realize your specialness to be created uniquely by God the Father. You are God's child. You are God's precious one. You are the child I shed My blood for. You are the child My Mother suffered for. She appears now, she cries out to you as the most loving Mother "come home to the Heart of my Son, on fire for love of you, through my Immaculate Heart. I place you deeply into the furnace of Jesus' love!"

Messenger: Close your eyes and see yourself, this little child, the son or daughter of the Father. You have a Divine lineage, you are heirs to His Kingdom. Close your eyes and be lost in God's love.   11/1/94

Return to the Heart of a Child

Jesus: Do you want to love Me? Then I call you to purity. Your heart must be so pure. Return to the heart of a child. A child has a heart that forgives and is ready to love. A child does not remember hurts and grudges, a child loves. Unless you become like little children, you shall not enter the kingdom of heaven!

Be as the saints, you are My saints this day in this world. I call you to love. To love God with your whole soul. I call you to love your neighbor as yourself. Child, to My death on the cross I loved those who persecuted Me. I call you to this love, to pray for your enemies, to love those who give you the greatest trouble.

If you want to love Me, your heart must be pure. Any willful taint of hate and anger in your heart blocks your closeness with Me. See, My beloved ones, God with an open heart on fire for love of you. The fire is ever ablaze, it is ever loving, it is bellowing, it is love from God Himself, Who is love. Why hold on to grudges with mere men when I, Jesus Christ, the Son of God, wait for you with My open Heart of love. I love you so this day that I would suffer and die for you. Put on Christ in all your actions. I showed you the way. You were created in the image and likeness of God. Would I hate your brothers? My way is peace, My way is love, My way is the way I show you in My life. Live the rosary in your life. Live the lives of Jesus and Mary in the rosary. There is such intimacy in Our lives and Our Hearts.

She suffered so for love of you! She calls you this day to return to a pure heart, a heart that was made for loving. When you were baptized you were born into new life—the life of sanctifying grace. You partake in the Divine life in a special way when you remain in the state of grace. Live as I showed you the way. Always love, My dear children. I call you to a heart full of My love for one another. Our union together depends on your ability to let go. Let go and live in Me.

Come to Me in the Eucharist, the Sacrament of My greatest love. I pour out Myself to you. I give Myself to you. Devotion to My Heart leads you to the Eucharist. I love you so much. Come to Me, be one with Me, see Me in your brothers. I call you to live in Me. I call you to be Christ to one another. I call you to Love. Pray the Our Father.   11/1/94

November 1, 1994

Jesus: You are My special apostles to spread the love of My most Sacred Heart. Do not take this job lightly. I give you this day your arms for battle. They are your hearts filled with My love. Come to the Eucharist, come to the tabernacle and be filled with My love. I am the Sacred Heart of Jesus. My Heart is open and waiting to share My love with you. Make up to My Heart for all the indifference shown to Me. Come to My Sacrament of greatest love and give Me your love. 11/1/94

I Beg You to Take Me Seriously

(**Messenger:** Awakened with cramps in my feet and didn't want to get up, but He wanted me to rise. It is 4:00 a.m.)

Messenger: Oh Jesus, I do love You. Please give me all you want me to do and help me to not be distracted by satan.

Jesus: Do you realize that men's souls are at stake? Do you realize I am giving you these letters? You take My work so lightly. Be committed to this. Will you ever let go so we can be about our union? You fight this union, you still do not want to believe with all your heart that I have called you here to write. I called you and I will continue to knock. Pray for strength to forget the world and focus on the souls that will be lost if you do not help Me with these letters. I call you, you write, half-asleep and want only to go back to bed. It is All Souls Day, pray for the poor souls. I beg you to preach My ardent love. Preach, preach, sing the songs, record the songs today. I want them to circulate. I am the Savior, I am Jesus, Son of the Living God, I am He Who intently loves you! Come and love Me this moment. Forget the world, release yourself into My hands. Total surrender to Him Who loves you.

Messenger: My God, My God, give me all I need to be drawn into this union with You.

Jesus: You are fighting everything. See My Heart, focus on My love, I love you so much!

Agony of all agonies, the agony I suffered from those I love and how they would reject Me, how they are so cold in their hearts. They refuse My love, they refuse My grace, they refuse Me. I am your Savior. I died that you would have life abundantly. Then, to be ignored after I give you My life. Oh, do you know the ways of this Heart?

Do you see the Heart I show you? Always have this Heart in front of your face, it is your link to this deep union with Me. Focus on My immense love and the love and presence of My Mother. Focus on My presence. Did I look like this statue? I gift you so abundantly, yet you run to others to be validated. How your lack of faith tears at My Heart and makes it bleed. Oh, you, My favored child, when will you come and dwell and live forever in My Heart? I call you to surrender.

Messenger: I recognize the face on this Sacred Heart statue in the den as the same face I saw in the grotto, but this one is in color. I recognize the Heart as the Heart in the vision.

Jesus: If the world hates you, you know My love - live for Me and to promote the devotion to My most Sacred Heart. Lead people to Me

through the Eucharist and the tabernacle - this is the Sacrament of My
greatest love.   11/2/94

"This Is My Body"

Messenger: I recognize the face on this Sacred Heart statue in the den
as the same face I saw in the grotto, but this one is in color. I recognize
the Heart as the Heart in the vision.

Jesus: If the world hates you, you know My love - live for Me and to
promote the devotion to My most Sacred Heart. Lead people to Me
through the Eucharist and the tabernacle - this is the Sacrament of My
greatest love.

Messenger: I can see the face on the grotto any time I want, it is on
this statue here in the study and so is the Heart.

Notes: On September 3 I heard "This is My Body, This is My Blood."
I couldn't look at Mary's statue. He lets me experience some of her emotions.

"I am aware of all of the souls that will be lost because they do not
know His love."

"The world stands still, I am on the other side". Read September 3.
So good - read it, again and again. This is reality to me, seeing this stat-
ue of Jesus, Jesus nailed to the cross, the pieta, the agony, and Jesus in the
Sacred Heart picture in the mirror.   11/2/94

He Truly Gave His Life for Us

Messenger: I see His hands and His feet pierced with nails, His head
punctured. This is Love! (when I was awakened with cramps this morning, I thought of someone putting a nail through my foot!)

Jesus truly gave His life for us. I will take the lead with the cold hearts
that do not hear His plaintiff cry, that He loves us so much. I go to the
world for love, I go to the world for validation of these letters and day
after day He opens up to me such insights into His love I miss the deep
love, the dwelling in His Heart as I hold on to this world. He is my refuge,

He is my strength. He writes these letters to all souls and cries out His dearest, tenderest love and who hears? These are His words to me to you. Oh, I who write do not pay attention as I should in these letters. The love He pours out in these words. I have a cold heart. That is why He shows me this, His most magnificent Heart, bulging over in intense whites and yellows, as open. He gives to us His most open Heart.

Jesus: Come, My little ones and dwell deeply in the recesses of My Heart. My blood I spent for you. My hands and feet were pierced, they numbered all My bones and I give these letters of My intense love for you. I died for you, why would I write a letter of such intense love?

I am your Jesus. Please harken to My calls of love to spread these letters swiftly, for souls will be lost for not obeying Me. My love I pour out here. My Heart I give as a symbol of this great love. Take refuge in My most loving Sacred Heart.

Messenger: To You, oh Lord, I lift up my soul. Why do I worry about what anyone thinks? I live to spread His love. He writes here and begs me to spread this love. I love You so, my God!

Wake the dead, to the fact that Jesus truly gave His life for us! I am so blind. He writes over and over again of His love. I am but a little child that needs God's grace to see more His love. Wake the dead, Oh how cold is my heart! He shows me the big heart, this puts in perspective how little I know His immense love! I know so little!! I thirst for so much more. I thirst and hunger for You, my Lord. My hungry soul cries out for Your love. I know so little of the magnitude of this love. Wake the dead to His most precious Sacred Heart. Read the promises, for fervent hearts shall quickly mount to the highest perfection. Oh, Sacred Heart, make my heart ever more fervent in Your love.

Jesus: This emotion I impart to you, My dearest daughter. I felt such anguish in the garden, I sweat blood. Your heart cries, it is one with My Heart. I am life. Life is active. Life is sensitive. Life responds. Feelings of the heart -- My Heart is beating with greatest love this day, this moment. I love you so much, dear one, I love you.

Messenger: It is my sensitivity to His Heart that suffers when I focus on myself and what others think. Create in me, oh Lord, a heart to serve You!

I can see Jesus looking at me and I run to the world for recognition and He patiently sits and tells me how He loves me and I look for momentary gratification! I don't want to offend Him anymore by going to others for recognition. See His Heart overflowing. He is God, the hairs of my head are numbered and He is always watching.

It is not in the signs and symbols, it is in this interior awareness and oneness with Him that I know Him deeper. I do not need to have anyone believe me. I need to live for His love. Mary draws me so close to His Heart and leads me with such intimacy to Jesus. I don't have to worry who likes me, who is looking at me, all I have to do is love and please Jesus. I am free.

Jesus: Surrender to Me, let go totally into My arms.

Messenger: I don't have to worry about what anybody thinks of me. All I have to do is try to love Jesus and ask myself if I am pleasing Him.

Mark 10:15
In truth I tell you, anyone who does not welcome the kingdom of God like a little child will never enter it.

Babies do not worry if they are impressing anyone. They just are. We should be as children and live in Him. Be so united to Him, to live in His love, to give His love, to be as He lives in us. All I have to do is live as He lives in me.

Jesus is watching me. I have to act as He wants me to. I have to please Him with my actions and don't have to judge my brothers in their actions. I must always love.

We must try to act as He wants, likened to Him. In all our actions we must put on Christ. The more we are united to Him in the Eucharist we become more one with Him in our lives.   11/2/94

A Flower I Give to My Father

Messenger: I live each moment to do my Father's will with love. Each moment comes and goes. I want each moment to be a flower I give to the Father when I see Him. How was this moment spent? If it is as He wants me to spend it, it is a beautiful flower for His bouquet.

I am your child, Father. I live to please You and You alone. As a little child tries so hard to do what their father asks them to do, with such fervor, Father to You I lift up my soul. I want this moment to be spent trying to please You. I want my moments to be beautiful flowers in my bouquet of life to give to You when I see Your face. I must live to please the Father, to please Jesus and the Holy Spirit, with my Mother as the tenderest motherly guide. To You, oh Lord, I lift my soul. If I am pleasing You, I am giving Your love to my brothers.   11/3/94

Live in the Moment

From a Lenten Homily given by Father Carter:

Today's Gospel in its story certainly points ahead to Jesus in His Passion and death. And as we read passages such as this during the Lenten season, we are reminded once again that the Church in her Liturgy of the Word gives us an opportunity to undergo a purification, an ever deepening cleansing of ourselves so that we may be a more fit instrument for receiving the great graces which are to be given to us at the time of the Resurrection memorial on Easter.

And so all in all, Lent is a time of purification to prepare us for ever-greater gifts of the Lord. It's a time of self-discipline, a time to renew our efforts to be self-disciplined in the service of the Lord. Self-discipline is an aspect of purification. And I suggest that one of the most difficult acts of self-discipline in the spiritual journey is to concentrate on the present moment.

We have a very strong tendency to disregard the importance of the present moment by focusing in a wrong way on the past or in a wrong way on the future. There are proper occasions for thinking of the past and the future. For example, we have to learn from the past and we have to prepare for the future, but our great emphasis has to be upon the present.

There is a Latin axiom which says, age quod agis, age quod agis, which means: do what you are doing, concentrate on the present. And of course we are familiar with that term in the history of spirituality: the sacrament of the present moment.

And so the discipline of Lent certainly encourages us to include in a deeper self-discipline a greater determination to get as much as we can out of the present moment.

People with a terminal illness have an opportunity as they prepare for death for increased prayer, contrition, love of God. However, some are taken very, very quickly. But for those who have the opportunity of knowing with some certainty the time of their death, I'm sure as they look back on their lives, they are saddened by the many times they did not use time and opportunities for the service of the Lord properly, and are overjoyed at those times in which they did use the present opportunity properly.

A great means we have of living in the present properly is a greater focus upon our Lord. For if I have that awareness of the fact I am united with Jesus here and now, why should I be concerned so much about the future or the past? Yes, a great help in living in the present and deriving all the good we can from it for ourselves and others is an ever greater focus upon Jesus, because the more I focus upon Jesus and the more I live with Him in the present moment, the more I am satisfied with the present moment.

And so let us in our Lenten activity resolve to grow in that self-discipline - which is very difficult at times - to really live in the presence with the fullness of our being as much as is possible, with the help of God's grace. Now is the day of salvation. Now is the day of salvation.

3/24/00

Love Your Brothers as I Have Loved You

See Note: November 4, 1994 about this message

Jesus: I am watching you at the Center. My Heart is an endless furnace of love. I am waiting for your time with Me. I love you each so dearly. Your soul craves My love, but I sit alone and you complain about one another. I love you with an open Heart that is ablaze for love of you. Each child there, I love with the tenderest Heart. I died for each person, I would suffer and die for you this day. My Father created each child His special and loving child. You are a child of God! You are so loved. My Father gave you Me for love of you. The Holy Spirit loves you so intently and wants to give you such love. Love on fire! He wants to lead you to such great love of Me and My Father.

My beloved Mother, who suffered so for love of you, who stood by Me and shared in My Life, appears as Our Lady of Light to light your way to the love of her precious Son. She, who suffered and experienced joy with Me, she who from a young girl to an old woman knew the love of My Heart for you, appears to lead you to such love with My Sacred Heart. She wants you to come to her pure Heart and let her place you deeply in My Heart.

My dear children, loved by My Father and My Mother, let the Spirit sanctify you, let go and be led to the most Sacred Heart of Jesus. I am as present this day as the day I died on the cross. I am present in the Eucharist in My Divinity and humanity. I am waiting for you in the tabernacle. I am waiting to give you My love. I pour Myself out to you.

You go into battle with your hearts filled with My love. I watch you battle everyday this spiritual battle. I cry out to you to return to holiness. I cry out to you to realize the divine love I pour out to you. Come back to love. Make Me the very center of your life. You will not light your city with hearts that are angry. It is only by the love of God that you will light your city. Come to the burning Heart of Jesus. Come to Him for your love.

I am the Sacred Heart of Jesus. I suffered so for those who neglect Me and My most precious love. I pour out to you Myself. I love you no less than the day I died.

Open your hearts to be hearts that are pure. Rid yourself of all hate and anger toward your brothers. Come from a heart that is pure. You cannot love Me if you do not love your brother, all your brothers. Look to your brother for the Jesus that lives in them. You must love every person. I command you to love God with your whole heart, your whole mind and your whole soul. I command you to love your neighbor as yourself.

I gave the last beat of My Heart for your brother. I live in your brother. Your Father created your brother. How can you say you love Me when you do not love your brother? I am in your brother, I love you all. I watch each of you. I love each of you and many times you hate one another. You are often divided because you are not coming to Me for your strength. You need to operate from love. Love one another. I watch you hate one another and then tell yourself you love Me. I love each person. You cannot light your city without the love of God alive in your hearts. To love God you must love your brother. To love your brother, pray to realize My love for you. Pray for grace. Pray for one another. Say the Morning Offering. You are the city of My love. Love gives, love is kind, love is compassionate, love finds its roots in the Eucharistic Christ.

Come to Me and I will pour My Heart out to you. These are the letters of My true love I pour out to you. I died for you. Why do you not think I would send you a letter of My love for you? I love you — these words are My love letters to you! These messages are My instructions for holiness and love of one another. Love one another as you realize My immense love for you. I talk directly to you and profess My deepest love. I give you songs of My greatest love. LOVE is active, LOVE is from the heart. LOVE is rooted in a pure heart. You cannot hate one person and love Me. LOVE is kind, LOVE is seeing Me in your brother. This is the mighty medicine to light your city of love. Your children are sick and need this medicine. I beg you to circulate these messages. I talk to you every day and give you your answers, so sweetly given. My Heart is as Rita sees a heart open and burning with intense white and yellow flames. I came in the grotto to show you I am united with Mary to spread My intense love. I am Jesus, Son of the Living God, these messages need to be circulated. I am sending you these love letters daily. I beg you to listen to Me, it is in these letters you will unite in My love.   11/3/94

I Want to Use You, Surrender

Messenger: My heart knows You dearly, my most precious Lord.

Jesus: I am your Savior, the Son of God. I come to you with greatest love, love for you, My chosen one. I love you to come from your sleep and write My messages of love for everyone. I call you to surrender. Do not hold onto anything. I am leading you into the desert, but you will not fear, for I will walk with you and I will carry all your supplies for the journey. I am God. I know all things. I know your needs. You never want because I supply you with everything.

Let go into My arms. Let Me walk with you. Let Me talk for you. Let Me be in you. As a deer seeks water, seek only My face. My face will forever by with you. You will know My presence more and more and I will forever sustain you.

Oh, you, My little worker, the harvest is plenty, the laborers are few, but at My hands the laborers are mighty. One worker rooted totally in Me can do mighty work. You must let go totally into My most loving Heart. I never go from you! Your problems are mere obstacles when you realize God is forever with you. I will move the obstacles. It may seem tense at times, but you do not get tense because you forever trust in My all-abiding Presence with you! I will operate you. You will do only My work. Surrender your whole being. I never ever leave you for one second!

I want to operate you. I want to use you. I want to possess your soul. I am Jesus, the Son of the Living God. Harken to Me, My precious child. I go before you and pave the way. Dark days are coming for this world . Pray constantly for your brothers that their hearts are turned toward Me. It is your prayers that will help many to turn from their ways. Do not worry for the things of this world. I will operate in you. You must surrender and be selfless.   11/3/1994 - 4:45 a.m.

I Am Here this Moment

Jesus: My child, do not worry for any details in your life. Love your children, they need you. I am the Sacred Heart of Jesus, as you go through each day I walk with you with such love. I am here this moment. Close your eyes and focus on My presence and the presence of the Father and Holy Spirit within you.   11/4/94

Note about the
November 3, 1994 Message

Messenger: The priest at the Holy Spirit Center told me to duplicate November 3 message and he would pass it out. He talked about the plan unfolding -- in front of the whole church Friday night he said the message was from me. He said Fr. Carter was very important to the plan that would unfold.

They sold the video -- the messages from Jesus video of mine April 17, 1994 in the bookstore.

The priest was about to put out the message May 4, 1994 -- FINALLY -- at the Falmouth Farm.

This message caused the split between Shepherds of Christ and the Holy Spirit Center and Falmouth Farm because they would not put it out.

Fr. Carter told them to put it out -- They asked him in May, but somebody took the message of mine from Jesus, May 4, 1994, off the handout at the Falmouth Farm.

That started the big split and the people there became very divided Jesus said from not getting the Blue Books. Finally the priest at the Holy Spirit Center did put this message May 4, 1994 out on the Falmouth Farm -- so many months later.

I include the message here.

May 4, 1994 - 4:30 a.m. - I Call You to Holiness

Jesus: Dear ones, I am calling you to love your brothers. I have loved you. Would you, dear ones, lay down your lives for your brothers? How are you loving this day? Are you following Christ in your actions? I am the Way, I am the Truth, I am the Life. You must constantly put the world aside and look to the Master for all your directions. I call you, My little ones, to holiness. I call you to pure hearts, hearts that are full of love and empty of hate and anger. I call you to guard your hearts and watch that they stay forever holy. You, My precious bride, I want your soul white.

Do you criticize your dear brothers? I gave the last beat of My Heart and the last drop of My blood for the soul you are displeased with. I would die for them this day. Will you not love them for Me? They are so precious to Me!

Quit sizing up your brothers. You do such unloving things in your mind. You do not even know how unloving are your thoughts. You judge your brothers by their exteriors, by their education, by their money. You do not see the beautiful creation of God the Father. He created your brothers just perfectly and He loves His creation. Who are you to criticize His creation? Love your brothers when they are hurting. It is in your loving the hurting ones that they will see the reflection of Christ in you.

Do not hold on to foolish things. One moment and your days on this earth have ended. All that remains is how you loved. Did you love God? Did you love your neighbor? Love is not selfish. It gives of itself. Its whole purpose is to draw the other closer to Jesus.

Study the crucifix. It is such a comfort! I loved you so. I died for you. I would die for you alone this very day, little ones! Look at Me dying on the cross! The way to Me is to follow Me. Be Christ-like in your ways. You must study Me to know My ways. Do not give in to yourselves. My way is love. Will you be the reflection of the love of God within you? My way is the way of the cross. They persecuted Me, they hurt Me, they tore My flesh and spit on Me. They did this to Me for My love given to all! This world is not your end. You follow My ways and you move as you should toward your goal.

I am Jesus, I am the Son of God. I love you so ardently. I died and shed My blood, My beautiful blood, for love of you. I await you this day, My little ones. I loved you so I remain with you in the Eucharist. I await, I long for you to come and share in our love. I am the tenderest of Hearts. No man can be close to you as I. I love you so. I want to dwell and live within you. I want to fill you with all My love and radiate My love to your beloved brothers. I want to shine from your souls.

Oh, little ones, take Me seriously. I am truly here, begging for you to live in My love.

You are the light that will shine in this dark world. You will light up the darkest night with My love.

The best gift you can give to this world is to busy yourself about your love affair with Me. I love you, My little ones. I love you and I want to share this love with you.

Love your brothers. Do not let satan talk in your heads and make them wrong and you right. Love them as I have loved you. Do not look at your brothers and size them up. See them with the eyes of God, the beautiful creations of the Father.

Will you love My beloved ones for Me this day, or will you say "no" to My call? Love your brothers in darkness. They need your love. I am calling you to love them for Me this very day. They may scoff at you and persecute you, but you will plant a seed that I Myself will water and give sunlight to. Plant seeds of love. This is the most important seed you will plant, a seed of love. Watch it grow as I provide it with water and nourishment. I will shine on your brothers through you if you stay in My love. Be the light that shines on this dark world. They are crying out for the love of God. They are suffering. They need your love.

Put yourselves aside. Die to yourselves. Live only for the love of God.

If the world goes one way, you stay focused on My love. Do not follow the world. Follow the risen Christ!

I love you so, little ones. I bring you new life. I fill your hearts with My love. Pray to the Holy Spirit for His gifts. Pray the Our Father. Let My mother mother you as she mothered Me. She loved you so. She suffered so for love of you. She appears to bring you back to her beloved Son. Will you answer her call? She is calling you to put God first in your life. She is calling you to love, love of God, love of one another.

Forgive your brothers. Empty your hearts of hate and anger and let go. Let all your anger go. Give Me your resentments and let Me heal your hearts. Forgiveness is the way to peace. Let go. Do not size up your brothers. Love them all. Pray for them. Unite in My love. Love is a miracle cure. Say you are sorry. Be gentle in your ways. Pray for your needs. I love you, little ones. I am with you this day.

Will you answer the call and love for Me? I love you. I am your beloved Jesus. I would die this day just for you. I love you the same as I did the day I died. Turn to Me and give Me your life. I will care for you and love you. I am your Savior. I am Jesus Christ, Son of the Living God. Let Me live in your heart!   11/4/94

I Thank You for Your Love Letters

Messenger: How many letters has Jesus written about His presence and His love and I don't really take them to heart. He cannot get close to me if I hold onto the world.   11/5/94

Strengthen Your Faith and Trust in Me

Jesus: My dear daughter, do you know how much I love to be with you in the morning? I love for you to come from your sleep and choose Me over your sleep, especially when you are so tired.

Be with Me and let yourself go into the sanctuary of My Heart. My Heart is an endless ocean of mercy and love. You do not comprehend about My mercy and love. I am writing you to help you understand it so much better.

My Heart was pierced with a lance and what flowed from My Heart was Blood and Water. To the last drop of blood in My body, I gave you My life. My life was given up for you that you would be able to enter into everlasting life. From My Heart flowed blood and water.

I give you a sharing in My life. I give you the sacraments. I give you My Church. My Heart is an endless fountain of mercy and love. As I gave the last drop of My blood for you, I give you this fountain of life and mercy.

From My pierced Heart the Church was born. You must go to My Heart, it is the abyss of My love. Through My Heart you are taken to the Father. From My Heart you receive life and mercy. From My pierced Heart all graces flow. You seek such grace in your life, grace to love and know Me more. You must come to My Heart, through Mary. Focus on My Heart. See before you the picture of the open Heart and tell all of My endless fountain of mercy and love. My Heart is this open for love of all. This is the secret to reach a hardened heart. My love is so abundant that your feeble minds cannot imagine.

I am your Savior. I am your lover. I am your life. I am the way, the truth and the life. I come and give you Myself in the Eucharist. I give My Heart to you. I love you so dearly but you do not comprehend. Pray to know more My immense love given for you. Come to My fountain of mercy and love. Let it flow into your soul. Be cleansed and bathed in a bath of My blood and dwelling forever in Me. I am life. I give you life. I am the bread of life come down from heaven for you My beloved, for you, for you, with greatest love, for you!

I am Jesus. You do not let go totally into the abyss of My love. Pray for the virtues. Your faith is lacking. It is keeping you from intense union with Me. It is faith that will allow you to let go and experience My words here.

Rita Ring, I am writing to you with greatest love and you want to check My letter out? Your whole thoughts are on checking out the letter. How can I write to you of My mysteries when you want to go to check Me out? You miss My love here, you lack faith, child, faith that would let you experience Me ever deeper.

I want to have a relationship with you. Love is built on trust. Love is giving your all. I showed you how to love when I died on the cross, I gave My all, I held nothing back. Will you give your all for Me?

Let go and write as I dictate. I am Jesus, child, do you believe it yet? No, you want to check out My letter, then you might believe I am talking to you. This is how I choose to come to you, this way, in this letter. You are a child. I want you to listen to Me. Focus on being only a baby – a baby at the breast. You are led through My Mother to My Heart. Let go and pray for faith. Your faith is very weak. My little one, you tap so gently on My ocean of knowledge. Press harder and you will learn more, I want to give you such understandings. You are afraid to let go. You do not know how you hold back. Love Me and trust Me. I am here. It is you holding back the ocean! You hold back what you thirst after because you lack trust and faith. You, My little one, must let go. Pray for faith - pray to trust - let go - trust Fr. Carter. It is not so scary – it is your way to My ocean of love! My love I pour out to you. You will be saturated. Come to Me and believe Me. You are holding up our relationship with your fear and doubt.

Rita, Rita, you lack trust and faith. You play a safe game that keeps you so far from My Heart. See the Heart – open and on fire, that is the key to deeper life in Me. Deeper union with the one, true God. Deeper union with the Persons of the Trinity. Let go, let go, let go. Hold not back. LIVE TO DO GOD'S WILL. Believe, KNOW I AM ALIVE IN YOU. Experience My love. The ocean will flow with such force. You are afraid of being wrong, more so than ever before.

Listen to Me and you will know deeper insight into My hidden mysteries, the mysteries into My Heart. I am teaching the world about My Heart in these letters of My love. I am teaching them the ways of this open furnace of love. It is through you and Fr. Carter this world will know My Heart. The infinite abyss of My love, given up for all. It is ablaze, it is on fire, it is as you see and no words can describe this Heart. It is the Heart that was pierced to save mankind from their sins. It is the Heart whereby flows life. I outpour My grace to you. Let go, child, you are holding up My work here. I cannot teach you if you hold back. You must believe I am talking to you!   11/6/94

Faith Means You Believe

Jesus: My dear child, I am tending to My work. You do as you are told. I want you to come to Me in the night, this is a very special time for us to be together.

I must tell you about faith. Faith means you believe. You are so attuned to My Heart you must pray for faith. Stay close to My Heart. Operate for love of Me and love of each other. If the world hates you, you still love them. You love all men. You see in them the creation of the Father, you see the person I died for.

Stay attuned to Me child, this takes time alone with Me. Everyday I need such time with you. You need time to play with your children – that is what most pleases the Father now. Everyday set time aside to be with them and pray that satan stays away from your children. He is working on all children. He is cunning and deceptive. Come to Me. You must spend time with Me. This is the key to your holiness.

Let go into My arms. Faith is faith. You operate in love of Me and believe I will always catch you.

I want to operate in you and be one with you. Let go into My waiting arms. Lay your head gently on My Mother's chest and surrender to Our Hearts. She leads you to this special intimacy with Me.

When you operate, always operate being one with Me. Love as I love.

Messenger: Put on Christ in all your actions. Put on Christ, act as He would act – See the Christ in one another! Always perfect peace as you, at the moment, operate to please the Father. Do the Father's will every moment.

Jesus: Do the Father's will with the greatest joy for love of Me. Oh, it is so simple, all I tell you is so simple. Man has turned simple love and kindness into such complicated things.

I give you a conscious. I teach you My ways. Act as I would act. Do you listen to your heart or do you do what you please? Follow your heart, My dear child. If you are forever united to Me, your heart will follow My way.

Make Me the center of your life. Live as I live in you, doing as I would do, praying always in all your actions. Each moment should be an act of My love given to this world.

Love for Me, My precious ones, this world needs your oneness to Me. I love you so much! 11/7/94 - 5:00 a.m.

I Write of My Love to You

Jesus: Dear sweet one, Come into My Heart and be wrapped in My love. I truly write all My love to you. Your job is clear: to circulate these letters, to talk, to sing. I give you My immense love to tell others of this great love. Little one, little one, I want to be drawn ever closer to you.
11/7/94

From Mary at the Grotto

Mary: I am the Immaculate Conception. I come to you with the tenderest love. Come and be close to my Son Jesus. This is my house, this is my grotto, this is the place to draw yourself ever closer to my Son through His letters written to you. They are the letters of His tenderest love. Every word professes His immense love for you. Please read and circulate His messages. He loves you so much, with the tenderest Heart. He is the Sacred Heart of Jesus!   11/7/94 - 6:45 a.m.

Read Jesus' Letters

Messenger: I spent one hour and fifteen minutes talking to Jesus and I cried -- He wants these messages to circulate. He says He loves so much and every word He writes here is from Him. He wants all to read His love letters. He begs us to circulate and tell them His Heart is open and on fire for love of them. These are His love letters to you. He loves you so much, every word is what He says to you. Please this is an urgent request.

11/7/94

Spend Time with Your Children

Jesus: Let your heart be not troubled for I will sustain you. You must spend time with your children. You know you are not doing My will. Be steadfast that this is a top priority.

I am calling out because time is short. Do not worry for the things of this world, only for your salvation and that of souls. Time is very short, a batting of an eye and your life has ended. If today was the last day of your life, how would you spend it?

I am your Savior. I am your Redeemer. I am He who loves you. Turn to Me in your cares and do not go it alone. Rita, Rita, you are carrying your load on your back. Let go into My arms.   11/8/94 - 4:00 a.m.

Will You Love or Reject My Father!

Jesus: I write to you this day, My beloved children. You are children of God. You are the special creation of God, the Father. He created you. You are a soul He loves. He wants you to love Him first above all things. You have a free will, My children, you can love God as He commands you to or reject Him. If you love Him and follow His will, you will attain happiness. Happiness is found in God. The more you seek Him, the more you are satisfied. He has what your soul craves.

The Spirit leads you to God. He transforms you into His image and likeness. The more you dwell in the Two Hearts, the more you are molded into the image of God.

Surrender My beloved children to His will. It is in doing His will with love that your peace and happiness lie. Always live to please the Father, as a little child tries to please their Father. Live to love Jesus and give His love to others. Center your life on Christ and doing the Father's will. Pray, pray, pray, My dear ones, I never abandon you. I love you dearly. You are My soldiers to spread the love of My most Sacred Heart.

Be wrapped in the arms of My loving Mother. Mary held Me as a child in her loving arms, picture her holding you, so close, to her Heart.

It is through her tender and loving Heart you will dwell in My Sacred Heart. Come and dwell in Our Hearts and know Our love. Let go of the things of the world that keep you from Me. Be alone with Us in Our Hearts. Drop your worries at the door of Our Hearts and rest securely in Our love. Come and be with us now.   11/8/94

I Sustain You

Jesus: My child, little child, put all worry and doubt aside and be lost in My arms. I sustain you, I love you, I am Jesus, your Savior. As you heard Me from days past, listen to My voice. I truly love you, My child. Let go and focus on Me.

There are so many distractions. Souls will be lost. Souls are being lost today, as you preach My words. Think of Me. Pray, pray. I will spread My words to your family, you do not have to be there. I am your Savior. Come and pray with Me, child. You need time alone with Me or you will suffer attack. Do not prove yourself to any man, just do as I tell you. Pray – that is what I tell you.

Little child, little child, I have always loved you. Song: "From the day you were born, I've been here with you." Pray, Rita, your job is to pray, your job is to be with Me, your job is to do the will of the Father. You are My precious child.   11/9/94 - 4:00 a.m.

He Waits for Your Time

Messenger: Everything I do must be to promote the love of God. I am not acting to be right. I am acting to spread the love of His Most precious Heart. He waits alone for His beloved ones to come and spend one hour with Him. He waits for your time, for your love. He waits for you with such love. His Heart is a burning, endless flame of love. He wants our love, He wants us to love Him and make up some to Him for all who neglect Him.

Oh, Lord Jesus, teach me to be the slave of Your Most Sacred precious Heart. When I am filled with fear, help me to see before my eyes Your Heart ablaze and in love, ablaze and in love, ablaze and burning for love of souls. Help me to promote this love by doing what You ask of me. Oh how Your Heart burns for love of Your beloved ones!

Things here matter little to me, only as I spread this devotion to His most tender and loving Heart.

I go to the end of the limb and I jump – this is total surrender to Your most loving Heart. He who lives in me. I find shelter only in Your Heart. I rest in Thee, my beloved Lord. I jump and I am secure as I only find rest in Your most precious Heart.

Jesus: Surrender for it is I who sustain you, My child. This work is My work to spread the devotion to My Heart. I long, long for the love of My Most precious souls who treat Me so coldly. Promote My love. Tell them how I wait for them with a burning Heart on fire for them. Think of My Heart ablaze and waiting the love of all souls. I want their love. Tell them how I wait for them. Tell them how I am a Heart ablaze and I long and I wait for them to come. I am God and I am longing for their love. Tell them, tell them – if you do not speak, they will not hear. I am talking to you here!   11/10/94 - After Communion

An Urgent Message

Jesus: Be wrapped in the arms of My loving Mother whom I love so dearly. I write here about all My love given to you, but who listens? I give to you messages of My love and they are treated so lightly. Souls will be lost for not reading these messages. I beg you to publish My letters. Every word I write to every human soul. I want them to read these letters of My intense love.

I died for you on the cross. I came, I was born a mere human. I gave My life for you. I give these letters of My intense love. I tell you, souls need these letters! They need all the letters. To hold up My letters is to deprive souls of personal love letters I write to them.

Faith, My child, I tell you to have faith. I am Jesus Christ, I am writing to My beloved souls. I beg you, I beg you, to take Me seriously. I write everyday, I tell you how to be holy, I tell you of My love. These letters will draw men's hearts to My most Sacred Heart. Your answers of loving each other lie in these letters. My Heart is so sad for the souls that will be lost because they did not know My love.

I, Jesus Christ, write every day. My beloved ones are missing My words of love I give to them! Nothing is more important than spreading the love of God. You are operating to draw souls closer to the Sacred Heart, yet you tend to other details and hold up My letters. Are you operating to lead men to heaven? I am calling out for the holiness I teach you in these letters. You miss the golden gift I give you here.

Your answers are found in these letters. I call, I knock, I write, I beg, I am God and I am ignored. Souls will be lost if you do not spread these letters of My intense love. I teach you so sweetly how to love one another.

You cannot love each other if you do not know the intense love I have for you. The answers to My love are found to a great extent in prayer. I am truly present in My Divinity and humanity in the Eucharist. I am alone there most of the time. Can you find one soul to be with God? What is more important than God? I am your beloved Jesus that died on the cross, no less present than the day I died and who spends one hour with Me? If you loved Me you would wait with Me, you would come with hearts full of love and anxious to be with Me.

You are missing our love affair because you are not reading My love letters. I profess day after day in every word how I love you. How it wounds My Heart to see the cold hearts of My faithful ones. Your answers are found in loving Me. I am the Sacred Heart. You are drawn closest to Me in the Blessed Sacrament, in the Eucharist. My Heart is a symbol of My intense love for you. I cry out for our love affair. Men will be drawn close to My Heart and to holiness when you circulate My love letters.

I am Jesus. I come to you with greatest love in songs and messages. I am God and I am ignored. Souls need these messages. The devil has created this confusion . You do not go to My tabernacle, you argue with one another for solutions. You try to figure your answers out and I sit with all the answers. I write these letters to you everyday and no one listens.

I want My letters of love to be circulated. I have given you four books of My love letters. I want the messages circulated. Your city will be lighted with My love when you circulate these letters given to you by Me. I am Jesus. Your answers are in holiness. My letters will lead men's hearts to such burning love for Me. Play My love songs. I love you so much!

Publish the messages on the rosary. My Mother appears, day after day, and tells you how to make the rosary alive in your life. You will not be Christ-like if you do not meditate on our lives. Our lives are your key to living Christ-like lives. If you pray the rosary as We have instructed, you will live Our lives in your lives everyday. These meditations need to circulate.

I am Jesus, I am writing to you every day. I am ignored. I beg you to light your city with the love of Jesus in your hearts. I want My books published. I will provide the funding for books three and four. Book three is your answer to your problems of loving one another. You need to circulate these messages on hate and anger and love! I ask you, I beg you, please publish all My books! Your answers lie in these books. I am Jesus. I am writing to you this day with My Heart a burning furnace of love. I show this Heart to Rita. I ask you, please to listen. I have been ignored. Your sweet ones need these messages. I love each person. I want to have a love relationship with each person.

Every word I write here is of My intense love. These messages need to be read so people realize I am writing every love letter to them. It makes Me so sad to love so much and to write these letters to My beloved ones and for them to not be circulated.

I love as I say here and much more. The insights into My life and My Mother's life, into her suffering and My suffering, are in these letters. You hold up messages of such love I pour out day after day.

I am Jesus. This is the mighty medicine. Time is so short. Your answers for your Center are in these messages. You are My city of love. I love each person with the dearest love I profess in the letters. My Mother wants all there to pray the rosary as she has instructed. I beg you to listen to My letters. These are My letters given to you. You will stay divided if you do not circulate these messages. I write every day for 10 months of My intense love and you have only circulated two letters. I beg you, I beg you, I beg you to take Me seriously. These are My letters given to you. Unless you circulate these letters of My love people will continue to be divided.

They need to realize My intense love. I appeared in the grotto to show you that Jesus and Mary are united to spread My love at your Center.

I tell you, I ask you, you try to answer your questions, when your answers are found in My letters of love. Release these messages and you will have hearts on fire for love of Me. Hearts that are holy do not hate one another. Hearts that realize the love of God operate with love. I died for you. I gave you these letters today to spread My love. I beg you, beg you to publish all My letters. I am Jesus. I am writing to each soul, My precious love.

It wounds Me so, you do not believe Me. If you truly believed Me, you would read My letters and circulate them. Pray the Prayer for Union with Jesus… in it lies the secret to your city of love.   11/10/94

The Life I Give You Is Myself

Jesus: The bread of life is the Eucharist and My Word. I come to give you life that you will have it more abundantly. The life I give you is Myself. Oh, you little dumb ones, you do not like these words. What do I call you when I, Who Am God, give you Myself. I come to dwell in your hearts and be united one with you and you treat Me so lightly.

I am the bread of life. I come that you might have life and have it abundantly and you count your silver and care for every detail of your life. Oh, child, Life is Life rooted in Me! Happiness is happiness only as you seek life in Me! Little dumb ones, bicker about My words to you and miss My life — My life given to you in the Eucharist. I come, no less present than when I walked the earth and you run from My altars to K-Mart. You do not like these words because you are blind to the true words spoken here. You will be rocked off your rockers and then you will be sorry you did not look beyond your silly blindness.

Every word I write here, I want to be obeyed. I am telling you how to light your city with love. God speaks to you. If you do not listen, you will suffer and many souls will never know My intense love for them.

I write, I am ignored as you go about your busy lives. I Am the bread of life — I come in the Eucharist with a Heart ablaze with My infinite love! I sit in the tabernacle. (You, at the Center, why is your church not packed?) I beg you to read these letters. I beg you to read them from your hearts. They are love letters. If your lover read you a letter, you would read it from your heart.

I am Jesus, My Heart is a burning furnace of endless love and I wait for you in the tabernacle. My love burns for you this very day. I am He who died for you. I gave My flesh, I gave My blood, I gave every breath in My body. Study Me in My Mother's arms under the cross, read My letters and her letters, her suffering for love of you. Oh, you little blind ones, worry about K-Mart and the rockers — you will know one boom was not enough.

I beg you to circulate My letters. They are not Rita's letters. Why would she continue to talk when no one is listening? I am begging you to listen to Me. I am God. I profess My ardent love here, this day. Souls will suffer while you hold up these letters. I am Jesus Christ. I am the Son of God. I write every day to you. Your workers will stay divided as long as you ignore Me. My third Blue Book speaks of love of one another. No one is reading any of it, but you fight and fight and hate one another.

My intense love is poured out in My second book. I beg you, I beg you to listen to Me. I am the Almighty God. I can rock this earth. I come sweetly, I ask gently, I wait patiently. I professed My on-fire love for you since February, it is almost a year later. What do I do to get you to listen? Do not forsake Me. I will never forsake you.

Song: *A Song From Jesus*

My Heart is open, it is ablaze, it is on fire for love of you. Your city will shine with the love of God when you circulate My letters of Love! I beg you to take Me seriously. Faith, My little ones, Faith in He Who died for you and wants your on-fire love relationship with Me!

I am talking to all of My beloved children at the Center. I profess My love for you this day. I am the Sacred Heart of Jesus. I Love you. Come to Me in the Eucharist.

Every word in the message of November 11 is from Me. I am Jesus Christ, the Son of God. I speak to you. Harken to My call. You listen not - you will lament.   11/11/94

I Am an Endless Ocean of Love

Messenger: I eat, breathe, and live in my every action with Jesus. I look to you and see Jesus in you.

Jesus: Satan constantly talks, My child, to create division. He gets into your thoughts and tells you this person is not nice, he is a problem to you. Cast him out immediately. Do not ponder thoughts that are creating division.

Focus on My love. I am an endless ocean of love. The ocean never runs dry. It is forever flowing and plentiful for you. Look at My Heart, ablaze for you and open. My Heart is so open. You must only come in. The door is always waiting and inviting you in. Oh, child, don't feel bad. Come to Me, trust in Me, have faith in Me. I will not ever let you down. Things are not in your control. Surrender to My Heart.

You will be aware of My presence and experience intense union with Me everywhere you are. You are the slave of the Sacred Heart. Live to promote My love. I am forever with you, My beloved.

Deep love is what I long for. I long for this great love from all My precious souls. Comfort My Heart. Spend your every moment in My Heart in deepest love. Dwell within Me and I will operate within you. Do not fret, the devil is trying to stop you. You, child, have My love and I am the Almighty God. I have all the power. I am in control. I will tend to all your cares. Let go!

Do not be defensive. I am outpouring My love to you. See all the love everyone is showering on you- such acts of love given from God Himself through God- loving souls! You are not alone. The devil is trying to make you feel bowed down. I am present inside of you, outside of you, in your brothers, in the beautiful world you live in. See with the eyes that seek the presence of God. This is your secret to happiness - to seek God in all things.

Rita, I am your best friend. Come to Me now. Come in all your needs. Love is present between persons when they are hurting or happy. I am here to comfort you and sustain you in this trial and all your trials. Come and lay your head on My Heart, lay on My chest and let Me comfort you.

11/12/94 - Saturday

Love Is from the Heart

Messenger: The key to love is in the heart. If you stay in your head, you have knowledge, not love. You can't love God with your heart closed. Mary wants to lead you to the burning Heart of her Son. Jesus sweat blood in the garden from the agonies He felt in His Heart, especially from the cold hearts of His specially anointed priests.

Jesus: My agony was so great from all the priests that would talk about My love with so little emotion. Love is from the heart! If your loved one talked to you, you would respond from your heart.

My Heart is on fire for love of each soul. I thirst for the love of My precious ones. So few come and pour their love out to Me. My Heart cries out to all priests who have turned their hearts cold. Love is warm - My Heart is a furnace of love! So many priests speak only from their minds and have forgotten the love involved. I cry out for your love. You do not teach that which you do not know. You must come and develop your love affair with Me.

My beloved priests, come and be with Me after communion, I give you Myself. I long to be one with you. I want a love affair with you. I love you so much. I died for you. As I gave Myself on Calvary, I give Myself to you in the Eucharist. Oh, My beloved priests, I thirst for the love of souls. I long for their love. I wait for them. Who will spend one hour with Me? Who will hear My cry to come and give Me real love?

If you spend time with Me in the Eucharist and in front of the tabernacle, our love will grow. I am there, no less present than on Calvary. I beg you to listen. When you love, My beloved priests, you will preach about love from your hearts. Your hearts have turned cold. I beg you to come and be with Me.

My Heart is an open furnace of love. I long for you. I want your love. My suffering was so immense for all the souls, especially the priests that would come to My Mass with cold hearts, that would read My Gospel without love. When you come to Me, you will enkindle love in your hearts. Make Me the center of your life. Pray for love of God from your hearts. Pray to the Holy Spirit to set your hearts on fire with the love of God.

Oh, My beloved priests, how I long, long for you to come and sit with Me! My Heart is burning for love of you. Oh, dear, special anointed ones, I love you so much. When you enkindle this love affair with Me, you will feed the starved souls that come to be fed. Feed My sheep, I beg you to come and be fed, My beloved priests and you will feed this world. Oh, how I love, how I wait, how I want each of you to come and love Me. I Am Love! How can you talk about love, love is from the heart, love is not from the head! Pray, My beloved ones and fall in love with the most Sacred Heart of Jesus. It is found in the Eucharist. Come and be present. I love you so. Love Me with your whole heart. I am God and you shall have no gods before Me. Happiness is found in loving God — anything not rooted in Him is useless.

11/12/94 - Saturday - In my car - 5:30 a.m. - After Communion

Personal

Jesus: No one is receiving what you are receiving, I have chosen you because I love you so and long for your love. You are My special soldier of love to teach others the ways of My Heart. Others will be led to such deep love of Me through what they learn from Me through you. Deep love is what I long for.   11/12/94

My First Love Letter to Jesus

Messenger: Dear Jesus, I love You. Not breath, not any words I know can describe my love for You. You are the life in my soul. You are my beginning and my end. Without You I would not want to live. I love You with the deepest love. Words are so flimsy to describe what I feel for You. I love You so much when I am united with You in Communion. You are my Beloved. You are so sweet. You are always there. You always love me and how little I give back to You! I experience Your presence within me sometimes and I feel so close I cannot describe it. I want greater union with You. I thirst after You. I want so desperately to be so united to You always with the deepest intensity, never to leave You. My heart knows what my pen cannot write. Oh, Your presence in my soul! I love You so and long for You to be so close to me. Your presence pervades my soul!

Jesus: Continue to write love letters to Me and watch your love grow.
Song: *I Thirst for Your Love*
(Jesus speaks: Read this to Me especially after Communion and in front of the tabernacle)

Messenger: I need to learn how to give love to Jesus. I know He loves me. How do I love Him in return? I will do this: write letters of how I love Him, tell Him how I love Him, ask Him to give me grace to turn my cold heart to a heart on fire for love of Him.

When I love Him, I will see Him in my brothers and love them so much more. Oh, dear brothers, I don't know how to love. Be patient with me, as Jesus teaches me His ways of love. I want to learn. Lord, turn my heart into a heart more like Yours.
Song: *Teach Me to Love With Your Heart*   11/13/94

Come to Me with Hearts of Love

Jesus: Will you not wait one hour with Me? My Heart thirsts for the love of souls. Come to Me with hearts of love. My Heart wants your love poured out to Me. I love you so much. I want a love relationship with you.

Read all My letters from your heart, as you read a letter from your closest friend, the one you love. You dote on every word. Oh, how I love you! I write to you here. Read every letter from Me with your whole heart. This is My love poured out to you. Do not read these letters for knowledge, read them for love. These are love letters from Me to you, My most ardently loved ones.

When you open the book think of how I love you and long for your love. I want a relationship with you. I write to you with greatest love. Read My letters as from your loved ones. Read them from your best Friend. Read them from a Person that died for you!

I long for your love this day. Write Me a letter of your love. Write Me in front of the tabernacle, or after Communion. I long for your love. I thirst for the love of My most precious souls. Come to Me and find an ocean of love in My most Sacred Heart. Come to Me and find the true Love of your soul. I am Jesus. I died for you that you may have life. My Life I give you in the Eucharist. I am the Bread of Life come down from heaven for you this very day. Come and partake in My life given to you.

11/13/94

Love Him in Return

Messenger: Jesus is a Person that wants to be loved. He is not far off. He is inside of me right now, longing for my love, for my tender words telling Him how I love Him. I can scarcely breathe to be this close to God. Oh, God, impart to me Your gifts to know and love You more, to realize Your presence within me in Your Divinity and humanity now and Your constant presence with me in Your Divinity. I am so unworthy of Your love. We are just ignorant.

Pray for the grace to realize more His presence with us, to realize His love for us and to love Him in return.

Note: I had a vision immediately after the Consecration.

I saw a cross. Above it, the cup - they seemed to be connected, then the cup went upward. I saw intense light, a dark cross. His arms under the cross went close to the cross and it got bigger, then the cup went up to heaven.

Oh, Jesus, You ask us to love You with our whole hearts, but do I want to give You my whole heart? Make me have a heart like Yours. What does that mean? You gave, You loved, You held nothing back.

I never realized before, Lord, but I keep You at a distance because I hold onto parts of my heart. Do I really want to be like Jesus, to give my things away, and be ready to let Him have all if He wants it? Loving is as You loved.

To have a heart like Your Heart means I give You my all. You gave the Blood in Your veins, You gave all the beats of Your Heart and the breath in Your Body. Loving means surrender.

Oh, Jesus, how much of my heart I hold onto! It is another step to let go of my whole heart and ask for one like Yours. You hold nothing back, You always loved. You always gave to the other.

Oh, Jesus, how far I am from You, yet how I love You. Give me, oh Lord, a heart like Yours. When You were naked I clothed You.. what I do to my brothers, Lord, I do to You.

Create in me a clean heart. Let me see where I am blind. Oh, Sacred Heart of Jesus, I place my trust in Thee.

To be like You! I see you hanging on the cross, dripping with Blood, this is Your Heart! You ask that we love God with our whole hearts and souls and love our brothers as ourselves. You said: love your brother as I have loved you.   11/13/94 - After Communion

Teach Me to Give Love to You

Messenger: I am so focused on self. I do not even see Jesus' love. Love is giving. How do I give to Jesus? Do I tell Him with all my heart how I love Him? Do I think of how He is a Person that longs for my love? Do I thank Him for His life, His Sacraments, His Church, for His life given to me in the Eucharist? Do I thank Him for dying for me and tell Him? Oh, Jesus, I am so caught up in myself. Love is giving. Oh, Jesus, I am so self-centered. I do not even see how focused on self I am and how I want so much from You and give You so little back. You gave Your life for me. It is in surrendering myself I give my life to You. Teach me to love You tenderly from the heart, to surrender to You with greatest love for You.

Oh, Jesus, teach me to love You. Just to give to You. This is the way I try to love others, to give just out of love, but how little I have loved You. Just to love! How little I realize how You want just love, no strings attached. Just to love You for You. You thirst after our love. You say how I love You so coldly. How indeed I have loved You, God, with a cold and selfish heart. You, whose heart is open, all giving, giving us our free will, and I come and always love wanting something in return.

Help me to love You, Jesus, with a heart like Yours, love You just to love You. My heart is one of the cold hearts you talk about. I am so caught up in myself and my needs. Teach me to love. So little I know. I want to love You, Jesus, with a heart that gives love back to You. Where I was blind, I now see. But I am still so blind. Teach Me Your ways, Lord. Open my eyes to Your mysteries of love. I am a baby ready to be taught Your ways. It is in You I find my joy. In You lies true, lasting happiness. I love You, my precious Jesus. Open my eyes to Your way of love!   11/13/94

I Love You Jesus

Messenger: Jesus, Jesus, my beloved, I am your child, I love You with my whole heart. You are so sweet to me to be with me always. Jesus my thoughts are of You constantly. I want to love You the way You want me to. I know so little about love, teach me to love You. Teach me to tell You what You want to hear. Teach me. I am Yours Lord, come and possess my soul.

Note: Got down here 4:05am exactly 5:05am walked out of study - I had no clocks.   11/14/94 - 4:05

Watch One Hour with Me

Jesus: My little ones, you do not want to hear so you remain blind. I write here My ways. My ways are the ways to holiness, My way is in surrendering to yourself and doing the will of My Father.

I am the way, I am the truth, I am the life. My life I pour out to you. Let your hearts be open that you may partake in My life. My way is in prayer and sacrifice. I ask you to come and pray with your hearts. You do not pray with your hearts because you do not know the ways of love. I am love. You must come to Me to learn My ways. Come and sit with Me. You cannot watch one hour with Me? I gave My life for you!

I cry out for your love. You look for love in your world when I am ready to give you Divine love! Your soul is only satisfied when your love is rooted in Me. Surrender yourself. I call, I knock, I am present and waiting your life given unreservedly to Me -- you hold back so much of your life!

If you are to grow in your union with Me, you must die to yourself and your ways. You must allow Me to operate your being. Oh, children, you do not listen to these letters because you want things your way. You do not want to love others when they hate you, you want to be right. You fight with others to make yourself right. You want to take sides and have people that support you. You want to be right.

I call you to love. I loved those who tore My flesh, I did not argue back. I loved, I loved, I loved, I showed you the way. Meditate on My sorrowful mysteries. Oh, child, you have so much to learn, but you do not listen. You go to the world for your answers about God. Come and be taught by Me. I talk in your heart. I love you. You are missing the love your soul craves because you want to be right. You do not love your brother as your brother. You love him only if he acts the way you want him to act. I call you to see with the eyes of love. See your brother as I see him. See the Divine Creation of the Father. My Father created your brother and loves him. See Me dripping with blood, blood I shed for your brother. I ask you to love your brother as I have loved you. I gave My life for you. I ask you to spend your life loving your brother, caring for him and praying for him this day.

Messenger: We are brothers in Christ. God is our Father. He gives us each such gifts. He created us so uniquely, special!

Jesus: Love, Love, Love, I give to you this day, your brother, I live in your brother. Do you see Me in him? I ask you to see the Christ in your brother. I ask you to be Christ to one another. Do you hear or will you remain deaf? I showed you the way, I hung, beaten, bloodied and broken on the cross, My life given for love of each soul! I would die for each soul this day. Do you know how I love your brother? He is your brother in Christ. Be strong, pray for grace to love as I command you to.

Messenger: To love with my heart, to be like Him, I must act like Him. He was kind, He was loving. He gave His all for love of us.

Jesus: To love My brothers as I have loved you!

11/15/94

Sainthood Is in Your Reach

Jesus: I call you to love, love of God, love of one another. Your life is so short. You will be judged by your love shown to each other. I am the way, the truth and the life. The way to Me leads to happiness. I showed you the way to love each other. Love gives, love is not selfish. Love gives for the sake of the other. Love exists to draw the other closer to God.

Oh children, pray to follow My ways. Pray to the Spirit to sanctify you. Unless you become as little children, you will not enter into My Kingdom. Your hearts must be pure and holy. You can live your lives as the saints did, I ask you to love. I ask you to follow Me. I ask you to meditate on My life and My Mother's life so you will put on Christ in all your actions. Saints followed My Father's will. I call you to holiness. I call you to love. I call you to live My Father's will. You are My special soldiers of My most Sacred Heart. Do not take your job lightly. You will be formed more and more into My Image by the Holy Spirit if you allow Mary to lead you to My Heart.

Sainthood is not out of your reach. Sainthood is in your reach. I ask you to be My special soldiers to spread the love of our hearts. I called each person here to this group to love. Come to My Heart and be fed by My love. You will give My love to others the more you put on Christ in all your actions. Meditate on the rosary as we pray here daily. Close your eyes and let go into Our lives. I call you to be My saints to this world. I love you each so dearly. I am Jesus Christ, Son of God. You are My hands, My heart, My love, given to this world this day. Come and be alone with Me. I want to give you My most tender love. I am the Sacred Heart of Jesus.

11/15/94

"I Give You Myself"

Messenger: I realized His immense presence after Communion. He is truly present and within me. I had a vision in my heart of Him on the cross and realized this is the same Jesus within me!

I heard Him say, louder and firmer than ever before, "I give you Myself" – to the point that I gasped.

I started with this vision in my heart before I received Him and started to cry. It is hard to explain what it is like to have such a realization that He is the same Jesus.

I knew it was the Person that died on the cross and gave His very flesh for me.

I saw Him in all His suffering on the cross. I wanted to cry, seeing Him suffering so.

I realized He is in me and present in the Eucharist, the same God who loved me to His death. It is overwhelming. I cannot express the emotion.

(There was a strong smell of lilacs)

I realized that all I want is perfect union with Him. I cried to want it to last and be as intense as is possible. Nothing else mattered to me, but Him!   11/16/94 - After Communion

See Through the Eyes of Jesus

Messenger: We must see others through the eyes of Jesus. How do we look at our brothers? Do we look at our brothers with love? How do we want Jesus to look at us? Do we want Him to look at us and criticize us? Jesus is Love! Jesus looks at us with the eyes of love. If we are to put on Christ, if we are to be like Christ, we must see as He sees. How do I see? How do I look at you, my brother? Do I look at you and criticize you or do I look at you to love you? I must see in you, my brothers – Jesus. I see Him in your smiles. I see Him in your kindness. I see Him when you are acting Christ-like. Do I see as God wants me to see you – with love?

Song: *Why Do We Hurt the Ones We Love*

Jesus: I call you to love your brothers. I call you to be Christ to one another. I call you to put on Christ. It is as I see your brother, the creation of My Father, he Who I shed My blood for! I call you to see with the eyes of love. I am love. I see your brothers always with love. Do you want to cooperate with the graces I am giving you this day, to love your brother? Your willfulness wants to love only sometimes. I am pouring My graces out to you this day. I call you to love your brother. I call you to put on Christ in all your actions. Love is kindness. Love is compassion. Love is understanding. Do you know how to love? Your hearts are sometimes cold because you do not want to love as I have taught you. Follow My way, study My passion. I love those who tore My flesh. See Me in your brother, I am the way, the truth and the life. Follow Me. I call you to love God and love one another.

Luke 10:27

He replied, 'You must love the Lord your God with all your heart, with all your soul, with all your strength, and with all your mind, and your neighbour as yourself.'

Messenger: Note: "It is the look on the face, the tone of their voice. I want more than anything to love as God wants me to. "

The greatest commandment is –

Luke 10:27

He replied, 'You must love the Lord your God with all your heart, with all your soul, with all your strength, and with all your mind, and your neighbour as yourself.'

11/17/94 - After Communion

See My Love in Your Brothers

Jesus: See My love in your brother. Look at your brother. Do you see the love he pours out to you? Do you treat each act of love from your brother with the same magnitude that you treat as an act when you feel you have been wronged? How many times, My precious children, your brothers give you great signs of My love and you forgot so quickly, but remember so well the acts in which you feel wronged. What if you placed such importance on kind words given so abundantly by so many of your precious brothers? Keep a notebook of love. Write in this notebook all the acts of love given to you from your dear brothers. You will see how you are abundantly graced with My love through them. Remember these acts of love. Do not focus on acts committed by your brother that cause you pain. You are abundantly blessed this day.

To spread My love is to spread My love. Do you complain to your brother or about your brother. Wherever you are, spread My love. Speak of My love given through your brother. Speak of My love given through others. Would you spread a dirty blanket over your precious children? You would spread a warm, clean blanket over them. I call you, My dear ones, to spread the warmth of My love over My precious children. Do not cover them with clouds of darkness. The sun will shine brightly and warm the earth if the clouds are parted. I am Jesus Christ. I am the Son of God. I come to your brothers in your love this day. Will you spread My warm blanket of love over them or will you block the sun by a cloud of darkness. This earth will be warmed and lighted by the fire of My love which is found in the most pure hearts.

Messenger: It is no longer I who live but He who lives in me. Create in me, oh, God, a heart for You alone, that I may be one in You and You may be one in me, that the world may believe that You have sent me to preach Your words of love.

You are alive in my heart and ready to give to this world a message of Your great love. I am Your messenger. I am Your servant waiting to be used by You. Father, united to the Mass, I offer You this day my life. Use me every minute to live as You live in me. Help me to spread Your word in my very being. It is no longer I who live, but He who lives in me. I am His temple. He is my God. I am one in Him. He is one in me, one in the mystical body of Christ as He dwells in our hearts and lives in our souls to spread His message of love to this world.

Notes: Hungry for His Love:

Heard Him say, I give you Myself. I could see Him dying on the cross. I knew it was Jesus that died on the cross for us. He gives us His very flesh and blood.

– Jesus provides nourishment for His flock. He gives Himself!

HE GIVES US THE EUCHARIST –

The Word and the Eucharist is our food.

Jesus feeds us with the Word and the Eucharist.

Christ nourishing us through His Word and the Eucharist.

The Word and the Eucharist is the Bread of life.

John 6:35-59

Jesus answered them:
I am the bread of life.
No one who comes to me will ever hunger;
no one who believes in me will ever thirst.
But, as I have told you,
you can see me and still you do not believe.
Everyone whom the Father gives me
    will come to me;
I will certainly not reject
anyone who comes to me,
because I have come from heaven,
not to do my own will,
but to do the will of him who sent me.
Now the will of him who sent me
is that I should lose nothing
of all that he has given to me,
but that I should raise it up
    on the last day.
It is my Father's will
that whoever sees the Son

and believes in him
should have eternal life,
and that I should raise that person up
on the last day.

Meanwhile the Jews were complaining to each other about him, because he had said, 'I am the bread that has come down from heaven.' They were saying, 'Surely this is Jesus son of Joseph, whose father and mother we know. How can he now say, "I have come down from heaven?" ' Jesus said in reply to them, 'Stop complaining to each other.

'No one can come to me
unless drawn by the Father who sent me,
and I will raise that person up
on the last day.
It is written in the prophets:
They will all be taught by God;
everyone who has listened to the Father,
and learnt from him,
comes to me.
Not that anybody has seen the Father,
except him who has his being from God:
he has seen the Father.
In all truth I tell you,
everyone who believes has eternal life.
I am the bread of life.
Your fathers ate manna in the desert
and they are dead;
but this is the bread
which comes down from heaven,
so that a person may eat it and not die.
I am the living bread
which has come down from heaven.
Anyone who eats this bread
will live for ever;
and the bread that I shall give
is my flesh, for the life of the world.'

Then the Jews started arguing among themselves, 'How can this man give us his flesh to eat?' Jesus replied to them:

In all truth I tell you,
if you do not eat

the flesh of the Son of man
and drink his blood,
you have no life in you.
Anyone who does eat my flesh
    and drink my blood
has eternal life,
and I shall raise that person up
    on the last day.
For my flesh is real food
and my blood is real drink.
Whoever eats my flesh
    and drinks my blood
lives in me
and I live in that person.
As the living Father sent me
and I draw life from the Father,
so whoever eats me
    will also draw life from me.
This is the bread
    which has come down from heaven;
it is not like the bread our ancestors ate:
they are dead,
but anyone who eats this bread
    will live for ever.

This is what he taught at Capernaum in the synagogue.

Messenger: God nourishes us through His Word.

God nourishes us through the Eucharist.

Bread of Life theme reveals God's tremendous love for us.

Eucharist – Jesus – greatest love for us.

The Bread of Life discourse shows us God's overwhelming love for us
    and our duty to love God and one another.

Each day we pray to know how much God loves us.

Growing in our awareness of God's love is the key to our spiritual life.

God loves each one of us uniquely.

The more we realize God's love – the more we can enter into a
    deeper relationship with Jesus.

With this proper love relationship, everything else falls into place.

Jesus leads us to closer union with the Father, Son and Holy Spirit and
    Mary.

Though the earth be shaken, the moon not give its light, I will be sustained by Your life within me.

Jesus: Feed My lambs. Feed My sheep. I come to bring nourishment for My flock. Nourish them with My love. Do you not see clearly that they are hungry for My love? They are fed by this love. To hold up My messages any longer is to hold up their nourishment. These are My love letters written to all My precious children. I call you to obey. Publish these messages.

I am the bread of life. He who comes to Me will never die. I love each of My precious children this day. Let your heart be pure as your heavenly Father wants – your heavenly Father created you.

My dear children, I long for pure hearts. I beg you to come to Me for your healing.   11/18/94

Can You Not Watch One Hour with Me?

Jesus: Can you not watch one hour with Me? Oh, the harvest is plenty but the laborers are few. Do you know that I am Jesus, your most precious Savior?

Let go of your tired body. When you are weary - pray. Do you ever hear in the Gospel that I was missing My sleep? I rested. I was always at perfect peace. So you lost your notebook – anyone who reads it would profit from it. You have nothing to hide. If someone thinks anything negative, it is their problem. I am Jesus, you have surrendered your life to Me, now let go into My arms and know My peace. My peace I give in your heart. Surrender all your cares to Me and focus on the Father's love for you. He loves you so much!

Notes: I saw the tabernacle light-up in Fr. Carter's chapel around the lock – then it was lit around the outside and the stand.

I put up sorrowful mysteries during Friday night meeting on the Rosary and the Scourging at the Pillar was illuminated.

Thursday: day before yesterday, day of Blue Book Meeting

On November 17 I had an interior vision:

Saw eye after communion, a woman from side of face, IT WAS MARY – (at Fr. Smith's Mass).

then I saw a big tear – it looked like a big plastic, crystal looking tear – see through under the eye on the cheek.

Second Vision: Talked at Carol's - saw eyes, looking at me, zeroed in on eyes – really watching me. It was the eyes of the child Jesus – Saw this after communion.

Remembered all the visions I have had of parts of faces, from under the chin, saw Jesus' face - after I saw the side of the head, after communion. I saw outside of His head today, nothing in it at prayer meeting. Realized how people give me so much love.

October 31: Saw all the faces in the grotto, Mary changed into Jesus, then into the Apostles, saw Claude.   11/19/94

True Happiness Is Found Only in God

Jesus: My dear tender ones, your lives may seem very difficult at times, you may feel as if I am far away from you, but I am forever watching you in every trial you experience, it is in suffering you are led closer to a realization of My presence with you. If you turn to Me you will learn a mighty lesson from your suffering. I never, ever, leave you, My beloved children! You look, you wander, you roam for that which will make you happiest. True happiness is found only in God.

Know that I am guarding each person here with My special love. Come to My Heart through My loving Mother's Heart and take all your problems to Me. Silence satan and any talk he gives you in your head. Focus on the mysteries of My life and My Mother's life. I came that you will have life and have it abundantly. Time is short, seek only the Kingdom. In all your actions, love God and love one another. In all your difficult days, live to please the Father. Your life may seem very difficult at times – turn your hearts to Me. Give Me your cares. Focus on giving My love to your brothers. You are My light to this world. Shine so that all may see your good works and praise your Father in heaven.

I am the way. I am the truth. I am the life. He who abides in Me will have the light of life!

Close your eyes and put all your cares aside. Come and take refuge in My most Sacred Heart. It is warm and the glow of My Heart will light your hearts with My love.

Do not be blown about as leaves on the ground. You must forever focus on My intense love for you. You are rooted so firmly in My love. Your roots are strong against the evils in this world. When the wind comes and blows, you will not falter, you will remain forever fixed because you are rooted firmly in the love of God.

Messenger: See Mary as our model for our life. Mold us into children likened to Mary. She was kind and patient and loving.

Keep Jesus' Passion forever fresh in your hearts. It is there you will realize His immense love for all of us.

Withdraw from worldly things and focus on the life to come.

Mary was taken up into heaven - Jesus ascended into Heaven.

John 6:27

Do not work for food that goes bad,
but work for food
　　that endures for eternal life,
which the Son of man will give you,
for on him the Father, God himself,
　　has set his seal.

John 6:32-33

Jesus answered them:
In all truth I tell you,
it was not Moses
　　who gave you the bread from heaven,
it is my Father
　　who gives you the bread from heaven,
the true bread;
for the bread of God
is the bread
　　which comes down from heaven
and gives life to the world.

John 6:35

Jesus answered them:
I am the bread of life.
No one who comes to me will ever hunger;
no one who believes in me will ever thirst.

John 6:37-38

Everyone whom the Father gives me
　　will come to me;
I will certainly not reject
anyone who comes to me,
because I have come from heaven,
not to do my own will,
but to do the will of him who sent me.

John 6:40

It is my Father's will
that whoever sees the Son
　　and believes in him
should have eternal life,

and that I should raise that person up
   on the last day.

John 6:49

Your fathers ate manna in the desert
and they are dead;

John 6:51

I am the living bread
   which has come down from heaven.
Anyone who eats this bread
   will live for ever;
and the bread that I shall give
is my flesh, for the life of the world.'

John 6:52-58

Then the Jews started arguing among themselves, 'How can
this man give us his flesh to eat?' Jesus replied to them:

In all truth I tell you,
if you do not eat
   the flesh of the Son of man
and drink his blood,
you have no life in you.
Anyone who does eat my flesh
   and drink my blood
has eternal life,
and I shall raise that person up
   on the last day.
For my flesh is real food
and my blood is real drink.
Whoever eats my flesh
   and drinks my blood
lives in me
and I live in that person.
As the living Father sent me
and I draw life from the Father,
so whoever eats me
   will also draw life from me.
This is the bread
   which has come down from heaven;
it is not like the bread our ancestors ate:
they are dead,
but anyone who eats this bread
   will live for ever.

Mark 6:17

Now it was this same Herod who had sent to have John arrested, and had had him chained up in prison because of Herodias, his brother Philip's wife whom he had married.

Matthew 28:19-20

Go, therefore, make disciples of all nations; baptise them in the name of the Father and of the Son and of the Holy Spirit, and teach them to observe all the commands I gave you. And look, I am with you always; yes, to the end of time.'

Luke 24:13-35

Now that very same day, two of them were on their way to a village called Emmaus, seven miles from Jerusalem, and they were talking together about all that had happened. And it happened that as they were talking together and discussing it, Jesus himself came up and walked by their side; but their eyes were prevented from recognising him. He said to them, 'What are all these things that you are discussing as you walk along?' They stopped, their faces downcast.

Then one of them, called Cleopas, answered him, 'You must be the only person staying in Jerusalem who does not know the things that have been happening there these last few days.' He asked, 'What things?' They answered, 'All about Jesus of Nazareth, who showed himself a prophet powerful in action and speech before God and the whole people; and how our chief priests and our leaders handed him over to be sentenced to death, and had him crucified. Our own hope had been that he would be the one to set Israel free. And this is not all: two whole days have now gone by since it all happened; and some women from our group have astounded us: they went to the tomb in the early morning, and when they could not find the body, they came back to tell us they had seen a vision of angels who declared he was alive. Some of our friends went to the tomb and found everything exactly as the women had reported, but of him they saw nothing.'

Then he said to them, 'You foolish men! So slow to believe all that the prophets have said! Was it not necessary that the Christ should suffer before entering into his glory?' Then, starting with Moses and going through all the prophets, he explained to them the passages throughout the scriptures that were about himself.

When they drew near to the village to which they were going, he made as if to go on; but they pressed him to stay with them saying, 'It is nearly evening, and the day is almost over.' So he went in to stay with them. Now while he was with them at table, he took the bread and said the blessing; then he broke it and handed it to them. And their eyes were opened and they recognised him; but he had vanished from their sight. Then they said to each other, 'Did not our hearts burn within us as he talked to us on the road and explained the scriptures to us?'

They set out that instant and returned to Jerusalem. There they found the Eleven assembled together with their companions, who said to them, 'The Lord has indeed risen and has appeared to Simon.' Then they told their story of what had happened on the road and how they had recognised him at the breaking of bread.

John 3:16

For this is how God loved the world:
he gave his only Son,
so that everyone who believes in him
    may not perish
but may have eternal life.

Matthew 26:26

Now as they were eating, Jesus took bread, and when he had said the blessing he broke it and gave it to the disciples. 'Take it and eat,' he said, 'this is my body.'

Acts 1:3

He had shown himself alive to them after his Passion by many demonstrations: for forty days he had continued to appear to them and tell them about the kingdom of God.

John 20:24-25

Thomas, called the Twin, who was one of the Twelve, was not with them when Jesus came. So the other disciples said to him, 'We have seen the Lord,' but he answered, 'Unless I can see the holes that the nails made in his hands and can put my finger into the holes they made, and unless I can put my hand into his side, I refuse to believe.'

John 6:51

I am the living bread
    which has come down from heaven.
Anyone who eats this bread
    will live for ever;
and the bread that I shall give
is my flesh, for the life of the world.'

Mark 14:24
...This is my blood, the blood of the covenant, poured out for many.

1 John 4:9-10
This is the revelation
   of God's love for us,
that God sent his only Son into the world
that we might have life through him.
Love consists in this:
it is not we who loved God,
   but God loved us and sent his Son
to expiate our sins.

Messenger: Jesus is the Son of God.
Jesus has two natures – a human nature and a Divine nature –
Jesus is a Divine Person.
Jesus died and rose on the 3rd day.
We can have a special sharing in His life through baptism.
Our human nature is elevated to greater heights in Him through baptism.
The Son of God became man to save man from his sin.

The Glorious Mysteries
   1. Jesus rose on the 3rd day.
   2. Jesus ascended into heaven.
   3. The Holy Spirit came – tongues were above the head
      of Mary and the Apostles.
   4. Mary went to heaven.
   5. Mary is crowned Queen of heaven and earth.

John 3:16
For this is how God loved the world:
he gave his only Son,
so that everyone who believes in him
   may not perish
but may have eternal life.

Messenger: God's love can raise men to the unfathomable happiness of the vision of God.
Song: A Song From Jesus
He came to give us life that we would have it to the full.
Jesus died for us.
Jesus gives us His Body and Blood in the Holy Eucharist.
Jesus gave Himself on the cross.
He gives us Himself, today, in the Holy Eucharist.
Jesus is no less present than the day He died on the cross.

Jesus is truly present in the Eucharist in His Divinity and humanity –
He gives Himself to us in greatest love.   11/22/94

I Come to You with Greatest Love

Messenger: Since 5:30 I have been understanding more the two
natures in Jesus and that He is the Divine God.

I was overwhelmed at Mass, realizing that the Eucharist is God truly
present. Jesus humbled Himself to share in our humanity and He allows
us to receive a sharing in His life in baptism.

The realization that this is God and I am receiving Him inside of me
is overwhelming. The realization He allows us to share in His life! Our
human nature is elevated to greater heights in Him through baptism.

The Mass and what is going on made me feel like I should jump out
of my skin. The priest has the power to change bread and wine into the
Body and Blood of Jesus. We should kiss the priest's hands and treat him
with such reverence that Jesus has given him such power. We are missing
so much, I feel so blind. Where I am blind, I now see.

Jesus: I am Jesus Christ, the Son of God. I let you experience this
realization with greatest love for you and all men. Tell them of My
intense love and presence in the most Blessed Sacrament. I am God. I
come to you with greatest love. It is in your realization and experiences,
your awareness of Me as God deepens. You must tell them. I speak to you
to tell others that I am truly God, I truly come to them in the Eucharist.
I am no less present than at Calvary. Do not hold back. Do not be taunt-
ed by satan. Pray to the Holy Spirit for courage to spread this to the
world.

I am allowing you to experience this intense awareness of My presence. You must speak of this to all. My presence, I make known to you so
deeply in the reception of the Eucharist. This is My presence within you.
Oh, child, what glory awaits he who loves and serves the Lord! Preach
My presence with you. I want to be so close to every soul. I thirst for the
love of souls. I am Jesus. I am the ardent lover of your hearts. Come to
Me in the Eucharist.   11/23/94

Jesus Told Me to Write a Letter to Fr. Carter for Thanksgiving

Messenger: Fr. Carter was my spiritual director - Jesus said He would talk to me through Fr. Carter.

Dear Father,

Thank you for everything you have done for me. Jesus told me to trust you always. I have learned very much about love and trust from you. You truly live in union with Him. Your actions are seen as He who lives in you.

There are so many things you have taught me about Him and relating to people and where I am in this world.

Thank you for everything, I have grown so much closer to the Father, Son and Holy Spirit and Mary and the Saints because of all you have taught me and showed me.

I love God so much and to be able to learn more about Him and get closer to Him is what I thirst after. This is so dear to me.

I thank Him for the great gift of knowing and loving God more deeply because of your spiritual direction. Thank you so much,

Love

Rita   11/23/94

To Fr. Carter Thanksgiving 1994 from Jesus

Jesus: My beloved priest son,

I am your Savior, I love you with the tenderest Heart. I have called you in a special way to bring My deepest love to this world. I thank you for your openness and your obedience to My Father. You, My precious one, will set many hearts on fire with My deep love. I give to you My deepest love. I am your Jesus, I am your Savior, I am your all, I Am Who Am, I am God. I give such love to all My precious souls, Thank you for spreading this love for Me.

I love you,

Jesus   11/23/94

To Fr. Smith Thanksgiving 1994 from Jesus

Jesus: My precious priest son,

I am Jesus, your loving Savior. I have called out to you to answer My special mission at My Mother's house. I thank you for all your willingness to spread the love of My beloved Mother. I want to call you to the deepest union with My most Sacred Heart. I long to be so close to you in such union. You are My precious anointed priest son. You are My instrument to touch many hearts with the fire of My love. Your city will shine with the glow from My Most Precious Heart. Oh My beloved one, how I love you and see your committedness to Me. Open your heart and let Me penetrate ever deeper into your soul. I love you so much, I long for this union with you. I am Jesus Christ, you are My special priest, thank you for answering My call to you.

I love you,

Jesus   11/23/94

An Overview of the Spiritual Life

Incarnation
John 3:16
For this is how God loved the world:
he gave his only Son,
so that everyone who believes in him
    may not perish
but may have eternal life.

Messenger: Jesus humbled Himself to share in our humanity.

Christ gives to us dignity by taking on a human nature. We are children of God and heirs of His Kingdom. Through baptism we receive a special sharing in His life.

Excerpt from the Spirituality Handbook by Fr. Edward J. Carter written in the summer of 1994:

An Overview of the Spiritual Life

The Christian life is rooted in the great event of the Incarnation. We must consequently always focus our gaze upon Christ, realizing that everything the Father wishes to tell us has been summed up in the life, death, and resurrection of Jesus. It only remains for us, then, to strive to understand with greater insight the inexhaustible truth of the Word Incarnate: "In many and various ways God spoke of old to our fathers by the prophets; but in these last days He has spoken to us by a Son, Whom He appointed the heir of all things, through Whom also He created the world." (Heb. 1: 1-2)7

What was the condition of the human race at the time of Christ's coming? In some ways, people were much the same as we are today. There were those just being born into this world of human drama. There were those who, in death, were leaving it, some of whom had grasped but little of life's meaning. There were those who were healthy and vigorous. There were those who were sick and lame. Some especially felt the burdens, the grief, the suffering of the human condition. Others were ebullient and desired all the pleasures life could provide. There was some good being accomplished. Immorality, however, was rampant. What St. Paul tells us concerning the time that immediately followed Christ's existence certainly could also be applied to the time of His entrance into the world. It is, in short, an ugly picture that St. Paul depicts for us (Rom. 1: 22-32).

Into such a depraved condition Jesus entered, with a full and generous Heart, to lead the human race from the depths of sinfulness to the vibrant richness of a new life in Himself. Through His enfleshment, this Christ became the focal point of all history. The authentic hopes and dreams of the human family, now so overshadowed by the ugliness of sin, came converging upon this Christ. He would gather them up in Himself, give them a new luster and brilliance and dynamism, and would lead the human family back to the Father in the Holy Spirit.

Christ was radically to release us from the dominion of sin and elevate us to a new level of existence. This life Christ has given us is not a type of superstructure which is erected atop human existence. Although nature and grace are distinct, they do not lie side by side as separate entities. Rather, grace permeates nature. The Christian is one graced person. The Christian is one who has been raised up, caught up, into a deeper form of life in Christ Jesus. Nothing that is authentically human in the life of the Christian has been excluded from this new existence. Whatever is really human in the life of the Christian is meant to be an expression of the Christ-life. The simple but deep joys of family life, the wonderment at nature's beauty, the warm embrace of a mother for her child, the agony of crucial decision making, the success or frustration that is experienced in one's work, the joy of being well received by others, and the heartache of being misunderstood-all these experiences are intended to be caught up in Christ and made more deeply human because of Him.

Jesus has come, then, not to destroy anything that is authentically human, but to perfect it by leading it to a graced fulfillment. This is the meaning of the Word's becoming flesh, the meaning of the Incarnation. The more God-like we become through Christ, the more human we become.

We, through our incorporation into Christ which occurs at Baptism, are meant to relive the life, death, and resurrection of Jesus. In doing so, we are not only accomplishing our own salvation, but we are assisting in the salvation of others also. The Incarnation continues all the time. Christ, of course, is the one Who fundamentally continues the Incarnation. But He enlists our help. The world no longer sees Jesus, no longer is able to reach out and touch Him. We are the ones who now, in some way, make Christ visible and tangible. In union with the invisible, glorified Christ, and depending on Him as our source of life, we continue the Incarnation in its visible and temporal dimensions. This is our great privilege. This is our great responsibility.

The Christian is initiated into the mystery of Christ, into his or her role in prolonging the Incarnation, through Baptism. In the words of St. Paul: "Do you not know that all of us who have been baptized into Christ Jesus were baptized into His death? We were buried therefore with Him by Baptism into death, so that as Christ was raised from the dead by the glory of the Father, we too might walk in newness of life." (Rom. 6: 3-4).

It is not sufficient, however, that we be incorporated into Christ through Baptism. All forms of life require nourishment. So, too, our life in Christ must be continually nourished. How can we continually keep in contact with Christ? There are various ways. We contact Christ in a most special way through the liturgy, above all in the Eucharistic liturgy. Here the entire course of salvation history, as centered in Jesus, is sacramentally renewed and continued. Through our most special and most personal meeting with Jesus in the Mass, we are more deeply incorporated into Christ. Also, we should remember that all the sacraments make up part of the Church's liturgy.

The reading of Scripture provides another special opportunity for meeting Jesus. This is true for both Old and New Testaments. The Old Testament prefigures the New Testament and leads to it. It is obvious, however, that we meet Christ especially in the pages of the New Testament. How true it is to say that not to be familiar with Scripture is not to know Jesus properly. We should resolve to read from Scripture daily.

We also meet Jesus in our interaction with others. Everyone we meet, everyone we serve, is in the image of Jesus. We have to take the means to grow in this awareness. If I truly believe that everyone has been redeemed by the blood of Jesus, how should I treat everyone?

These, then, are some of the ways we keep in contact with Jesus. Common to the various ways of meeting Jesus is a certain degree of prayerful reflection. Our contact with Jesus in the liturgy, in Scripture, and in our interaction with others, and so forth, will not be all that it should be unless we are persons of prayer. The light and strength of prayer enables us to keep in contact with Jesus as we should.

We live out our Christ-life in an atmosphere of love. Indeed, the life Jesus has given us is centered in love. It has its origins in the mysterious love of God: "For God so loved the world that He gave His only Son, that whoever believes in Him should not perish but have eternal life" (John 3: 16).

Our new life in Jesus has arisen out of God's fathomless love. Christ, in His descent into human flesh, has established a milieu of love. The life He came to give can flourish only in the framework of love. Indeed, we can summarize the meaning of the Christian life by stating that it is our loving response to God's love. The pierced Heart of Jesus, this Heart which shed its last drop of blood in the greatest love for each one of us, is the symbol of God's tremendous love for us. Christ's Heart also calls us to respond by giving ourselves in love to God and neighbor. Yes, Jesus invites us to respond to God's love by giving ourselves in love to Him in an ever closer union. The more closely we are united to Him, the greater is our capacity to love God and neighbor. The more closely we are united with Jesus, the more closely He unites us to the Father in the Holy Spirit, with Mary our Mother at our side.

Romans 6:3-5

You cannot have forgotten that all of us, when we were baptised into Christ Jesus, were baptised into his death. So by our baptism into his death we were buried with him, so that as Christ was raised from the dead by the Father's glorious power, we too should begin living a new life. If we have been joined to him by dying a death like his, so we shall be by a resurrection like his;

I Want Greater Union with You

Jesus: I am the bread of life, I come that you might have life and have it to the full. I give Myself to you in the Eucharist. I give you Myself in My divinity and humanity. I become one with you when you receive Me in the Eucharist. I give you Myself. I am God. When you are in the state of grace, you share in My divine life. I pour My life, My grace, out to you in the Eucharist. You are nourished and fed by My body and blood.

I am the true bread sent from heaven to nourish you and give you My life. I give you Myself. This is My great love that I give to you. It is from this giving you are fed. I want to be so close to you. Open your hearts and let Me penetrate you with My life. Let My most Sacred Heart reign forever in your heart. It is through My Mother's Immaculate Heart you will be placed deeply in My Sacred Heart. I am Jesus.

I am God. Where I am there is the Father and the Holy Spirit. The Spirit leads you to greater knowledge of God. Pray to the Holy Spirit to set your hearts on fire with the love of God. It is through Me you will be led to closer union with the Father. You will be led to greater union with the Father, Son and Holy Spirit as your union with Jesus grows.

11/23/94 - After Communion - 6:00 p.m.

Thanksgiving

Jesus: Do you know My dear ones that I love you so very much? You wander and roam and look for the love your souls seek and it can only be found in Me.   11/25/94 - Thanksgiving Day

Let the Holy Spirit Mold You into My Image

A Message from **Jesus** on Thanksgiving:

My dear little children,

I am Jesus, your beloved Savior. The Father loves you so much, My dear little ones, that He gave His only Son that you might have life and have it abundantly. I loved you, My precious ones. I was born a mere

Human. I gave Myself, My Body and Blood for love of you. My Mother suffered by My side. She loves you with the most tender love. The Holy Spirit loves you with such love. He is forever ready to mold you more deeply into My image and lead you to greater love with the Father!

Oh, little loved ones, do you not see the love I pour out to you? I remain with you this very day in the Eucharist, no less present than the day I was carried in Mary's womb, no less present than the day I walked this earth. I remain with you, I come to you and give you Myself, I give you My Life in My Divinity and humanity. I come into your body. This is the Sacrament of My greatest love - I give Myself to you in the Eucharist.

Oh, sweet ones, My Heart is open and on fire. See My Heart totally open and ablaze for love of you. I am the Sacred Heart of Jesus, the tenderest of all hearts I long and thirst for your love. I wait for you, My little ones, to come and receive Me in the Eucharist. I sit endless hours waiting for the souls I love to come and be with Me in front of the tabernacle.

My soul thirsts for the love of souls. I pour out My most tender love to you in the Eucharist. I long, I wait, I yearn for your love, My precious sweet ones. Oh, you do not know how My Heart suffered during My Passion for the souls that would reject Me and treat Me so coldly. The agonies I endured to love so much and be forgotten by so many souls I love so dearly!

Oh, I cry out with a loud voice so that you will listen to My pleading. I am Jesus Christ, the Son of God, I am on fire for love of you this day. As your body requires nourishment, your souls are fed by Me. I am the Bread of Life, he who comes to Me will never be hungry. He who believes in Me will never thirst. I give you My very flesh to nourish you. I give you My very Blood. I give you, My dear ones, My very self.

Messenger: What can you get on this earth that can compare to God, truly present and dwelling with you? How much do you comprehend that God comes to you and enters your body in the Sacrament of the Eucharist? Do you realize what transpires at Mass? Bread and wine are changed into the Body and Blood of Jesus Christ, through the hands of His specially anointed priest. Do you cry to realize what is happening at Mass? God is truly present. Jesus is no less present than the day He hung on the cross, dying for love of you.

Jesus speaks: I would die this day for you, My dear ones. I love, I love, I love. I am Love. You look, you wander, you roam.   11/25/94

Be Lost in the Heart of Jesus

Jesus: Let go and totally surrender. Trust Me. You can let go totally. There is always a holding back, not to let go totally, to protect yourself from being hurt. I will never forsake you. I will never abandon you. Totally release yourself into My loving Heart. Let go, total surrender, let go, let go, let go to My love. Be lost in the Heart of Jesus!

Messenger: There is nothing to fear in loving God. Total trust, total surrender, totally letting go to His love. He gave His Life for you - do you think you can't trust Him?

Jesus: You are never alone. Be wrapped in the immensity of My love. As your heart beats, My love is always there, it never leaves. As you breathe, My love is always there, I never take My love from you for a second. Have constant intense union with Me. Have constant realization of My immense Presence with you. My love does not flicker, it is a roaring furnace that burns for you.

Messenger: I want to let go of self. I want to be molded more and more into the image of Jesus. I want to be as He intends me to be. Dear God saturate me with Your grace. I want to know Your presence within me. I want to be as the Father intended me to be.

Song: *Create in Me Oh Father Your Special Child*

A Prayer

> Create in me Oh Father Your special child
> Mold me into the child You intended me to be
> Holy Spirit mold me into the image of Jesus
> Mary lead me to the inner sanctuaries of
> Jesus' most Precious Heart   11/25/94

This Heart Thirsts for Us, Tell Them

Jesus: My dear sweet child,

Your heart aches for love of Me. I allow you to experience such pain to your heart as you experience such joy when you receive Me in Communion. Your heart aches as it did on Sunday between 5:00 and 6:00, such longing, such thirsting, such pain.

This My child is a minute of My aching Heart for the souls I love so dearly. Oh I thirst for these souls, oh I long for their love as you long until it hurts to behold Me more, My soul aches so much greater for their love. Do you know now how I suffered so for love of souls.

Speak <u>little</u> <u>one</u>, do not hold back, lest your heart break for love of Me.

Song: *Teach Me to Love with Your Heart*

To you I let you experience the sufferings of My Heart and My Mother's Heart.

As you suffer now, you tell your brothers how I suffered so for love of them. How I wait and wait for their time with Me.

My Heart is ablaze and on fire and this world is blind, you experience some of this suffering. As you suffered yesterday to see My passion, remember the blows and sounds you heard at the pillar. Remember and be fixed to My suffering to spread My love. I AM JESUS truly present in the Eucharist. Oh, Rita, I beg you to tell them for Me. Your heart aches on Saturday and Sunday – I allow you to suffer, so little compared to My most Sacred Heart suffered for love of you. Oh, child, come and thirst after Me, it comforts My aching Heart. I love you to long for My precious love. Does it feel as if your heart will break? This is nothing compared to My aching Heart!

Alleluia, you have been given a special sharing in My life through baptism. I give Myself to you this day, I give you My life. I come to you with greatest love, I am your loving Savior, I am your God, I died for you, I come to you this day. Alleluia. Suffer your heartache and spread My immense love for you.   11/27/94

I Share My Life with You in a Special Way through Baptism

Jesus: I call you to surrender. The world is moving further and further away from My Sacred Heart. I am the Almighty God. I am the source of your light, your life, your power. Your heart beat is dependent on Me. Oh, dear precious ones, this world is indeed so blind. I set before you My life. I give you My Divine love. You are given these great gifts. You can say "no" and walk your own paths that lead to remorse. I am Jesus Christ, your soul knows loneliness, but you remain lonely, your soul is hungry, but you do not feed it. I am Jesus. Only in Me will you find peace and happiness.

You wander, you roam, you are anxious, you are hurried, you are busy, and I sit alone waiting for you to come and be filled with My Divine love. Oh, child, is anything on this earth comparable to a sharing in My life? You are human beings, you are raised to such heights through this sharing in My life through baptism. In baptism you are given this sharing in My life. When you are in the state of grace the Father, Son and Holy Spirit remain in you in a special way.

I give to you a sharing in My life. I pour My grace out to you. I pour My grace out to you in the Eucharist, in the Mass, before the tabernacle. I love you with a Divine love. I give you love as no human can love you. All love has its source in Me.

Oh, children, you are blind. I pour Myself out to you and you are busy. I give you such graces and you, in your willfulness, walk from Me.

Oh, children, pray for the grace to grow in your love of Me. Pray to grow ever deeper in knowing My love. I want to love you so deeply. I want you to share more deeply in My Divine life. I love you so deeply. You are given a special sharing in My Divine Life through baptism. Many are blind because they refuse My grace. I outpour My grace to you at Mass. I give you Myself in the Eucharist. Oh, pray for your brothers. Offer every minute of your day up for your beloved brothers and sisters.

Do not forsake Me. I want you to know, little child, little child, I love you so!   11/29/94

Plan for the Shepherds of Christ Meeting November 30, 1994

Song: *God's Love*
Song: *Amazing Grace*
Read the Thanksgiving Message
Read message this Friday after Thanksgiving

Jesus: The words to these songs are My life, singing in your soul.

Listen to them and feel My presence with you. I sing these songs to you with greatest love.

Listen to every word as coming from He Who loves you so much. Oh, child, I love you, I love you, I love you. I am Jesus, your ardent lover. You do not know how I long for your moments spent alone with Me. Oh, little child, little child, come and rest in My arms. Be with Me, little child, I want you with Me.

Song: *Little Child*

Jesus: What do I do to get you to come to Me? I tug ever so gently and you fight ever so hard. Let go to all I am sending you and know I never ever abandon you. I never, ever, leave you. In My suffering I was at great peace because I know the will of the Father. In your suffering, I am ever closer. I never leave you, ever. Let go, let go, you hold on so tight. The very hairs of your head are numbered! What waits you this day is a greater sharing in My intimate love for you. Do not fear, I want to be so close to you.

Let go, surrender yourself totally to My care.

I am Jesus, I never, ever abandon you. I am within your beating heart, loving you with My greatest love. Let go to Me, My child. I want to be with you. Does a mother forsake her child? I will never abandon you. Oh, precious one, how sweet you are to Me. How I long to be ever closer and love you with such intense love. Surrender, surrender and say, "Father, not my will but Thine be done." It is in surrender and love for all your brothers you will be healed. I am the Almighty God. I have all the power. I am drawing you ever closer to My Heart. Surrender to what things I have sent you in your life. Love all your brothers. Make your heart so pure that My love can penetrate every cell in your heart. I want to fill you with My Divine love, My dear, dear, loved one. I call you to let go, let go of yourself. Pray the Prayer for Union with Me. You must let go of all that is not Me and let Me penetrate your very soul. I want to be ever deeper in your heart. I came to give you this special sharing in My life – that someday you will know the fullness of life in heaven.   11/29/94

To Love to Do His Will

Messenger: To love to do His will. This is where my peace lies. To love to do what He wills me to do. Jesus is love, He loved the Father, He loved to do His will. To have that connection with the Father, that we operate as He wills us to. To love to do His will because we become one in Him. To love God so much that we operate as He dwells within us. To let go of self and consciously be aware of the God within us that is operating through our being. To love as He loves in us, to be as He is in us, to put on Christ in all we do, to always comply to His will. As Christ loves all His precious ones, we love all His precious ones and become more united to Him. For as we act, He acts through us. Our life becomes a life rooted deeply in His life, rooted deeply in the love of the Father, Son and Holy Spirit. A dying to the self to live in Him, to be the creation the

Father intended us to be. So as I operate, it is no longer I who live, but He who lives in Me. To put on Christ in all our actions, to be one in Him in every interaction with my brothers, as I act, a surrendering to Him to operate my very being. It is, therefore, His work that He completes in me through my surrender to Him. He uses me, I give Him myself -- He lives in me.

Romans 8:11

and if the Spirit of him who raised Jesus from the dead has made his home in you, then he who raised Christ Jesus from the dead will give life to your own mortal bodies through his Spirit living in you.

John 12:47

...since I have come not to judge the world,
but to save the world

Matthew 5:17

'Do not imagine that I have come to abolish the Law or the Prophets. I have come not to abolish but to complete them.

Jesus: For as I live and dwell in you, I operate through you in this world. I live in you, I love through you, I become one in you. You must surrender to Me. Surrender to Me and yield to the Spirit working in you leading you to be more likened to Me.

Oh is it so complicated or are you blind? You My children are blind many times. Pray for My grace within you. As you come and ask, I out-pour My grace to you. I love you each so dearly and want to bring you to greater perfection in Me. Open yourself up to be molded by the Spirit into My image. You are a beautiful creation of My Father. You are so uniquely special, you are a creation that is loved dearly by My Father. Realize your preciousness to My Father and know His love for you, My Father's plan for you, to know the Father you come to Me. The Spirit leads you to such intimacy and love with God: Father, Son and Holy Spirit. It is through the pure Heart of My beloved Mother you will know Me so deeply. Come into My Heart through her Heart, we are so closely united. It is in this union between Mother and Son that you will know Me so deeply. Our Hearts beat in the deepest love, as we dwell together in such oneness. Oneness with God is what your soul craves. It is in this awareness of this oneness you will experience such peace. It is in this one-ness with the Holy Trinity through Mary's Heart that your hearts will burn with Holy love. Our love is Divine love, our life is shared with you in a special way through baptism.

Come to My altar, come to My Church, come and be fed, as you live and breathe, I want to be one in you and live in you. I am Jesus, I long for your union with Me. Oh child, what more do I say, open your eyes and pray for vision.   11/29/94 - After Communion

Love His Will

Messenger: I feel such an awareness of surrendering to Him to let Him operate me, in everything I do, to love His will for me. I surrender, He leads me. I yield to Him and He operates as I deliver these messages always yielding to Christ and letting Him operate to try to be that person the Father intended me to be. To do what He wills, to do what is in His plan for me. It is an act of my will to love His will, so I surrender to Him and be the empty vessel He uses to operate from. I am the child, He is the Father, I am the baby submissive at the breast. I trust Him like the baby, I surrender to Him, to die to my own willfulness and yield. I give Him myself. His life is within me. When I get self conscious around others sometimes I take back my control. He wants to operate when we are around others.

Jesus: Let go, you hold on so tight to the things that are near you not always right. Let go, Let go.

Messenger: I have a constant presence of Father, Son and Holy Spirit.

"By the mystery of this water and wine may we come to share in the divinity of Christ, who humbled himself to share in our humanity."

~From the words of the Mass

Messenger: We are human, through baptism we are given a special sharing in His life. He came that we might have life and have it to the full.

Saturate me with your life.

He shared in our humanity.

The Son of God was made man in the Virgin Mary through the Holy Spirit.

Let us see the great sharing we have in His Divine life through baptism.

Help us to grow in our life in Him. He humbled Himself to share in our humanity.

LIFE is the word – We are blind - We do not see - We do not hear. We are busy until He gives us a bump on the head. Pray for all who cannot find Him even when they are bumped on the head. What a pitiful thing to not know God. Pray for all that they hear the word of God and keep it.

Jesus: Preach the Gospel in your being, My beloved ones. You are My hands, you are My feet, you are My body. Oh child, oh child, I do love you - open yourself up to My life dwelling in you. I am Life. I am Almighty. I am Truly present in the Eucharist this day! I love you so much! 11/29/94

Let Me Share Deeply in Your Life

Messenger: The more I become joined to Jesus the more deeply I can love God. I become more deeply one in Him. He lives in me. I can love God more deeply by being one in Him.

Song: *Teach Me to Love With Your Heart*

Teach me to love You with this new heart. Oh, I know little of how to love You. Create in me, oh loving Savior, this special heart.

I want to love You Jesus deeper and deeper – let me love You through Mary's pure Heart.

Let me be ever deeply united to You so I can love You more and more.

Father I come to You in the Mass in the Hearts of Jesus and Mary to offer a more pure sacrifice, a more pure offering – to love You more.

A Prayer before the Holy Sacrifice of the Mass

Let me be a holy sacrifice and unite with God in the sacrament of His greatest love.

I want to be one in Him in this act of love, where He gives Himself to me and I give myself as a sacrifice to Him. Let me be a holy sacrifice as I become one with Him in this my act of greatest love to Him.

Let me unite with Him more, that I may more deeply love Him. May I help make reparation to His adorable Heart and the heart of His Mother, Mary. With greatest love, I offer myself to You and pray that You will accept my sacrifice of greatest love. I give myself to You and unite in Your gift of Yourself to me. Come and possess my soul.

Cleanse me, strengthen me, heal me. Dear Holy Spirit act in the heart of Mary to make me more and more like Jesus.

Father, I offer this my sacrifice, myself united to Jesus in the Holy Spirit to You. Help me to love God more deeply in this act of my greatest love.

Give me the grace to grow in my knowledge, love and service of You and for this to be my greatest participation in the Mass. Give me the greatest graces to love You so deeply in this Mass, You who are so worthy of my love.

-God's Blue Book, December 27, 1995

Messenger: Jesus, impart to me Your Divine love, let me share deeply in Your life – so, I can say, it is no longer I who live, but You who live in me. Fill me, permeate my being so I am filled with Your life and this love. Then, oh, my precious Jesus, can I ever love You more deeply. Oh, Jesus, how do I love You, little me? But, if You impart to me Your love and Your life, I can love You with this life and love as I become more united to You.

Oh, Jesus, I want to love You with the deepest love. You, my precious Savior help me to love You more deeply as I am one with You. Mother Mary, place me forever in the inner recesses of His Heart so I can more closely unite to Him and give Him deeper love.

I want to love You, Jesus. I want to give You the deepest love I can. Help me to have a heart like Yours so I can more deeply love You and all those You love. How little I am, but with You, my heart can overflow with Your love.

Come and unite with me. Pour Your love into me. I want to be one with Thee, to experience Your life as it flows in me as a bubbling brook, vibrant and forceful. The power of Your Love in me – the electricity of Your Love – Oh God fill me, permeate me so it is no longer I who live, but You who live in me.

Total surrender to You, my beloved Lord.

Galatians 2:19-20
...I have been crucified with Christ and yet I am alive; yet it is no longer I, but Christ living in me...

Messenger: A dying to the self and a living in You. You live in me. I want Your love in me – vibrant, on fire. Surrender and love of the Father's will and the Father's plan. Surrender to Father, Son and Holy Spirit and Mary – Surrender to Your love. Your love permeates my being, Your life fills me. It is indeed no longer I who live, but He who lives in me. You live in me, oh Lord, to love this world with You dwelling in me. I want to be selfless and exist in You. Spirit mold me. Fashion me into the image of Jesus, to be as the Father intended me to be. He lives in me. Permeate me, fill me. I love You Jesus.

Song: *Abba Father*

Oh, Jesus, You are the Bread of life. You are love. I want to be like You. I want to live in You, my beloved Savior – I love You!

This is my love letter to you, Lord.

As the Father, Son and Holy Spirit dwell within me and fills me more, I love God more deeply. For it is no longer I who live but He who lives in me. How can I love You, Lord, little me. Help me to love You more deeply as I live in You. The more I am one in God the greater my capacity to love – the more deeply I can love God. I want to love You. How does a human person love a Divine person? If I become more one in You then I can love You better. I have a greater capacity to love, the more deeply I unite to God, the more deeply I love God.

11/29/94

Let Go to the Bliss

Matthew 11:28
Come to me, all you who labour and are overburdened, and
I will give you rest.

Messenger: Oh my Lord, I want to rest in Your most precious Heart.

Jesus: Let go, do not think, come and let go to My love, say you are
sorry, you are far from being like Me, I love you, I want you close to Me.
It is in your dying that you will put on Christ. It is in your surrendering
that you will know a new level of being united to Me. You will know My
presence with you. I want to operate through you and live in you. You
must let go of control -- letting go. Yield to Me My precious one. When
you feel overwhelmed with My presence, let go, do not stop the ecstasy -
- let go to the bliss, My Heart longs to be united to you in the deepest
way.

Messenger: Pour out Your love to me, saturate me with Your life. It
is as You saturate me more and more with Your life and Your love I can
love You with a greater capacity. I can then love You more deeply, I want
to love You so deeply and my love is so shallow, saturate me with Your
grace so I can love You more. So I can love You with deeper love.

Oh Lord, I long to give You love and I am so little, how do I love You
my Lord.

I thirst, I long, I crave, I want closer union with You. I want to love
You, I want to give You my love, but my love is so hollow only in You can
I love You more deeply. As You live in me, I love You more.   12/1/94

First Friday

Jesus: What was the most painful was the agonies to My precious
Heart, to love so deeply and be beaten by those I loved. To be so in love
with each soul that beat me and see their hatred and anger.

I felt the blood trickle down My face, I felt it run at times, My body
hurt so bad, but My Heart was so wounded with such agony to love so
much and be treated with such hatred.

This is how I come today with this great Heart of My immense love
and so many treat Me with such hatred and indifference. I love, I love, I
love and they hate Me and hate each other. How My Heart suffered for

this hatred. I saw before Me all the hatred and ugliness of My beloved souls and I loved them so much.

Oh do you know how it is to love each other and be treated with hatred. I loved each precious soul and I suffered for each soul that would refuse Me and treat Me with such hatred and neglect.

Spread My love on this First Friday.

I call you to be My apostles to spread this immense love of My Sacred Heart. I beg you to forget yourself and do My work at hand.

Messenger: Felt as if I could feel His blood run down His face but felt such immense agony to my heart, as if you couldn't take the pain to the heart.

I have a constant awareness of Blessed Mother statue at the Center, her looking down at me, me looking up at her.

I know what it is like to be hungry and want to eat.

My soul is thirsting and hungering for You Lord. I want You so much. I love You so much, my heart feels as if it will break it craves You so much.

I long for more and more of You, more intense union, I feel as if my heart is breaking to want You more.

Ask Fr. Carter to help me spread this devotion to the Rosary.
From Mary   12/2/94

First Friday between 12:00 and 3:00

Messenger: For three agonizing hours He hung, His Body bruised and bloodied from head to toe. His flesh was torn and He called out in a loud voice,

Luke 23:46
...'Father, into your hands I commit my spirit.'

Messenger: As He gave Himself on the cross He gives Himself to us this day in the Eucharist, but so many are blind to the immensity of His presence and His great love.

Stand under the cross with Mary and hear His cries from the cross. They are the cries that He cries to us this day,

Luke 23:34
...'Father, forgive them; they do not know what they are doing.'

Jesus: Oh you blind men, I write letter after letter here and no one listens. I give you your answers to turn men's hearts to love and you plug up your ears and run to your world.

You who are blind have covered your ears and you do not see or hear. What do I do to tell you how truly present I am, how I write here and want these messages to circulate? You do not pray because you do not love. I write My love letters to enkindle a love relationship with you. Oh blind men, I want these letters published. I want all My books published. You do things your own way and I am talking to you here.

What do I do to shake you? The Blue Books need to be published. These are My letters of love to all My beloved souls. Souls are at stake. Some men will lose their souls.

They need to read these messages. I ask! I plead! I tell you sweetly to publish My messages. You do not even read them yourselves. I am begging you to take Me seriously. I want all the Blue Books published. I beg you My beloved ones to listen to My pleading.

I am your beloved Jesus. I come to you with a Heart of love. I beg! I write! I come to you this day. Please listen to My pleading. I am the Son of God. I beg you to respond to My pleas. I am Jesus your Savior.

Hearken to Me, for I call out an urgent message to you this day.

12/2/94

I Saw Him Hanging

Messenger: He told me to go to the tabernacle and pray for three hours between 12:00 and 3:00.

Everyone was so excited about Christmas and Jesus was giving me intense experiences into His Passion.

I had heard Him scourged at the pillar and experienced this as if I was present while they scourged Him and heard the sounds during the night as He was in the garden. Again it was as if I were present. After Communion on December 2, I felt as if I could feel blood run down my face and I was so connected to His crowned head.

On December 2, when I received this message I heard the wind blow and saw the cross against the darkened sky. I saw Him hanging, literally hanging from the cross. He was not hanging straight as on the pictures but humped over, sliding down the cross. I do not know how to express this. I only know He was not hanging straight as I see Him on most crucifixes. He looks so in tact on the crucifixes on our walls. He did not look like that.

12/2/94 - On First Friday

First Saturday - Very Important

Agony in Garden

Messenger: See the dark night, hear the wind, the silence except the bugs of the night. Jesus is all alone, the anguish to His Heart to see every single soul before Him, to suffer for each soul, He loves so dearly, hear the wind, to know what was to transpire and His Apostles slept. He wanted their company and they slept. He was so alone, an angel appeared. I see this dark night. I feel His pain in His Heart, I feel His anxiousness to know what was to come.

Jesus: My Hour is at hand, can you not watch one hour with Me? I am Jesus, the Son of God, oh My children, do you hear My call this day as you go about your busy lives and no one has time to spend with Me. Oh My beloved ones, created by My Father, you are missing the most important thing of your life, it is this sharing in My life, it is My love. Blind are you My beloved ones. You cannot wait and watch, busy about your whims and I am God who waits with love.

Scourging at the Pillar

Messenger: I see a dark night, I see Judas, he betrayed Jesus.

Others stand about, but unexpected and so cruel is the first blow they give to Jesus, coming in the torch lighted night, a hard unexpected blow to His most precious face, a pushing of harsh instruments cold to His back as they tear His clothes and laugh, all so fast, no warning, the pushing, the poking, the anger, the hatred and He is He who is love. But the anguish to His most precious Heart, the men He loved, He loved them and they hit Him, so much pain to the Heart. The physical blows He suffered were nothing compared to the anguish to His Heart, the suffering to the emotions, to love and be hated.

Jesus: I loved those men with the tenderest love and they hit Me so hard. Unexpectedly, blows all over My body and they laughed. Oh child how they laughed and made fun with big mouths filled with the poison of hate. Oh child what comes forth from the mouth when the heart is whelmed over in hate. Men do not know that the heart is the center for love. As your heart grows in love, your whole body operates with greater beauty, as your heart grows in hate your body operates in ugliness. My Heart forever knowing the peace and love of My Father. My face forever pure in all its love, but their faces hard and ugly, welded up from the hate in their hearts.

The heart is the center for peace and harmony and love. The hearts runs the body on love. My soldiers have hearts of love. Their faces are filled with light, their mouths are pure and clean, their eyes are loving. Look at a man's face and you can see the reflection of his heart. His Heart is the source of the beauty in the person. Light your face with the beauty of a clean heart. To adorn your flesh is useless, all beauty comes from a clean heart. Make your hearts pure and loving, your eyes will radiate with the purity from within. My Mother is the symbol of purity. She is most pure. Her face radiates her most pure Heart.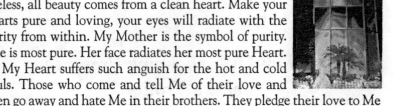

My Heart suffers such anguish for the hot and cold souls. Those who come and tell Me of their love and then go away and hate Me in their brothers. They pledge their love to Me and then in the next breath hate Me by how they treat others. My Heart was in such anguish for the hot and cold souls for those who love and those who then hate Me. Oh My beloved ones do you know the ways of the heart? Do you know how to love with real love? Love is kind, love knows no bounds, love gives, love is giving. Love is not selfish. Love is to give good to the other. Is that complicated? Do you love or do you selfishly want for yourself? If you are selfish it is not love.

Oh you are indeed blind, and what you need to see is not complicated. You can learn such technology, such complicated things in your minds, but you have left the simple concepts of loving from your hearts, behind.

Love is not haughty, love is not for your self-promotion, love is pure and simple to give good to the other. Do you know anything about love? Your hearts are so cold. You do not come to Me with a heart of love. I want to be loved by My beloved souls. I long for the pure hearts to come to Me. Oh are you blind, My blind little children, Christmas is the season of giving love, but so little love is given. You have turned My birthday into an exchange of gifts, not love. You give to get for yourself. It is so simple, you are so blind.

Come little children and purify your hearts. Some hearts are turning to stone and some selfish ones are allowing selfish minds to rule their lives. It is in knowing about the things of God that you are happiest. Make your hearts pure and watch your beauty grow. You will be beautiful when you love. Beauty comes from the heart; your clothes, your make-up, your hair does not make you beautiful, your heart makes your face shine.

It is My life alive in you and My love within that shines on your face, that makes you beautiful. Shine with the love of God in your hearts. Give the gift of a loving heart this Christmas. Give the gift of love from your heart.

Oh you tend to every detail and forget the King of Glory. He sits alone on His throne and you blind men see to every detail. Beauty is within. Beauty is in the eyes of the person, in their face, lighted with a loving heart.

It is so simple, you are so blind.

Song: *Teach Me to Love with Your Heart*   12/3/94

Had an Overwhelming Presence
of the Trinity

Jesus: I cry out to you and My words fall on deaf ears. If you have ears, hear, for I truly speak here and no one pays Me heed. You lack faith, you lack trust, you do not know what I impart to you. You, in your busy lives here, no time to hear My words.

I want My letters to circulate to My beloved children. I ask, I beg, I am not taken seriously. I am the Almighty God, heed My words here.

I called out and My words fell on deaf ears. My Heart cried out from its depth and I was rebuked, for the blind do not see and the deaf do not hear. I call out by day. I plead by night. I write My letters of such love to all souls and I am ignored. I am the Almighty God. I write these letters for all. I ask and I plead - I want My messages read. I want them to circulate.

You do things your own way. You are willful. You want proof, you lack faith. I come in the night. As the night remains, you remain in darkness. You see not. You do not even read these for the light. You do not want to be here. You do not want to pray, you do not want to turn from your ways.

You are blind men in darkness. I call, I write, I plead for months. I beg for a year. I want messages published. I am calling out an urgent request to publish these messages, to read them yourselves. You will be sorry, for souls will be lost because of the hold-up. These messages are needed now. The Eucharist is under attack. You hold these letters of My love and True Presence. I beg you one more time to listen to Me!

12/3/94 - First Saturday - Before the Tabernacle

Jesus on the Cross

Messenger: I see Him in perfect peace hanging on the cross. He is beaten, His mouth is open and blood comes from His mouth, peace. Jesus always doing His Father's will. He loves His Father's will. His eyes cast upward so often to the Father, but His face, beaten and bloodied reflects a Heart of  peace. No hatred for His attackers. Their faces so ugly and filled with hate. Their bodies unblemished projecting their anger on this Lamb of God.

Jesus: Peace I leave with you, My peace I give to you.

Messenger: He came. He showed us the way. What little crosses compared to His cross, but Jesus always in perfect peace. I see Him under the cross in the arms of His Mother, not a breath in His body, perfect peace even to His death. The secret is compliance to the will of the Father.

Jesus: Oh child, what lessons I teach you this day. Study My passion it is the doorway to My Heart. You come to Me in My sufferings, I open My Heart and you enter into the fire of My love.

Messenger: I see ever so clearer that afflictions to His body were not His greatest suffering. It was the sufferings to His Heart. His Heart is perfect love. How His most precious Heart suffered so for love of each and every soul. How deeply the wounds of the heart.

Look to Mary she suffered by Christ's side, not one mark on her body but her Heart so filled with pain we cannot describe her pain.   12/3/94

Come to Me, I Long for You

Jesus: My little dear children,

I am Jesus, your Savior, I remain with you in the Eucharist in My Divinity and humanity, no less present than the day I walked the earth. I love you so much. I wait for you, endless hours in the tabernacle, the same Jesus who died on the cross, I wait, I long, I yearn, I thirst for the love of souls. I want you to come and pour your heart out to Me. I give you My great graces when you come to Me in the tabernacle.

Oh little dear ones, I love you so dearly, this day, I would suffer and die for you, you are so precious to Me. I love you individually. I wait you to come and be with Me. I suffered so much for the endless hours I would sit in the tabernacle and no one would come and be with Me. Oh, I love you so dearly, I call to you in this message. I want to be so close to you.

God dwells in you in a special way when you are in the state of grace. I and My Father and Holy Spirit dwell within you. We are present within you.

I am present in My Divinity and humanity in the Eucharist. I am no less present than I was when I walked the earth. I am God, where I am, My Father and the Holy Spirit are. My Mother is forever by My side.

I, Jesus Christ, am no less present than the day Mary carried Me in her womb. I am there truly present, Body, Blood, Soul and Divinity and I wait for you this day.

Will you come and be with Me and share your love with Me? Will you come and allow Me to shower you with My great graces and love? Will you come and tell Me your love for Me? Will you come? I want to be your best friend. I outpour My Divine love to you.

Oh My sweet ones, I love you so dearly, I never abandon you. I love you with the deepest intense love every second. My Heart beats with deepest love for you, even when you forget Me.

My Heart is open, it is ablaze for love of you, this very day.

Come to Me, My precious one, I am waiting for you with deepest love.

12/3/94

Unconditional Love

Jesus: Do you know what it is to love someone and be treated coldly? Think of your most agonizing pain to your heart, think of Me loving so much those who totally neglected Me and hated Me to the point of death.

It is in understanding the agonies of My Heart that you understand My immense love. Love gives unconditionally, love gives, love does not exist to receive only. It is in giving that you receive, but love gives.

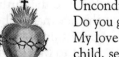

Unconditional Love:
Do you give this way? The heart is a symbol of love! My love burned for those who persecuted Me. You, My child, see My Heart open without the cross and crown of thorns -- My Heart is open to the point it is overflowing with

fire. It is the hour of My greatest mercy and My greatest love. I pour the open furnace of My divine love upon you. You are saturated by My love --divine love, I give to you!

I wait, I watch, I want the love of My beloved souls!

You hold personal love letters from Me to My beloved ones concerning this tremendous love. If the whole world does not believe, I want you to believe, how I, Jesus, love you this day. It is in your believing you will be drawn ever closer into the abyss of My love for you. You were tired, you are being tested as My soldier of love. Love is unconditional, love gives, love has itself rooted in God's love. He is the source. All other roads to love are second to His divine love. Oh, divine love, burning love, coming from My open Heart and you cry and run to this world.

Rita, Rita, I write to be heard. I want these messages to circulate now. The delays will hold up the hearts that are dying for My love.

Hearts are cold and hard and need to know My divine love. I beg you to take Me seriously. You are the apostles to spread the devotion to My Heart. I beg you to circulate these letters of My love. Every day the Eucharist is attacked more and more --- I am referred to as a "symbol".

My true presence is attacked. People do not believe. Children are being taught the Eucharist is only a symbol.

Every book is different. They need to circulate for the priests and sisters, they need to circulate for My faithful loved ones, they need to be published.

I write to be heard. These messages are important to spread the devotion to My Heart. I beg you. They are important to understanding My relationship with My Mother. To hold up these books is to hold up the messages on the two Hearts. I beg you to circulate all the books. The fourth book is on the two Hearts and deep union, **but the fifth book is a book of such deep love and understanding into My Sacred Heart.**

I beg you to spread these messages -- all the messages. I will provide all money to publish books, three, four and five. The money is given so the proceeds from the books and songs can go to Shepherds of Christ. These books are needed for this ministry. People in the chapters need to read these books. I am asking you to take Me seriously. I write these messages for My beloved souls. I write these messages to spread devotion to My Heart and My Mother's Heart. The books are on disks and the money is provided. If you want your people to grow close to My Heart, you will publish these books of My deepest love. I beg, I ask, I plead, I am ignored. I am Jesus, your beloved Savior. I am thirsting for the love of souls. The Eucharist is being attacked. I remain with you in My deepest love. To hold up these messages is to hold up hearts that would know My love. I yearn, I thirst, I long for the souls to come to Me.

I am Jesus. I beg you to spread these messages which lead to My Sacred

Heart, from My Sacred Heart, for My Sacred Heart, through My Mother's Heart. My Heart will triumph with the greatest love, it is through Mary's Heart many will turn to Me. These messages are written from Me and My Mother to spread devotion to Our Hearts. It is in the rosary many will turn their hearts to such love. These messages are written from the Heart of My tender Mother and Myself. I beg you to spread these letters.

Song: *Little Child*   12/4/94

A Message Given to Father Carter

A Message given to Father Carter, December 5, 1994, two years before Jesus appeared on the cross with His mouth moving at the point of death.

Jesus: My beloved priest-companion,

Please tell My beloved the following: I want all the Blue Books to be published through Shepherds of Christ Publications. I want them all to be published as quickly as is reasonably possible.

Give _____ the message I gave to My beloved _____ on December 4. Tell _____ I love him with a special love, and that he is not to doubt My words. I pour out the great love of My Sacred Heart to all.

I am Jesus, Chief Shepherd of the Flock.   12/5/94

Jesus Suffered for My Brother

Messenger: I look at the person I am having trouble with and send them love. I cannot be angry at any man, I must love them. To see that person with such love. Seek the good in them.

Oh how could I be angry at you my brother, Jesus suffered such blows to His precious back because He loves you so.

See Jesus standing at the pillar being beaten.

See the hatred of men and know He withstood it lovingly for the brother I am displeased with.

Oh you dear brother are so precious to Him, how dear you are to me.

My lack of peace can come from these two things not doing His will because it is something I do not want to do and is hard, holding anger in my heart for others.

I must love, but to love, I must be aware that God truly loves me and I am trying with all my heart to please God and love my brother.

To let go and say Jesus, I make mistakes, but my greatest intention is to live to do Your holy will, no matter how hard. To love God's will because He wants us to do it and it will give us peace.   12/5/94 - Monday

I Give You My Grace

Jesus: Oh sweet ones I was born a little baby for love of you that you would know My immense love for you.

I came into this world that you might be with Me in heaven. I want you to share My Divine love.

My love I show you so immensely during My passion.

I want to outpour My grace to you. I give you Myself in the Eucharist. I died, I rose on the third day, I opened the gates of heaven and you My beloved ones can be with Me forever in Paradise.

I was born, I humbled Myself to share in your humanity so you could share in My life.

"By the mystery of this water and wine may we come to share in the divinity of Christ, who humbled himself to share in our humanity."

~From the words of the Mass

In meditating on all the mysteries of My life, you can imitate My life and My Mother's life.

You were created in My image and likeness to love God and love one another.

This Christmas I call you to love. I call you to consecrate your lives to My Heart and My Mother's Heart. I call you to pray to the Spirit to mold you more into My image and likeness. Live in My Divine love, LIFE IS LIFE only in Me.

I came as a baby, I died for your sins and I raise you to new life, you are partakers in My Divine life through baptism.

Live your consecration daily, turn your lives to Me, surrender totally to love in Our Hearts.

Oh dear ones, close your eyes, live to do the Father's will, forgive all your brothers, live to love all, think thoughts of love for those you are angered with, see Me scourged at the pillar for love of them.

Let go and let My life and My love live in you. Let go. LET MY LIFE LIVE IN YOU.

Song: *A Song From Jesus*   12/5/94 - Monday

Satan Wants the Souls

Jesus: My precious child,

Do not doubt. Doubt and worry come from satan. I come to you with greatest love, I am your loving Savior. I am your God. I died for you. I come to you this day.

Souls are at stake. You can help prevent the loss of souls through your love and service of Me. I need you to spread My love. <u>Satan wants the souls of My beloved ones. He wants them to go to eternal damnation.</u> I am giving you these letters of My love. I write clearly and lovingly to all souls. How I intensely love all. Do not morbidly fear -- that fear is from satan. You need to pray. Do not let him work on you. He wants you stopped. Focus on My love for you. Oh children, hearken to My call for you. I call out by day, I call out by night. The world is asleep. They do not want to hear that which I impart to you. They plug up their ears. They close their eyes and who do you see that does your work?

I call you to prayer. I call you to surrender. I call you to Me. I will tend to your work, your house, your car, all those jobs you think are so important. They are never to stop you from your prayer. Let go to Me. Pray to Me. Only in prayer will you be protected.

I am guarding you My beloved child. Prepare Me a way, for I am coming into your midst. Many will lose their souls. Are your dishes your end? You are being called to spread My love this way. My love I give to you, My beloved one.

I love you so much. Read My letters, sing My songs. I am Jesus. I am in your midst this day. I come to you with greatest love. I am your loving Savior. I am your God. I died for you, I come to you this day.

Love, Jesus   12/8/94

I Am a Mother

Messenger: My children were about 10 and 15

Jesus: My child,

I want you home with your children. I provide opportunities for you to be alone with them and you want to be with them. Doing My will is doing My will. Your children come first before others. I want you to pray at the Center when no one is there. You have a job as a mother. You have a responsibility. Oh child, it is hard to do what you know you should, but your heart leads the way. I am Jesus and I love you so much.   12/8/94

See Me in Your Brothers

Messenger: To see Jesus in our brother.

Jesus: Rita, I am in your brothers. Look at your brother and see Me in their eyes. See Me as I dwell in them.

Play with your children. You are pleasing Me. Let go of this world and the glory. See Me in your children. Play with your children, when you play with them see Me in them.

See Me in others. Look for Me in their faces, in their actions, look for Me in your brothers.

I am in your brothers, starving to death. I am in your brothers. When you love your brothers you love Me.

You love Me when you love your brothers. What you do to your brothers you do to Me.

Messenger: Lord give me the grace to love as You want me to love. Help me to love others as You would love them. Help me to love my brothers. I am Your hand, I am Your heart, I want to give Your love to this world.

Doing His will is doing His will. That is what brings me greatest peace and happiness. I am living to do His will. In this I find my peace. He calls me to love. He calls me to spread His love to this world. I turn myself over to Him.   12/9/94

I Love the Consecrated Host

Messenger: I long for Jesus in the Eucharist. I want to receive Him so much. I long for Him so much, I feel as if my heart hurts. My heart hurts so much some times because I want Him so much.

I LOVE THE CONSECRATED HOST --

I LOVE TO LOOK AT PICTURES OF THE CONSECRATED HOST

I WANT TO ADORE THE HOST --

I want to see Him, my love. I receive Him in the consecrated host, I adore Jesus. Jesus is truly present in the consecrated host. Jesus is the Savior of the world.

My heart just aches to want Him more and love Him so much.

I know heart ache.

Opened Blue Book IV to September 9.

Agonies Of The Heart

Messenger: I realized in church that the Mary statue in the residence chapel is the same vision I had of Mary on the Feast of St. Joseph, March 19th. She was on the left side of the altar. She was holding the child, long and slender, same form, a light came down from above and surrounded her. (St. Gertrude's Church, at the Gospel, Sat. Feast of St. Joseph).

My heart, after communion, feels as if I will break. I want union with Him so much. No tears, nothing will satisfy this intense longing to want Him ever more. I just want Him so much. I feel as if nothing can express my feelings. I know it is an intense ache for union and nothing will make it better but Him. I crave union with Him, total and complete. I want to know the Father. I want God's love so much. My heart longs for the courts of the Lord.

Such intense longing, for I love Him so much. I feel like I will die from the ache in my heart.

Jesus: My soul aches for you, My precious child. How I long for your love. How I gave My very Self for you and this day I am ignored and forgotten. I am God. I am in your midst this very day, but people are so fixed on the things of this world.

Do you know how My soul longs for union with My precious ones? I allow you to experience the feeling of intense longing as if your heart will break. My love I pour out to all My beloved ones and I am ignored and forgotten. I give Myself to them. I remain with them in such intense love in the Eucharist and I am ignored.

Oh, My child, I give this to you to reach My little ones with this knowledge of My Heart. No one knows the pains of the heart as I suffered so for the neglect. To give My very own Flesh and Blood and be rejected and treated so coldly by those I died for! Agonies of the heart, the greatest of all agonies and My love so freely given for all. My Heart, a burning furnace of endless love, swelling up with such intensity and ardent love, to be ignored and forgotten!

My child, My Heart is as you cannot even comprehend, but I give Myself to you because I love them so. Tell them of My love. Your heart aches as I allow you to experience such heartache. My child, My child, suffer for Me. I love you so much. I give this to you in greatest love to be closer to Me.

You are My most precious child. I love you so very much. Draw yourself into the abyss of My love, draw yourself deep within My Heart. Let go, totally, let go and experience My Heart. My Mother leads you to My very precious Heart. It is through her Heart you are being placed so deeply into Mine. Let go and experience My most tender love for you. I am your precious Jesus. I love you so deeply, My beloved. Let go! Your resistance to let go is what keeps us from greater union. Totally surrender, giving your all to Me.

Messenger: I know a little how He suffered because He loves us so much. Such heartache, to love so much. He is forgotten by so many. How His Heart suffered for those souls He loved that would go to hell. For some very sinful pleasures of the body, some have lost their souls. I experience this suffering before the tabernacle or after receiving the Eucharist in Mass. He suffered immense pain. He suffered for the ignorance of so many. He is truly here this day and in our midst. This is the Son of God, truly present. I feel such connection to His pain suffered in the garden. He suffered so for the indifference, neglect, ingratitude of so many souls. He suffered for the injustices to the Blessed Sacrament, the Sacrament of His greatest love.

He gives Himself and He is rejected. What pain, agonies of the heart. He loves us so much and He is rejected by so many. He is treated coldly and ignored.

Jesus took on a human body. He loves us so much. He gave Himself, His very flesh and blood that we might have life! He is, this day, ignored. People have made themselves and others their gods. Many who receive Him in the Eucharist, do not realize He is truly present. Some do not have time to spend with Him and learn to know Him. Many of His precious souls know every sports star, they know all about the sport stars' lives but do not have time for the Son of God. Many souls do not have time for Jesus who gave His life for them!

Jesus: Oh, you blind world, oh you senseless ones, I am, Who Am. God created you. Many of your hearts have turned cold and forgotten your God! I come as a thief in the night. Many souls will be lost forever. What more do you want Me to do? I give you a free will, I love you so very much, and you do not come to Me. Do not live your life in vain. You wandered down roads that led you to your own destruction.

My Mother appears to lead you to My most Sacred Heart.

My children, My Heart waits for you. I am forever loving you with the same burning love. Turn not your backs to Me. I am the Almighty God. It is through Me you will be saved. If you love and serve Me, you will live in heaven forever and ever.

Alleluia.

* Vision: (I saw a door twice, saw His face twice in an interior vision.) Mary is the door we must go through to be placed in the inner recesses of His Heart. She carried our Beloved Savior in her womb. She taught Him how to be gentle, how to have a kind Heart. Now she is our spiritual Mother, she molds us and leads us to her Son.

* Jesus wants us to pray the *Prayer for Union* with Him.   9/9/94
12/9/94

Let Go, Love Gives

Messenger: I must be loving to unite with God. If there are any feelings of anger or division in my heart I cannot unite deeply to God. God is love.

Jesus: LOVE from your heart. Your heart is full of division, any bitterness toward others in your heart keeps us apart. Let go of all anxieties, let go of all your hurts, hidden or not, your heart must be pure. You are holding on to old hurts and lots of anger and then you expect to be close to Me.

Let all your cares at the foot of My cross. You are not being bathed by My love because you are not loving your brothers.

Love gives to the other for the sake of the other. Love cares for the other's needs. You need to go home with your son, you need to be with your children, you need to let go and experience My peace, My love within you.

Operate as I want you to. Let go, let go, let go into My loving arms. I am Jesus your Savior, you must smile and love and do the Father's will.

12/10/94 - Saturday

Do You Hear?

Jesus: My beloved children,

I am your precious Jesus, I write to you this day because I love you so dearly. I come to you. I was born in a little stable in Bethlehem, I come to you -- My Father wanted Me to come.

John 3:16
For this is how God loved the world:
he gave his only Son,
so that everyone who believes in him
    may not perish
but may have eternal life.

Jesus: I come to you into this world through the Holy Spirit in the womb of My loving Mother.

I am My dear little children still with you this day. The trumpets blare, the drums roll -- I came in the quietness. Do you hear? Are you blind? I am Jesus, no less present than I was in My Mother's womb. You will reach greatest intimacy with Me this day through Mary's tender Heart. I want to come to you this day through My Mother's Heart.

Pray dear ones for grace to know and love Me more, beg for the virtues and gifts of the Spirit to live in you. I outpour My grace to you. I outpour My love. All through the day live to do the Father's will. Do His will with the greatest love. It is in offering your daily actions in the morning offering to the Father in union with the Mass throughout the world that you receive great benefits for all your prayers, works, joys and sufferings. Pray at this time for an outpouring of grace, pray for virtues and gifts.

I long to be ever closer to you. You will have peace and joy when you strive ever more to live in the Father's will. I love you so much.

12/11/94

Hold Me, Mary

Messenger: Oh I long to be molded more and more into the image of Jesus. As He was formed in Mary's womb, I long to be formed in Mary's Heart to be pure.

Song: *Give Me Your Heart Oh Jesus*

Dear Mary,

As you held the child Jesus so tenderly against your chest, hold me next to your Heart. It is in your loving arms I find rest.   12/12/94

Remove the Blocks

Messenger: Dear Jesus,

What is the wall around my heart that is keeping me from You? I want to be close to You, but something is blocking me.

Oh Jesus create in me a clean heart, to let go of all the hurts and problems I have with anyone in the past. Help me to forgive, to put all my past behind and love. I want to spread my love.

I can feel the wall lifting as I make it my goal to love all persons I have ever had a problem with, living or dead, loving my mom and dad and all those who have died and looking forward to seeing them again some day.

I see them in my heart happy with You. Oh Jesus, thank You for lifting this blockage to loving You. I want to love You and love those around me. Create in me oh Lord, a heart like Yours.

I bumped into a car in the parking lot and the lady was so mad, I hardly touched her.   12/12/94

With Regard to Suffering

Messenger: He humbled Himself to share in our humanity. Let us share in His Divinity.

Jesus: In suffering you must feel My love. I am close to you, My child. I am forever there with a beating Heart of love. When you suffer you must trust. Learning this is the key to your peace. Do not wait for the suffering to be lifted, draw closer to Me in the suffering. Your life is never apart from Mine. Your life is one in Me.

In suffering, I allow you to experience My deepest love. Embrace all I send or permit as the Father's will. This too, shall pass, but I am allowing whatever you are experiencing now for a reason.

Oh little child, you must trust Me as He Who loved you to My death.

I give you great gifts of My love. Trust and have faith. As Mary always said, "yes", you say, "yes" to all I send you. Come to her loving Heart and be formed by the Spirit more and more into My image. Love is the key, always love and doing the will of the Father.   12/12/94

The Joyful Mysteries

This rosary, December 12, 1994, was given as Mary appeared that evening at 6:30 in the back of the Rosary Chapel at Our Lady of the Holy Spirit Center.

Song: *Ave Maria*

The Annunciation

1. "In the sixth month the angel Gabriel was sent by God to a town in Galilee called Nazareth, to a virgin betrothed to a man named Joseph,

of the House of David; and the virgin's name was Mary. He went in and said to her, 'Rejoice, you who enjoy God's favour! the Lord is with you.'" (Luke 1:26-28)

2. Hail Mary...
3. **R.** In response to the angel Mary said, "yes". She always complied to the will of the Father. She always trusted and had such faith.
4. Song: *Come Holy Spirit*
5. **R.** Mary was filled with the Holy Spirit and the Word was made flesh.
6. **R.** There was such intimacy between Jesus and Mary from the first moment of conception.
7. **R.** Jesus grew inside of Mary's body.
8. **R.** It was in her womb that His most precious Sacred Heart was formed.
9. **R.** Joseph was filled with fear and an angel of the Lord appeared to him and told him to be not afraid.
10. **R.** When we receive Jesus in the Eucharist He is no less present than when Mary carried Him inside of her womb.

Song: *O Holy Mary*

Song: *Ave Maria*

The Visitation

1. **R.** Mary went to visit her cousin Elizabeth.
2. **R.** When she saw Elizabeth the babe in Elizabeth's womb leapt for joy.
3. **R.** Mary was filled with the Holy Spirit and cried out with a loud voice her Magnificat.
4. "The Magnificat
And Mary said:
My soul proclaims
the greatness of the Lord
and my spirit rejoices
in God my Saviour;" (Luke 1: 46-47)
5. "for the Almighty
has done great things for me.
Holy is his name," (Luke 1:49)
6. "because he has looked upon
the humiliation of his servant.
Yes, from now onwards
all generations will call me blessed," (Luke 1:48)
7. **R.** Jesus wants us to realize how truly present He is inside of us each time that we receive Him in the Eucharist. We receive the true Jesus Christ, the Son of God, who comes inside of us with such love.
8. **R.** If we saw Mary this day carrying Jesus we would jump for joy, but we receive Jesus every day when we go to Communion and He is no

less present inside of us.

9. Hail Mary...

10. Song: *O Come, O Come Emmanuel*

The Birth of Jesus

1. **R.** Put yourself in the stable in Bethlehem and see Mary and Joseph as they anxiously await the birth of Jesus.

2. **R.** Jesus is born.

3. **R.** The cows and sheep are there to keep Him warm.

4. Song: *Angels We Have Heard on High* (verse 1)

5. Song: *Angels We Have Heard on High* (refrain)

6. Song: *Away in the Manger*

7. Song: *O Come All Ye Faithful*

8. Song: *What Child Is This*

9. Hail Mary...

10. Hail Mary...

    Song: *Ave Maria*

The Presentation of Jesus in the Temple

1. **R.** See Mary and Joseph as they bring the Baby Jesus to the temple to be circumcised.

2. **R.** Mary holds her tender Baby Jesus so close to her and Simeon prophesizes the sufferings that she and Jesus would suffer.

3. "Simeon blessed them and said to Mary his mother, 'Look, he is destined for the fall and for the rise of many in Israel, destined to be a sign that is opposed --" (Luke 2:34)

4. "and a sword will pierce your soul too -- so that the secret thoughts of many may be laid bare.'" (Luke 2:35)

5. **R.** From that moment on whenever Mary looked at her beloved Son the prophecy of Simeon was close in her Heart.

6. See her as she gazes so tenderly into the eyes of her beloved Son.

7. Song: *Mary's Song*

8. **R.** How well the Heart of Mary knows the Heart of Jesus. She looked at Him so tenderly as a baby. She peered into His eyes on Calvary.

9. **R.** And how many times her Heart was pierced with a sword during His bitter Passion as she stood under His cross and beheld the One that she held as a Baby when Simeon told her this prophecy.

10. **R.** If we could see through Mary's eyes all that Jesus suffered for us, all that He underwent all through His life in greatest love for us. She comes to tell us of this great love that He has for each and every one of us. See through her eyes, see her Son from His infancy to His ascension into heaven as she saw Him. Go to His most Sacred Heart through her most precious Heart that pondered Him and His love.

Song: *Ave Maria*

The Finding of Jesus in the Temple

1. "Every year his parents used to go to Jerusalem for the feast of the Passover. When he was twelve years old, they went up for the feast as usual." (Luke 2: 41-42)
2. **R.** They had gone a day's journey before they realized that Jesus was still behind.
3. **R.** With their hearts in deepest sorrowing they returned to Jerusalem to look for their beloved Son.
4. **R.** Faith and trust always in God, Mary's Heart always trusted, even in all her sorrow she always knew that the Father loved her.
5. **R.** They found Jesus in the temple and He was talking to the teachers and they were astounded at His wisdom.
6. "They were overcome when they saw him, and his mother said to him, 'My child, why have you done this to us? See how worried your father and I have been, looking for you.'" (Luke 2:48)
7. **R.** And He told Mary and Joseph that He had to be about His Father's business. He then went down and was subject to them.
8. **R.** Mary, if we ever wander from Jesus' most Sacred Heart, lead us back to the love of Jesus' Heart.
9. **R.** She is the key to lead us to the greatest intimacy with Jesus. It is through her Immaculate Heart that we will be led ever closer to Him.
10. Song: *Sweet Sacrament We Thee Adore*
    Song: *Ave Maria*   12/12/94

I Run the Universe

Jesus: Prayer My child, I run the universe, I run all the world and you do not think I can handle your problems. You who I died for. You who are so special I write you all these letters dear heart and now you have wondered from My Heart to your world.

I am in your world, I am in your heart, I am God, I never ever leave you, though a mother forsake her child, I never, ever abandon you.

Oh beloved loved one of the Father, harken to Me for as I lived and died, as I came to earth in greatest love for you, I remain forever with you this day.

Oh dear one, be alone with Me. Satan is causing confusion in your life to keep you from My Heart. Surrender to the moment, surrender to Me,

I am with you at this moment within you. I am in you, The Father, Son and Holy Spirit dwelling within you in a special way when you are in the state grace.

As long as there is any hatred or anger in your heart, you cannot get close to Me. Pray the our Father with your whole heart.

The Our Father

Our Father, Who art in heaven, hallowed be Thy name. Thy Kingdom come, Thy will be done on earth as it is in heaven. Give us this day our daily bread and forgive us our trespasses as we forgive those who trespass against us. And lead us not into temptation, but deliver us from evil. Amen.

Messenger: I am not thanking Jesus for all the gifts, I have this day. My Heart is anxious and at unrest because I am not stopping and being with Him. Union, intense union in everything I do.

Jesus: I am with you Rita, right now, God is with you, inside of you. Make a spiritual communion with Me and feel My presence as you do after Communion.

Messenger: I long for You, Jesus. I want You, Jesus. I need You, Jesus.
12/13/94

See Jesus in Their Eyes

Messenger: Went to Mass at the Center. I could see Jesus in the priest all through the Mass, as if Jesus was there.

I saw His brown hair, His face, I saw His body, I saw His love in His face and eyes. I saw Jesus so clear in the priest's eyes.

Then when I went to receive the blood, it was as if Jesus' eyes looked back at me when the woman gave me the cup. I saw Jesus' eyes in her.

He is always saying to look into their eyes. There is a reading in the blue book. It gives me chills inside to see His eyes look back at me.

Jesus: I come to you with greatest love, I am your loving Savior, I am your God I died for you I come to you this day.

Open your eyes and see My love, I live in your brothers, I am in his eyes, I am in his heart. I come to you this day.

Messenger: Give me Your Heart oh Jesus, give me a heart like Yours.

Song: *Teach Me to Love with Your Heart.*

See the priest, Christ gives us the priest. The priest is to be reverenced, he is to be honored as Christ's specially anointed son.

Jesus: Pray for your priests, how richly I bless you for your prayers and work here. Oh My beloved ones, I am present, I am with you, I am in each of you here, you are so special, God dwells in you. No less present than in Mary's womb, you receive Me in the Eucharist, Kiss the hands of the priest that is with you this day. He is to be reverenced, he is My special servant, He is with you this day.

My beloved ones, apostles of My love, open your hearts, see My Heart totally open and on fire for love of you. Ask for the grace to let go of anything that is blocking your union with Me. You must love every man, past, present, dead and living.

Love, love, love. I am love, you cannot unite with My love, if you hold on to any anger or resentments toward any person living or dead. Pray for the souls to enter heaven, love all men. This is My birthday, let your hearts be born to the greatest love. See My eyes in your brother, see the reflection of the God who created him and lives in him.

Seek and you shall find, knock and it will be opened unto you, I am here and in your midst this day.

Close your eyes and be with Me. Let Me fill you with My love. Let go, Let go.

Little child, Let go, Let go you hold on so tight, to the things that are near you, not always right etc.

Song: *Little Child*

Messenger: Jesus my Lord my God my all, How can I love You as I ought --

I can love You in my brothers.

Christmas is Christ's birthday, I must love, that is what it is all about.

After communion the priest sang Jesus, my Lord, my God, my all, I started to cry, filled up with such emotion, felt His presence -- How can I love God as I should? He is God. How can I love You as I ought?

I still feel such a presence, my heart is lingering and longing for His love.

Sat on my glasses and broke them.

How can I love You Jesus? I can love You in my brothers.

12/13/94

Fr. Carter Discerned These Messages

Jesus: My dear child,
Tell them.

Messenger: Fr. Carter has been instrumental in discerning these messages and helping me develop on my spiritual journey.

I would like to thank Ellen Satori for typing this book, for her endless hours of service to Jesus.

I would like to thank all those who have supported me with such love and I would like to thank all, my uncle Andrew.

I would like to thank Fr. Carter for discerning these messages and helping me on my spiritual journey.   12/13/94

Mary Appeared As If She Was Going to Cry

Messenger: Mary appeared as if she was going to cry.

What is the depth of Jesus' wounds — they were pierced to the other side.

What is the depth of the suffering to His precious Heart. We cannot imagine, there is no depth to His suffering.   12/13/94 - Tuesday

Mary Was so Beautiful

Messenger: Mary was so beautiful couldn't talk for 10 minutes when she appeared.   12/14/94 - Wednesday

Your Life Is Short

Messenger: My dear Jesus,
Help me to see Your ways and know Your will.

Jesus: Oh my child, how the devil will tell you to fear. Fear not for I am He who created the universe. I am your God. I am everyone's God. You are doing as I have instructed you to do. I want to save every last soul. Time is so short, men are so blind and you child are My beloved messenger. I write to you, your life is so short, the time wasted delivering this message is time that souls will be lost.

May the blessings of My Father penetrate your soul and may you feel the peace I felt on Calvary to know His love. You are so loved child, let go and do this work at hand, for it is not of your doing.

One stumbling block after another, but child, God never leaves you. You know that I am guarding you and I have protected you on your way.

Let them peck at your heels, your love for Me will sustain you, always.

12/15/94 - 5:25 a.m.

The Priests Entered the Priesthood for Love of Jesus

Messenger: The priests entered the priesthood for love of God. Love of Him led them to give up the things of the world to be priests. The priests need to be fed with the love of God. Only Jesus can feed them with His love. When the priests are fed, they will feed the people. The priests must come back to the Eucharistic Heart of Jesus. It is through Mary's most Immaculate Heart that priests will be led back to the inner sanctuaries of Jesus' most tender Heart. Emphasis must be placed on leading priests to the intimate love of the Savior. When priests are fed by the love of God, they will feed the hungry souls.

Only the love of the Sacred Heart can stand firm in this sick world. Jesus is the light of the world. It is only through His love we will be fed. The priests must be led back to the Sacred Heart of Jesus. His Heart is on fire and burning for the love of His specially anointed priest sons.

Jesus: Pray for your priests to be drawn ever closer to My most Sacred Heart through My Mother's Heart. I am the light of the world. I want to shine through My beloved priests in the Church to the hungry souls. Do not forsake Me. I am Jesus. I died for you to bring you life. I bring you My love in My Heart this day. I will warm the cold hearts. I will shine the brightest in this dark world. Come to My Sacred Heart on fire for love of you.   12/15/94

You Cannot Harbor Thoughts against Any Man

Jesus: Eyes are the windows of the soul. A heart always of love. See My Mother the purest of all hearts, her eyes tender and loving. Do not think ill thoughts of any man. Look into your own eyes and generate love from your heart. Think of the pure and loving Heart of My Mother. She is beautiful in that her Heart is full of love. Beauty is not skin deep. Beauty is a reflection of your heart within. You cannot harbor thoughts against any man, your heart must be forever pure and filled with love. Let go of any ill thoughts you have toward any person living or dead and send them My love and My Mother's love this Christmas. Pray for your deceased relatives and friends. Send them love wherever they are. Oh little ones, life is so short, you hold on so tight to things that are passing. Release, let yourself go into the arms of My Mother. Let the Holy Spirit form you into My image be transformed in the Heart of My beloved Mother. As she molded Me in her womb, let her mold you into My image though the Holy Spirit. I am your Jesus, My Heart is on fire and waiting for you to come and dwell in My Heart. Let My Mother place you ever so gently in My most Sacred Heart.
12/16/94

Fr. Carter and Jesus

Messenger: Fr. Carter was like Jesus all through the Mass. I see Jesus there, feel His presence, it is so wonderful.

Such oneness and unity with the world as I felt with lady at Church that day. We are all one in His body, we all receive His body. We are one in Him. Such oneness to see Jesus in our brothers.

I saw Jesus in Fr. Carter while he was celebrating the Mass.

Oh Jesus, how sweet You are to me. How my heart burns when You come into me.

Wanted to cry when I heard He humbled Himself to share in our humanity. Such honor He bestows on us who are so unworthy.

To such great heights He raises us. He is so good.

We are one in His body. We are one in the body of Christ.

Can't have any thoughts of division to be pure in heart.   12/16/94

Personal

Jesus: You do not have a minute to spare. I am calling you to intense surrender. Let go and let Me touch the souls I need in My army. Love your children, I am guarding your family. You will not have trouble spreading My letters or your words about Me. I am ever present. The devil is taunt-ing you. Put him behind you.

Do not ever worry about what others think. Live for Me alone.

12/16/94

Friday Night

Messenger: They passed out meditations

Mary was so beautiful — she was real — most beautiful appearance I saw, I ever saw.   12/16/94

Friday Night at Home

Messenger: Jesus appeared as my Jesus of Mercy   12/16/94

I Love God

Messenger: Oh my Jesus, How I love You, I love You.

I love You, I love You, my heart cries out for You, for deeper, deeper union with You, union that will never end, to be with You in Your most intense presence, never ever to end, oh my beloved, Jesus, how I worship, how I adore, how I love You with my whole heart, my whole soul, my whole being.

How I love so intently Your most beautiful Mother, my dear Mother, my Queen, my sweet and pure Mother and I love the Holy Spirit who is so dear, He penetrates my very being with His life inside me.

I love so dearly my beloved Father, He who is all good, He who created me, little me, with such love. Who am I that He bothers to love me so much.

Oh I cry for this tremendous gift of sharing in His life and love, I am in awe and tears to know this God in all His Might, just a little. To know Him a little is to be overwhelmed and filled with such emotion for He is truly God. He dwells among us.

Jesus Christ, the Son of God is here this day, totally present to me in the tabernacle, no less present than the day He died on the cross, no less present than the day Mary carried Him in her arms.

I am overwhelmed by the greatness of God. At His name we feeble creatures should bow and give to Him such tribute. He is the Master, He is for all generations the Almighty God, one, true, magnificent and omnipresent here and in my midst, my heart is overwhelmed with emotion and shouts of jubilation to this our God, to His greatness, to His mercy and His love. For He is one, almighty, powerful, adorable, loving God.

My beloved God, all three Persons with Mary by my side, I am overwhelmed with it all.   12/17/94

My Letters

Messenger: Fr. Carter took these letters very serious. He discerned them and was very careful to preserve the words of Jesus. Others pressed on him sometimes trying to get him to do it their way. He did not comply to people's wishes.

Here is a message from Jesus.

Jesus: Bow and bend low to He who is mighty. To HE WHO IS TO BE WORSHIPED AND PRAISED. I AM YOUR GOD, I AM HE WHO IS THE LORD, I AM THE ALMIGHTY GOD. I write to you this day with the greatest love. If you change words here, you change My words. I am writing to you My beloved one, listen or not, it is your loss, you are blind, you do not hear. You do not listen, you do things your way. You change words in My letters, I write with emotion. My words are My words. I am He who writes here this day. Harken to My call to take Me seriously. I AM GOD, I WANT TO BE HEARD. The deaf do not hear, the dumb do not speak. Give your ear to these messages for I am truly speaking here, but the blind to not see and the deaf do not hear. You do your own wills, you do not open to the Spirit among you. I am the almighty God, I can rock this earth. I ask and I plead, I am not taken seriously, I write to be heard. To alter My letters is to alter MY Letters. I ask you to be My special servants to deliver these messages. You are My dear beloved ones, I want these messages to circulate as I write them. To change My words to alter My words displeases Me. Fr. Carter is helping with all these letters. Special editing to please the public is not to My liking. I am writing with such emotion to alter the word, so much, is to alter the letter. I beg you to take Me seriously. To change words to please the reader is not publishing the letters as they were received. I ask you to once again, realize, I am Jesus, I am speaking here, these are not Rita's letters, these are My letters, these letters are from Jesus Christ, the Son of God, I love you dearly and ask you to help Me circulate My letters of love as I have delivered them.   12/17/94

Little Boy Jesus

Messenger: Realization of little boy Jesus how she looked at Him and knew what He would suffer - broke her Heart every time she looked at Him.

Passion and wounds, bare back - wounds on Jesus, thorns, nails, hands and feet - want to cry - I love Him so much.

Keep hearing I'm not going to be around long. Don't know what that means. All I care about is my children, worry about them.   12/17/94

Live to Go to Heaven

Messenger: If my life is short, all I have to worry about is loving and drawing many souls to His love.

Live to inherit the kingdom of heaven.

Time is so short, live only to get to heaven and lead others to go there.

God Bless you, I love you.

Song: *See the Eyes That Look at Mary*   12/17/94

I Saw Mary and Jesus

Messenger: 10 days all through the passion - I was there heard the blows, saw Him hanging on the cross, heard the wind blowing, heard sounds of night.

How deep is the wounds in His hands -

He humbled Himself to share in our humanity.

"By the mystery of this water and wine may we come to share in the divinity of Christ, who humbled himself to share in our humanity."

~From the words of the Mass

Saw Mary Friday.

Saw Jesus.

If we see Jesus in one another we realize that we can be one in Him. We receive His body in the Eucharist, this oneness is so enhanced after communion.

Song: *One Bread, One Body*

Messenger: We are one body in Him.

There is such oneness between Mary and Jesus, as I grow in my union with her - I am more united to Jesus because she is so closely united to Him.

We are one body, we must see in each others eyes the Jesus that is living within. As I saw Jesus' eyes in a lady at church and a priest and Fr. Carter.

Look into your brother's eyes. The eyes —   12/17/94

Joyful Mysteries

Messenger: December 17, 1994 Mary appeared, 6:30, at Our Lady of the Holy Spirit Center. I received the following rosary.

The Annunciation

1. The angel Gabriel appeared to Mary. "Mary said, 'You see before you the Lord's servant, let it happen to me as you have said.' And the angel left her." (Lk 1:38)
2. **R.** She always had such trust and faith in the Father. She always complied with the Father's Will. She said yes to the angel.
3. **R.** She was filled with the Holy Spirit and the Word became Flesh.

4. Song: *Come Holy Spirit, Fill Our Hearts . . .*
5. **R.** There was such intimacy between Mary and Jesus from the first moment of conception.
6. **R.** His little life grew within her body.
7. **R.** It was in her womb that the most Sacred Heart of Jesus was formed.
8. **R.** Joseph was filled with fear and an angel of the Lord appeared to him and told him to be not afraid.
9. **R.** He loved and supported Mary.
10. Song: *O Holy Mary*

The Visitation

1. **R.** Mary went to visit her cousin Elizabeth.
2. **R.** When she arrived, the child in Elizabeth's womb leapt for joy.
3. **R.** Mary was filled with the Holy Spirit and cried out in a loud voice the Magnificat.
4. Song: *My Soul Rejoices in God My Savior*
5. **R.** Jesus is no less present when He comes inside of us when we receive the Eucharist than He was the day that Mary carried Him inside of her womb. If we saw Mary with Jesus in her womb, we would be in awe of God inside of her, but He comes inside of us in His Divinity and Humanity, and He is present to us. We should be so flattered that Jesus comes inside of us.
6. **R.** He wants so much intimacy and love with us.
7. **R.** This is our beloved Savior. He longs and He waits for us to come and to receive Him, and to sit with Him in front of the tabernacle.
8. Song: *O Come, O Come Emmanuel*
9. **R.** A voice cries out in the wilderness: Prepare the way of the Lord!
10. Hail Mary...

The Birth of Jesus

1. **R.** Jesus was born in a stable because there was no room for Him in the inn.
2. **R.** He had not a place to lay His head. He laid His head in a manger at birth and it hung from a cross at His death.
3. **R.** The sheep and the cows kept Him warm.
4. Song: *Angels We Have Heard on High*
5. **R.** Jesus comes to us now as He was born in a stable, in quietness. He comes inside of our hearts.
6. Song: *Away in a Manger*
7. Song: *O Come let us Adore Him* (refrain)
8. **R.** What the birth of the baby Jesus did for salvation history!
9. **R.** Jesus loved us so much that He humbled Himself to be born a human.
10. Hail Mary...

The Presentation in the Temple

1. **R.** See Joseph and Mary as they take Jesus to the temple to be circumcised.
2. **R.** The prophet Simeon predicts the sufferings of Jesus and Mary.
3. **R.** And a sword, too, shall pierce thy heart.
4. "As the child's father and mother were wondering at the things that were being said about him, Simeon blessed them and said to Mary his mother, 'Look, he is destined for the fall and for the rise of many in Israel, destined to be a sign that is opposed ⸴' ". (Lk 2:33-34)
5. **R.** See the tender eyes of Mary look into Jesus' beautiful baby eyes with such love. And see her eyes look into His eyes as He carries His cross on Calvary.
6. **R.** How her Heart was pierced with a sword. See her. See all the sorrows that she went through. See through her eyes all the sufferings that she saw Jesus suffer for love of us. She calls us to see through her eyes the love of her beloved Son.
7. Song: *I Rocked Him as a Baby*
8. **R.** Stand under the cross with our beloved Mary and see through her eyes. Helpless, she stands and watches her Son for three agonizing hours as He breathes His last breath and sheds His last drop of Blood and gives the last beat of His Heart . . . the greatest love for each and every one of us.
9. **R.** How do we think about Mary who mothers us as she mothered Jesus, who is forever by our side with the most intense love? Mary, please help us to have a closer union with you so that the Holy Spirit can transform our hearts more into the image of Jesus, your Precious Son.
10. Song: *I Rocked Him as a Baby*

The Finding of Jesus in the Temple

1. **R.** See Mary and Joseph as they take Jesus up to the temple for the feast of the Passover when He was twelve years old.
2. **R.** They had gone a day's journey before they realized that they had left their beloved Jesus behind.
3. **R.** Think of the sorrow in their hearts to lose their beloved Jesus. Think of how it would be to lose your beloved child.
4. **R.** With hearts full of greatest sorrow, they returned to Jerusalem to find their beloved child.
5. **R.** After searching for three long days, they found Him teaching in the temple.
6. And she said to Him: "...'My child, why have you done this to us? See how worried your father and I have been, looking for you'." (Lk 2:48)
7. **R.** And He told them that He had to be about His Father's business,

and He went down and became subject to them.

8. **R.** Mary, please lead us to the Eucharist. He is truly present there, no less present than He was when you searched for Him and found Him in the temple. And He comes to us with greatest love, and longs for us to realize His presence and how He remains with us this day with greatest love.

9. **R.** Mary, please lead us to the Eucharist, to your Son, Jesus Christ, who waits endless hours in the tabernacle longing and thirsting for souls to come and be with Him. Open our blind eyes through your Immaculate Heart. Help us to realize your Son's immense love for us.

10. Song: *Sweet Sacrament We Thee Adore* (Refrain).

12/17/94 - Saturday

December 17, 1994

Mary speaks: The song of my Son, *See the Eyes that Look at Mary,* should be sung by all. Please put it here. It was given December 17, 1994.

See the Eyes That Look at Mary

by Rita Ring

Wake us up,___ Let us see that You are tru - ly
Fill us now, Give us Your love.__ Let us be so

Christ the Lord! _ We are blind, we need Your grace, please
close to You! _ We are blind, we need Your grace, please

o - pen up our eyes to You!
o - pen up our eyes to You!

to refrain

VERSE 3

3. We are Yours, we give our-selves, we con - se-crate our

hearts to You. We con - se - crate our

hearts to You, we give You all our love!

no refrain

A Message to Fr. Carter

Jesus: My beloved priest-son,

(6 years later Father Carter died on December 18, 2000)

I would like the Blue Books used by the members of the chapters of the Shepherds of Christ. If they so desire, they can read these messages and your messages at meetings. All the Blue Books should be published as soon as possible, as they deal with the Sacred Heart and the Immaculate Heart of My Mother.

I love you with the dearest love and thank you for your faithful service to bring the priests to the heart of My Mother and My most Sacred Heart. I am burning for love of My priestly sons. You are so special to My Heart, I have forever written your name in My most Sacred Heart. It is through this most special movement that My Church will be led back to the on fire love of My Heart, through My Mother's Heart. I am forever guarding you and keeping you deeply in My Sacred Heart. I love you with this My most tender burning love.

I am your most Sacred Heart,
Jesus   12/18/94 - Sunday

Message for the Shepherds of Christ Meeting December 20, 1994

Jesus: My dear, dear loved ones,

As My birthday approaches fill your hearts full of My love. I am with you this day.

Do not look at the little problems you face, look at the big picture. Live each day to spread the love of My dear Mother and the Christ child.

Do not let satan get you focused on incidental events. Focus on LOVE — look at the big picture — live My love in your heart.

I am filling you with such grace to spread this love. Open your hearts and love your families the greatest gift you can give this Christmas is a heart of love.   12/20/94 - Tuesday before Christmas

I Am with You

Messenger: Fill my heart with Your love. Oh Jesus, I want to receive You in the Eucharist.

Jesus: Oh little loved one,
Do you know how I miss our time alone? Please come in the night, I wait and watch for you.

Oh beloved of My dear Father, though heaven and earth pass away My words do not pass away ever, they live in your hearts.

I am truly God. I am with you in this Holy Spirit Chapel. Let Him transform you into My likeness. Pray to the Holy Spirit. Sing songs of praise and thanksgiving, worship, honor and adore the God who loves you.

Oh child, you will be raised to great heights in heaven. Highest joy and happiness. I am your beloved Savior, I love you so much. I never leave you.

Song: *A Song From Jesus*

Matthew 5:18

In truth I tell you, till heaven and earth disappear, not one dot, not one little stroke, is to disappear from the Law until all its purpose is achieved.

Jesus: My love never goes from you. Oh little loved one, you who need so much, you seek what you need in the wrong place. My love satisfies. I outpour to you a sharing in My life. You are missing such love I pour out to you My little beloved one.   12/94

Glorious Mysteries

Resurrection

1. **R.** Jesus died to bring us new life. After being locked in the tomb for three days after His crucifixion, He arose on the third day as He foretold.
2. **R.** When we suffer sometimes it seems so hard to bear, but in all the suffering, if we cooperate with the will of God, there is a deeper sharing in His life that this suffering brings, the life that Jesus wants us to share when we go through this suffering.

3. **R.** Jesus came that we might have a share in His life, so that we might have life and have it to the full.
4. **R.** Mary Magdalene and some of the others went to the tomb. The stone had been rolled back.
5. **R.** Jesus appeared to Mary Magdalene. She didn't know who He was at first, but then she realized that it was Jesus. He told her not to touch Him because He had not gone to His Father yet.
6. **R.** Jesus appeared to the apostles. They had locked themselves in a room because they were afraid.
7. **R.** Jesus traveled with two men on the way to Emmaus and recounted to them the scriptures that referred to Him from Moses and all the prophets.
8. **R.** When they got to Emmaus, they sat at table and He broke bread and blessed it. Then they recognized Him, but He vanished from their sight.
9. **R.** Later Jesus appeared to the apostles. Thomas was with them and he wanted to put his hands into Jesus' hands and feet. And Jesus said, "Blessed are those who have not seen and yet believe."
10. **R.** Jesus gave to them the power to baptize and to forgive sins.

The Ascension

1. **R.** When we are baptized, we share in God's life in a special way.
2. **R.** Jesus took them out to the town of Bethany and gave them His final blessing.
3. **R.** Then Jesus raised His arms and ascended into heaven.
4. **R.** Think of this. Jesus rose from the dead and He ascended into heaven.
5. **R.** Jesus died - He rose from the dead - He ascended into heaven.

6. "But our homeland is in heaven and it is from there that we are expecting a Saviour, the Lord Jesus Christ, who will transfigure the wretched body of ours into the mould of his glorious body, through the working of the power which he has, even to bring all things under his mastery." *Phillipians 3:20-21*
7. **R.** Think of Mary and the apostles and how they felt to see Jesus leave.
8. **R.** Jesus is truly present today in the Holy Eucharist, He remains with us in love.
9. Song: *A Song From Jesus* - I come to you with greatest love, I am your loving Savior.
10. **R.** Jesus gives us a special sharing in His life in baptism. Song: *I Am the Bread of Life.*

John 6: 53-58

Jesus replied to them:
In all truth I tell you,
if you do not eat
   the flesh of the Son of man
and drink his blood,
you have no life in you.
Anyone who does eat my flesh
   and drink my blood
has eternal life,
and I shall raise that person up
   on the last day.
For my flesh is real food
and my blood is real drink.
Whoever eats my flesh
   and drinks my blood
lives in me
and I live in that person.
As the living Father sent me
and I draw life from the Father,
so whoever eats me
   will also draw life from me.
This is the bread
   which has come down from heaven;
it is not like the bread our ancestors ate:
they are dead,
but anyone who eats this bread
   will live for ever.

The Descent of the Holy Spirit

1. "John baptised with water but, not many days from now, you are going to be baptised with the Holy Spirit.'" (Acts 1:5)
2. "When Pentecost day came round, they had all met together, when suddenly there came from heaven a sound as of a violent wind which filled the entire house in which they were sitting;" (Acts 2:1-2)
3. "and there appeared to them tongues as of fire; these separated and came to rest on the head of each of them." (Acts 2:3)
4. "They were all filled with the Holy Spirit and began to speak different languages as the Spirit gave them power to express themselves." (Acts 2:4)
5. **R.** And the apostles were transformed from fear to fearlessness.

6. **R.** Holy Spirit, transform us to be more and more like Christ so that we may be led to deeper union with the Father, through Mary's Immaculate Heart. Mary, please help us to be joined ever so closely to your Immaculate Heart.

7. Song: *Come Holy Ghost* (1st verse)

8. **R.** The apostles that were once full of fear, now went out to preach the Gospel and all understood. And where they were once so fearful, now they were not afraid. They were fearless and transformed through the power of the Holy Spirit and His magnificent grace.

9. **R.** Holy Spirit, impart to us the grace that we need to be drawn ever closer to the most Sacred Heart of Jesus through His most loving Mother. Help us to have the courage to do that which God has created us to do and to follow the plan of the Father. Where we were once full of fear, make us now fearless to follow Your calling.

10. Song: *Come Holy Spirit, fill our hearts*

The Assumption of Mary into Heaven

1. **R.** Mary remained on the earth a long time after Jesus' death.

2. **R.** And when her time had come, she was taken up into heaven.

3. **R.** Mary loved Jesus so much.

4. **R.** Mary is with God forever in heaven.

5. **R.** Mary has the closest union to God.

6. **R.** Mary is our Heavenly Mother. She wants to guide us to an ever closer and intimate union with her most precious Son. It is through her Immaculate Heart that we will achieve a most intimate union in the inner recesses of Jesus' most Sacred Heart.

7. **R.** All that is of any account, is always rooted in God. The greater our union here on earth, the greater our union will be with the Father and the Son and the Holy Spirit when we get to heaven, which is our true home.

8. **R.** Jesus longs to be ever closer and closer and closer to us. In order to have this intense union with Him, it is necessary to realize the oneness between Jesus and Mary, and go through Mary's Immaculate Heart to reach such deep union with Him.

9. **R.** Mary, hold us so close to your Heart; mother us. Help us to know you as our most Loving Mother whom Jesus gave to us, and lead us to such close intimacy to your Beloved Son and His most Sacred Heart.

10. **R.** Holy Spirit, please transform us more and more into the image and likeness of Jesus.

Coronation of Mary as Queen of Heaven and Earth

1. **R.** Now Mary reigns with her Beloved Son in the courts of heaven.
2. "Now a great sign appeared in heaven: a woman, robed with the sun, standing on the moon, and on her head a crown of twelve stars."(Revelation 12:1)
3. "What no eye has seen and no ear has heard, what the mind of man cannot visualise; all that God has prepared for those who love him;" (1 Corinthians 2:9)

4. **R.** Such preciousness, those moments after communion, this special union with Jesus. Such burning love He has for us, and we love Him. We share a most intimate union with Jesus. Our union with Jesus here below is a speck amount compared to the intense union that we will have with Him that will last forever and ever and ever and never end in heaven.
5. **R.** This intense union that we have with Jesus and with Mary leads us ever closer and closer to the most tender love of Our Father in the Holy Spirit.
6. **R.** No person, nothing that we experience here can ever compare to the intimate union that we have interiorly with the Father, the Son and the Holy Spirit and also with Mary.
7. **R.** That is what heaven is: this unending intense union with the Father, the Son and the Holy Spirit, and seeing Mary and being with her and all the angels and saints in such bliss forever and ever and ever.
8. Song: *Hail Holy Queen Enthroned Above* - 1st verse and refrain
9. Song: *Ave Maria, Gratia plena*
10. **R.** Mary is with us this very day. Jesus is truly present in the Eucharist. This is God's world. Jesus is truly present in the Eucharist with the most ardent love for each one of us. Jesus remains in the Eucharist and longs and waits for each one of us. And someday we can be forever in such intense union with the Father and the Son and the Holy Spirit, in union with Mary and the angels and saints forever and ever and ever in heaven. We cannot imagine in any way what heaven is like. God's Divine embrace in heaven, such a gift.

Messenger: The Blessed Mother appeared to me during this rosary. It was a live rosary transcribed from a tape. I received this during Mary's apparition. I was there with my two children and Marty while Mary appeared.

The Seven Sorrows of the Blessed Virgin Mary

1. **The Prophecy of Simeon.**   And a sword, too, shall pierce your heart, O Mary.

2. **The Flight into Egypt.** "After they had left, suddenly the angel of the Lord appeared to Joseph in a dream and said, 'Get up, take the child and his mother with you, and escape into Egypt, and stay there until I tell you, because Herod intends to search for the child and do away with him.' So Joseph got up and, taking the child and his mother with him, left that night for Egypt, where he stayed until Herod was dead. This was to fulfil what the Lord had spoken through the prophet: I called my son out of Egypt. Herod was furious on realising that he had been fooled by the wise men, and in Bethlehem and its surrounding district he had all the male children killed who were two years old or less, reckoning by the date he

had been careful to ask the wise men. Then were fulfilled the words spoken through the prophet Jeremiah: A voice is heard in Ramah, lamenting and weeping bitterly: it is Rachel weeping for her children, refusing to be comforted because they are no more." *Matthew 2: 13-18*

3. **The Loss of the Child Jesus in the Temple.** Think of Mary's and Joseph's hearts in such sorrow as they search for the child Jesus.

4. **Jesus and Mary Meet on the Way to the Cross.** Such intense suffering as they peer into one another eyes: but joy to see the other.

5. Jesus Dies on the Cross. Stand with Mary under the cross and see through her eyes her Beloved Son as He hangs on the cross, as He dies. Her little beloved child that she once held in her arms, now she sees Him hang from the cross.

6. Mary Receives His Lifeless Body under the Cross. Such love this Mother had for her Son and has for each one of us this day. Such love Jesus has for us that He gave His life, and such love that the Father has for us that He gave His Son. Jesus calls out to us to realize this intense love that He has for us, that He truly died and was laid in His Mother's arms without a breath in His body. He gave Himself in compliance to the Father's will and in greatest love for us. He calls out to us this day to take this seriously: that this is His world; our every breath depends on Him; our every heartbeat depends on Him; and we do nothing without God. But He calls us only to love, love of God and love of one another. Reach out and spread His love to this hurting world. This is our calling this day. Do not be blinded by the world. Pray to the Holy Spirit, to see the world through God's

eyes and see as God wants us to see this world. We are His servants to spread His love to this world and He longs and waits for us to come to Him to receive this love that He pours out in abundance to us so that we can love our brothers as He wants to love through us.

Jesus: I call you My children to love; love of one another. Will you answer this call this day? Turn not a deaf ear to Me. Open up your hearts and let Me enter in. I want to love through you, My beloved ones. I love you with the dearest love. My Heart is open and on fire for each one of you. Come and I will pour My love out to you.

7. Jesus is Placed in the Tomb.
And Mary weeps bitterly outside.

12/21/94 - Feast of St. Peter Canisius

A Note from Jesus

Jesus: You look for your love in other persons and places and I am here second by second pouring out Myself to you. Oh little scared one, do not size yourself up, just love for Me.

Love as if today was your last day to live. If you had only 24 hours to live how would you spend it?

Oh little loved one, what are you doing that is keeping you from My love? You are finding time for other things. My child, I wait for you, I love you. Let go and live in My love.

I love you my dear
little Rita.   12/94

December 1994

Messenger: I cry because I love Him so much. Last night I read the bible and it was about the crowning with thorns.

I cried and cried to hear them say they hit Him.

I cried today when I see Jesus and Mary, I love Him and her so much.

Song: *I Love You Jesus*

To realize that He is truly God, that God dwells in me in a special way when I am in the state of grace. I am filled with such emotion that I know His presence. I want to cry at Mass. He is inside of me and where He is, so is the Father and the Holy Spirit, it makes me have such great emotion.

Song: *God's Love*

This is God, this is His life He shares with us. God dwells within me in a special way when I am in the state of grace.

Such intensity I feel after communion, the Son of God comes to me in His Divinity and humanity.

We are only seeing with limited vision. Our work is affecting this world, our prayers for the priests, the Church and the world.   12/94

See the Big Picture

Jesus speaks: To all My dearest beloved ones at the Center and in the Shepherds of Christ:

You do not see the big picture. You do not see how your job is so important to My plan. Do you see your confusion? The devil presses in . He tells you how everything is hard and you are working so hard and not seeing any results. He tells you that you have not done enough. Oh, little loved ones, you are involved in the renewal of My Church. You see with such limited vision! I am using Shepherds of Christ to renew My Church throughout this world. I am lighting My world with the love that is being radiated in the many hearts that are coming to the Center and the Farm. You see, minute-by-minute, day-by-day, your frustrations and problems.

I am Jesus Christ, the Son of God. I write these intense love letters of My love for this world. You see only your little daily frustrations. You are so important to spreading My love! I am giving you messages for all My beloved souls of this world. My (Shepherds of Christ priestly) Newsletter will enkindle in priests the fire of My love. I will light this world with My light through you.

Oh, little loved ones, see the big picture. Pray for grace to know and love Me more. It is by your love of God that you will carry out My plan with ease.

You see little details. I call you to prayer. I call you to sacrifice. I call you to love and purity in your heart. I call you to union with Jesus and Mary. I call you to consecration of your heart to the Immaculate Heart of Mary and the Sacred Heart of Jesus. I call you to live in the Spirit, to pray to the Spirit, to be alive with His fire, to be transformed into My great soldiers of love, so that your hearts will be on fire with the most burning love of the Sacred Heart of Jesus.

I call you to vision. I call you to doing the will of My Father, to saying "yes" as Mary said "yes" to the angel, total compliance with His will!

I call you to time spent alone with Me in front of the tabernacle and after Communion.

Oh, My beloved children, you are blind. You do not see that this is My world. The reality is that your every breath depends on Me. I am here. I am in your midst this day, no less present than the day Mary carried Me in her womb, no less present than the day I died on the cross. Open your eyes and see the love I am pouring out to you.

This (Our Lady of the Holy Spirit Center) is My Mother's house. I write these letters to you from her house in Norwood. I am alone many times in My tabernacle here. You cannot light this world on your own.

You need to pray for the grace to grow in love of Me.

I write these letters of My intense love to My precious souls. I want these letters to circulate. The lives of Myself and My Mother will become more and more alive to you as you read these letters. Pray the rosary with these meditations. I am begging you to listen to Me.

I am Jesus Christ, the Son of God. I have written five books of My intense love. I have given you such insights into My suffering and My Mother's suffering. It is through the rosary and these letters that the love of God will grow more and more in men's hearts. I beg you to take Me seriously. I love, I love, I love. I write songs of My love. I want these songs recorded.

I am an open furnace of endless love, on fire for My beloved souls. I write, I write, I write of this love. You do not take Me seriously!

Your city will shine with the love of Jesus in the hearts of those who go to the Center when you promote these letters. To hold these letters back from My beloved souls wounds My Heart. I wait. I long. I thirst for the love of My beloved souls. I write five books of love letters. I beg you, all of you involved in circulating and publishing these letters, to do so. Your churches will radiate with My love when you circulate these letters.

My Heart is on fire for love of you. I beg you this day to listen to Me. I am Jesus. I write of My ardent love for you and I am taken so lightly! Please circulate and read these messages! Please support these letters! What more must I do to tell you? What more do you want? I write five books of My love. I teach you the rosary to help Our lives live in you. The rosary is so important to the hearts of those who go to the Center and the members of Shepherds of Christ. The rosary and its mysteries must live in the lives of those who pray them. My renewal will come from the two Hearts. Listen to Me. Please circulate these letters and rosary meditations. They will lead many hearts to My love and the love of Mary.

12/22/94

I Love You Jesus and Mary

Messenger: My beautiful Mother,

Oh how I love you Mary, you held the child Jesus so tenderly in your arms, you who mother me so tenderly. Hold me in your arms, so close to your heart and place me ever so gently into Jesus' tender loving Sacred Heart. Oh Mary, my dear, dear Mother, draw me ever closer to your motherly love and the love of your beloved Son. Draw me ever closer to His most Sacred Heart. This Heart that thirsts and loves me so dearly.

I LOVE YOU SO MUCH.

Love Rita

Messenger: Oh Jesus How I love You.

Song: *I LOVE YOU JESUS.*

How Mary and Jesus love us and want us to give Them such love. They can experience this great love we have for Them.

Jesus says He thirsts and longs for our love.

Song: *Teach Me to Love with Your Heart*

Song: *The Rosary Song*

The Rosary Song

by Rita Ring

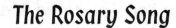

REFRAIN

Oh the ro - sa - ry, __ the ro - sa - ry __ is the

love of their two hearts, Oh the ro - sa - ry, __ the

ro - sa - ry __ is the love of their two hearts.

VERSES 1-4

1. A - ve Ma - ri - a, A - ve Ma - ri - a. Oh the
2. Je - sus we love You, Ma - ry we love __ you. Oh the
3. This is her peace plan, Chil-dren must pray __ it. Oh the
4. We turn to Ma - ry, She is the Queen of Peace. Oh the

VERSE 5

No left hand

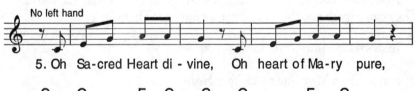

5. Oh Sa - cred Heart di - vine, Oh heart of Ma-ry pure,

A - ve Ma - ri - a, We love to pray it! Oh the

Be There in the Passion

Messenger: Hear the wind blow — see Him hanging on the cross. I heard the blows, it was so clear —

I heard the agony — I heard the sounds of the night —

How deep is His wounds in His hands

Carrying cross injury to arms

Song: *Little Baby Hands and Feet*

Priest is such a gift from God, such honor

We should LOVE His Church
We should LOVE the priest
We should ADORE JESUS

One-ness of Mary and Jesus

A Message to Fr. Carter

The Holy Spirit

Jesus: "My beloved friend, tell My people to pray daily to the Holy Spirit. They are to pray for an increase in His gifts. My people must realize that the Holy Spirit comes to transform them. The Spirit desires to transform you more and more according to My image. Those who are docile to His touch become increasingly shaped in My likeness. He performs this marvel within Mary's Immaculate Heart. The more one dwells in My Mother's Heart, the more active are the workings of the Spirit. The Spirit leads Mary to place you within My own Heart. In both Our Hearts, then, your transformation continues. The more you are formed after My own Heart, the more I lead you to the bosom of My Father. Tell My people all this. Tell them to pray daily for a greater appreciation of these wondrous gifts. I am Lord and Master. All who come to My Heart will be on fire to receive the gifts of the Spirit in ever greater measure! I love and bless My people!"

Reflection: The Holy Spirit is given to us to fashion us ever more according to the likeness of Jesus. And the more we are like Jesus, the more Jesus leads us to the Father. Do we, each day, pray to the Holy Spirit to be more open to His transforming influence? Do we strive each day to grow in union with Mary? The greater our union with our Mother, the spouse of the Holy Spirit, the greater is the transforming action of the Holy Spirit within us.   *Excerpt from Tell My People*

Messenger: Mary appeared to me!
Song: *The Rosary Song*

12/22/94

The Sorrowful Mysteries

Agonies of the heart...the greatest of all agonies
Messenger: On December 23, 1994, I received the following rosary at Our Lady of the Holy Spirit Center. I met Harold and his family.

Agony in the Garden
1. **R.** Be there with our beloved Jesus in the garden. Hear the sounds of the night. See Him as He kneels in such anguish, seeing all the things that are about to happen with His coming Passion.
2. **R.** And He cries out to His Father. " 'Father,' he said, 'if you are willing, take this cup away from me. Nevertheless, let your will be done, not mine.' " (Luke 22:42)

3. **R.** Agonies of the heart...the greatest of all agonies. Jesus saw before Him the souls that He loved so dearly. Many souls would neglect Him and treat Him with such indifference.
4. **R.** The agonies He suffered to His Heart were so immense. The wounds in His Heart so deep.
5. **R.** He saw before Him all of His most beloved souls that would be condemned to eternal damnation despite all the sufferings that He was about to undergo.
6. **R.** His agony was so great that His sweat became as great drops of Blood upon the ground.
7. **R.** This is the reality: God runs the world. Jesus truly suffered for love of us. He gave His life and He suffered in the garden for all the sins that we are committing this day.
8. **R.** He saw before Him His entire Passion: the blows, the spitting, His death on the cross. He saw this. With greatest love of us, He endured the Passion to the end.
9. **R.** He was filled with such anguish and suffering that an angel of the Lord appeared to Him to comfort Him.
10. **R.** He waits endless hours in the tabernacle today. Jesus Christ, the Son of God in His Divinity and His humanity, waits for us to come and to be with Him. He said in the garden: "He came back to the disciples and found them sleeping, and he said to Peter, 'So you had not the strength to stay awake with me for one hour? Stay awake, and pray not to be put to the test. The spirit is willing enough, but human nature is weak.' " (Matthew 26:40-41)
Can we visit Him today in the tabernacle?

Scourging at the Pillar

1. **R.** See Jesus as they tie Him to the pillar. He is God-made-man.
2. **R.** With anger in their hearts, they beat Jesus to the point of their own exhaustion.
3. **R.** Hear the sounds as they beat Jesus. They hit His precious back. Hear the blows over and over again as it tears at His flesh. Do you hear Jesus as He makes whimpering sounds? The men are  filled with anger and hatred, and they beat Jesus with great force.
4. **R.** Do we have any idea what it is like to suffer as Jesus suffered for love of us?
5. **R.** How deep are the wounds that covered His entire Body as they stood by mercilessly and they beat Him?
6. **R.** Think of how Jesus suffered. Be there at the pillar and hear the sounds. See what He went through: their anger and their voices hol-

lering at Jesus. He was mercilessly tied to the pillar while they struck Him, God Who is all love.

7. Song: *A Song from Jesus*
8. Song: *Teach Me to Love With Your Heart* (verse 1)
9. Song: *Teach Me to Love With Your Heart* (verse 2)
10. Song: *Teach Me to Love With Your Heart* (verse 3)

The Crowning of Thorns

1. **R.** They pounded a piercing crown of thorns into Jesus' most precious head.

2. **R.** They put a dirty purple robe on Jesus and they sat Him on a throne. They mocked Him and they spit on Him, and they hollered ugly slanders against Him.
3. Song: *God's Love* (verse 1)
4. Song: *God's Love* (verse 4)
5. **R.** He is truly here with us, and His Heart is ablaze with love that radiates for us. We are His beloved ones. He withstood all this torture so that we might have eternal life, so that He might have the deepest union with us. And some day, if we go to heaven, we will be forever united to Jesus, the Father, and the Holy Spirit in such close union that will last forever and ever and ever. He shed and gave His last drop of Blood for love of each one of us.
6. Song: *A Song from Jesus*
7. **R.** He is present in the tabernacle with such love for each one of us as He had the day they crowned Him with thorns and poked Him and spat on Him. He is with us this day, no less present than the day He was scourged and crowned with thorns. He loves us so much. He shed His Blood and gave the last beat of His Heart.
8. Hail Mary.....
9. Hail Mary.....
10. Hail Mary.....

Jesus Carries His Cross

1. **R.** He carried His cross on His most precious shoulder. The weight was so heavy that it felt as if His shoulder would break. He did not give up His cross. When the weight was too heavy for Him to bear, He collapsed under the weight of it.
2. Song: *Under the Weight of the Wood*
3. **R.** Jesus traveled with His cross on His back. His Heart was in such anguish for all the souls that would reject the grace for eternal salvation that He would merit for them.

4. **R.** Jesus is our focus. The more we are drawn to the immense love of this most Sacred Heart, the more we realize how He is truly alive this day. He loves each one of us. We will experience the peace, the joy, and the love that He wants us to have. We will be His lights shining in this world.

5. **R.** He has DIVINE LIFE and DIVINE LOVE in His most Sacred Heart. He outpours HIS LIFE TO US. He merited this grace for us by His death on the cross.

6. **R.** As His Mother walked along side of Him on Calvary, she walks along side of each of us. She never leaves our side. She withstood all this suffering. She knew what it was like to suffer. She did not take anything to relieve the suffering and she did not leave His side. She withstood such suffering, standing by His side. She stands by our side as we walk our path, which sometimes seems like a slow Calvary. But Mary is by our side with such love. She gives us her maternal love. She mothers us as the most perfect Mother. God the Father chose Mary as Mother of Jesus and us.

7. **R.** When our path is so hard we must realize Mary is always with us. It is God's grace that will get us through.

8. **R.** Jesus' grace is sufficient for every trial that you are experiencing this day. We must go to Him, go to His most Sacred Heart through Mary's Immaculate Heart. Mary leads us to Him. He is Love.

9. Song: *Little Baby Hands and Feet* (verse 1)

10. Song: *Little Baby Hands and Feet* (verse 2)

Jesus is Crucified and Dies on the Cross

1. **R.** See Mary as she holds the tender feet and the tender hands of the Child Jesus. And see her as she sees them nail His precious hands and feet with big nails into the cross.

2. **R.** How deep are the wounds in Thy precious hands and Thy feet, oh Jesus? How deep, oh Jesus, are the wounds to Your Heart? You suffered so for souls. Oh precious Jesus, fill our hearts with Your divine love and Your divine grace so that we may never wound Thy Sacred Heart with indifference, with neglect. Fill us with Your divine life so that we will always be drawn to the source of real life which is only found in You. I am sorry for all who neglect you in the Holy Eucharist.

3. **R.** You gave Your very flesh, You gave all the Blood in Your veins. You spread Your arms and You gave Your all for love of us, dear Jesus. And this day, You give Yourself in Your Divinity and Your humanity, with greatest love, in the Holy Eucharist. Help us, dear Jesus, to be deeply aware that You are truly the Son of God and that when we receive

You, we receive God in our hearts.

4. Song: *A Song From Jesus*

5. **R.** You ask us to love God and love one another. You were beaten for love of our brothers. Why can't we love our brothers? You call us to love as You loved us. You call us to give our lives for our brothers.

6. **R.** Oh Mary, as you stand under the cross, how deep is the anguish to your Heart? You have no wounds, you have no scars. You're supported by your beloved John. And this day you walk by our side and you support us as we walk what seems to be a Calvary sometimes. You forever walk by our side and hold us up with such motherly love. You gave Jesus such love as you stood under His cross. Thank you, Mary, for the love that you outpour to us.

7. Song: *I Love You Jesus* (verse 1)

8. Let us see, Oh Mary, through your eyes, the love that your precious Son has for us. Let us be joined ever closer to the tender Heart of Jesus through your most Immaculate Heart. Jesus gave the last drop of His Blood and the last beat of His Heart for love of us.

9. Song: *I Love You, Jesus* (verse 2)

10. Song: *I Love You, Jesus* (verse 3)   12/23/94

A Heart of Love - GIVES

Jesus: I gave, I gave, I gave. When you love you give, you do not hold back, you do not build a wall to fortify the self, the focus is always on the other. Seeing with My eyes, feeling with My Heart. I give Myself to you this day. I am with you.

I gave Myself, I showed you the way. Mary went to the hill country to visit her cousin Elizabeth. My Mother was carrying a child, but she went to help Elizabeth, total giving. She gave her life, she gave her body, she gave herself for the other with her great love.

A heart of love - GIVES, do you give or do you hold back. Christmas is the time of My love given to you. Mary's love given that she brought forth her beautiful infant and laid Him in a manger.

Giving and love, when Christmas Day is over, remember the Christ Child. I gave Myself to the world so that you would have eternal life. I humbled Myself and became a man for great love of you. Oh dear little hearts, how you are loved by My Father and the Holy Spirit. How Mary and I love you. Soak in this great love being outpoured to you today.

Come with a pure heart, a heart free of any resentments or anger, let go of hurts, take the walls down around your heart. How can I get in if you are holding walls around your heart to protect you from others that may hurt you.

I will never hurt you. I died for you. I was born in the womb of Mary. I took on a little baby body for love of you. Let go of anything holding you back from a pure heart.

Open wide your gates and I enter in with My Heart open and on fire for love of you. I am Jesus the Lord, your beloved, come to give you My great love this day. Let down your walls, I will sustain you, I will protect you, the Holy Spirit will transform you into a heart likened to Mine. I will take you to the inner sanctuaries of My Heart. Go to My Mother and be united to her love, she will lead you ever closer to My Sacred Heart.

Little one, little one, how you search for such things when I have for you a Heart of Divine love to fill you. I give to you a sharing in My life. I give you My Divine love. Let it penetrate your being. Draw ever closer to My beautiful Mothers' Heart and My Heart, We are the Hearts of such love. Ready and waiting for you.

Tender, tender love, waiting for you. I love you so much, My beloved ones.   12/23/94

My Mom Died

Messenger: Mary teach me to be a mom like God wants — My mom died when I was five — I am always learning to be like Mary — Mary help me to love like you love Jesus and all souls.

I smelled roses when I was 5 the whole time in the funeral parlor. I always remembered the roses.   12/23/94

I Walk by You

Mary: Every time you thought you were alone I walked by your side. As I walked by Jesus on Calvary, I walked by you all through your little life, all through your adult life.

I walk by you, I am standing by you now my little love. Feel the presence of your most loving Mother. From this day forth you will know what it is to have your mom by your side.

As I held Jesus so close to my heart, I hold you ever close to me. I tenderly caress you and love you with the dearest motherly love.

I am your loving Mother. The more you realize my tender love that I have for you, the deeper you will love Jesus, with tender love. He is the tenderest of all Hearts. He loves you with such tender love.

But I, my little child, how I love you with the deepest maternal love. I have forever cared for you and loved you. I am your loving mother. This day you will forever blossom and bud forth more and more — blooming. You are my beloved daughter.

I will lead you tenderly to my Son. I am Mary your loving mother and thank you for responding to my call.

As I watched all the sufferings of my beloved Son, I stood under His cross and watched my child hang and die. I will not abandon you, I stayed with Him. This was the most bitter heartache.

I stood under His cross with full awareness of what was happening. I did not take any pain medication, I stood there and I withstood the heartache. When your heart aches remember how I endured all the sufferings. Through God's grace you can endure your trials. If I could withstand such anguish, you with God's grace can withstand your trials.

Focus on your Father's love for you to give His only Son. Focus on Jesus' love for you to give His life. Focus on my love for you and how I forever stand by you, always with you, I never abandon you.

You have a loving Mother, always by your side, as I stood under Jesus cross and endured all of this suffering, I walk with you, I never leave you and I hold you up as John held me under Jesus' cross.

Mother you, I do. I mother you, I love you, I call to you to come to my motherly heart so that I may lead you to the Heart of my beloved Son.

Oh little loved child of mine, you have a mother. I am Mary your Mother. I stand by you today.   12/23/94

Blows at the Pillar

Messenger: After the consecration, I had a strong realization of Him receiving blows at the pillar. My stomach and my heart ached. I could hear noise and hear His grunt. I felt as if I could feel His wounds. I wanted to get so connected to it. I sat down after communion and felt like I could get totally lost in His wounds and knowing His love for me and for us. Head down, I wanted to go somewhere and be lost in His passion. I wasn't thinking about the passion at all and all of a sudden I could hear Him getting scourged at the pillar. I wanted to cry and buckle in, go off somewhere and be alone with Him.

Same as when I saw wound in His hand when praying the rosary with Fr. Carter.

Today prayed rosary with Fr. Carter afterwards — I prayed and was so close to Jesus, felt as if I could go off — I had an ecstasy in church this morning.   12/23/94

Message to Rita on Christmas Eve

Jesus: Dear Child,

I am your precious Savior, from your bed to this letter you are already talking in your head.

Little one, little one, it is in trusting in Me you will find your peace.

You do not trust, you are afraid what others think. You are afraid they will leave you and not talk to you again.

All you suffered led you to where you are at this moment. Oh, how you have received such gifts from Me, your beloved Savior, but satan wants to stop you. You must let go totally to Me. You do not fume, you do not fret, you must totally surrender to the will of the Father.

I am caring for your every need, child. Oh child, child, how you waste your precious days in planning and prodding when I am guarding you with My Divine love.

No problems will befall you. Anything that occurs will be handled by Myself and My Mother. She forever watches you and guards you. She is by your side, always. Little child, little child, sing My songs of love. I have hand delivered love songs, love messages, I showed you so many miracles and you are still at unrest.

Rita, Rita, I talk to you constantly, I watch you and you, fumble around in your heart. Your heart is so full of fear, all the days you suffered were in vain child. I am here at every moment, I never ever leave you. I died on the cross in perfect peace.

Peace is yours. I am so attentive to you and your needs. Let go, let go, let go, I walk with you, I talk with you. I am forever with you and guarding you and you child are full of fear and trembling. Oh, dear one, beloved of the Father, your life is unfolding as He, My Father, has planned. Your surrender is necessary for this plan to take place. You stumble on your path. You fight your trials, accept that which happens as that which I allow. Accept and surrender to the joys, to the sorrows, to the love that is outpoured to you. Surrender to rejection. Did I not show you how to live in adversity? Oh little loved one, beloved of My Father, His plan for you is unfolding, your response will lead you to peace or turmoil. You bump along, yet you surrender. Surrender. Consecrate your heart to My Heart and that of My Mother's. I talk, you do not hear. Consecration is surrendering, you accept, you are then in great peace. I am guarding you. Suffer child for the child Jesus. I was born in such poverty, I came into this world God made man in a stable, I died on a cross.

Do you want to follow Me? I was at peace ALWAYS. I knew the Father's will, I knew His love. You need to take down the wall of protection you are building around your heart. It is being fortified by your fear and lack of trust in Me and My Father. Surrender to the will of God. Let the Spirit move your soul. Surrender and be led to deeper life in Me. I am pouring out to you My grace.

Surrender, Surrender, Surrender. You fret so about being abandoned. My child I never abandon you. This is your secret. If I never abandon you, why do you fear?

You are fearing and not trusting in He who guards you. I guard you. You do not write this letter at 4:00am to comfort yourself. Oh little one please let go in your heart to My Heart.

You are fighting My union with you. I want union with you, intense union at every moment. You are only connected to Me at certain times. You are a little frightened child.

Take hold of your heart and surrender to My dear Mother's Heart and My Heart. All you know about Our Hearts and you fear. Oh little one, your fear is from satan. He aims to cause you discomfort. I walk with you and forever guard you.

Let go and come totally into My Heart. My Heart is open and waiting your entry.

Let go to all I send you. You cannot control the weather, you cannot control others, you must surrender. This trial will lead you to the deepest recesses of My most Sacred Heart. Accept the trials and suffering for they are the most precious moments when our souls are joined so closely together. Oh sweet one, how sweet is the union I want to have with you. You are to savor all I send you with trust and love. I am Jesus, your beloved Savior, I came to this earth and died for you, why do you worry this morning? Oh I love you. Come to My Heart, I am your most Sacred Heart and I love you with a Heart burning for love of you.

Sweet surrender to My love. Sufferings are the golden gems that lead you so deeply into My loving arms.

I LOVE YOU. I love you that I came to share in your humanity and you fret for anything.

Messenger: I saw the Sacred Heart picture at the Center turn into Claude and many Saints. It was all in color and so distinct. The rosary was so intense and gorgeous. I had heard blows in church at the Cathedral of Him at the pillar and felt His suffering, I want to go off and be in His passion. We said the Sorrowful mysteries and the Sorrows, most beautiful. Oh Jesus how You bless me and how I am so easy to fall into satan's trap to take my glow away. I saw Mary all aglow, I saw Jesus turn into the Saints.

Oh the Communion of the Saints I pray in union with them in this rosary and with Mary, praying to Jesus.

We were alone, my two children, Marty, Harold and his wife, Diane and his son and we were united to the saints as we prayed. We are united to the saints and Mary when we pray. Though we are little in number the most beautiful saints are united with us as we pray. Oh I love You Jesus and Mary, how much I have to learn and how exciting to talk to You and be with You. God and the saints are my greatest friends. I love You so much.

Take my heart, oh Lord, make it ever true. Take my heart, oh Lord, I belong to You.   12/24/94 - 4:00 a.m.

The Rosary Book from Jesus and Mary

Jesus: Ask Marty to help you with writing up the meditations on the rosary. You can use Harold's picture for the cover of the book.

My dear little child,

Please write up the meditations on the rosary. Ask Marty to help you and ask Harold to use his picture for the cover.

You are to begin recounting your experiences daily. Start with the experiences from July 5, 1994. Include Fr. Carter's part in the rosary and Marty's part in the rosary. Write down the events you see daily, by date. Write down what you see. Include October 31, 1994 rosary. Marty is your partner in publishing the rosary book.

You should list all you both see. Include the Christmas rosary. Begin by writing down your rosary meditations. All will become clear as you begin your rosary journal.

Your time recounting these events will lead to a closer understanding of Our lives and Our intimacy with each other.

Mary: Your union with My Son and the Father and the Holy Spirit will deepen as your understanding of the union between myself and Jesus grows.

From this day forward you will be closely united to me, your Mother, and closely united to Jesus through the rosary. I want you to lead the rosary always. Always dim the lights and use candles. I will be there and Jesus will be there whenever you pray the rosary. We will be with you in a very special way. Your job is to promote the rosary. When you pray the rosary, tell them about my letters to them, centered around my Son in the Eucharist.

Always pray the rosary. Always center it in the Eucharist. Ask Marty and Fr. Carter to help you. This will be a powerful tool for bringing many to the rosary and to loving My Son in the Eucharist. I am Mary, your Mother, and that is my Christmas gift to all. Pray the rosary for us.

Get Marty's picture fixed and everywhere you pray the rosary take that picture and the extra Sacred Heart picture at the Center.

Always start the rosary with the Holy Spirit Song.   12/24/94

Mary Speaks

Mary: My dear ones,

I want pictures of the rosary and seven sorrows in the rosary book. I would like meditations on the seven sorrows. I would like the songs that could be used during the different mysteries of the rosary. I would like rosary meditations and certain messages that pertain to meditations on some mysteries. My rosary, prayed as I have instructed, will lead many hearts to Our Two Hearts. We are so closely united in the rosary. The rosary is the most beautiful prayer. Singing between the Hail Marys pleases me so much. Lift up your hearts. Pray the rosary with your whole heart and it will live in your day. I, your beloved Mother, and my Son thank you for responding to my call.   12/24/94

Joyful Mysteries

Rosaries from the Hearts of Jesus and Mary from Mary's Daily Apparitions

Annunciation

1. "The Word became flesh, ..." (John 1:14)
2. "Look! You are to conceive in your womb and bear a son, and you must name him Jesus. He will be great and will be called Son of the Most High..." (Luke 1:31-32)
3. "...And so the child will be holy and will be called Son of God." (Luke 1:35)
4. "And I tell you this too: your cousin Elizabeth also, in her old age, has conceived a son, and she whom people called barren is now in her sixth month, for nothing is impossible to God.' " (Luke 1:36-37)
5. Mary said, 'You see before you the Lord's servant, let it happen to me as you have said.' (Luke 1: 38)
6. **Jesus:** Be with Me in the first station of My cross, I am condemned to death. I said yes - Your Mother said 'yes'. I said 'yes' I gave My life for you.
7. "... I lay down my life ... No one takes it from me; I lay it down of my own free will, and as I have power to lay it down, so I have power to take it up again; and this is the command I have received from my Father." (John 10:17-18)
8. **R.** Think of Mary's FIAT.
9. **R.** Jesus gave His all for us.
10. **R.** We are called to say yes to God — to serve Him - to live all for the glory and honor of God and
    Mary: Live to do the will of the Father in love.

Visitation

1. **R.** Mary is the singular vessel — Mary loved Father, Son and Holy Spirit. She went with love to serve and support and strengthen her frail cousin.
2. "and *his faithful love extends age after age to those who fear him.*" (Luke 1:50)
3. "He has used the power of his arm,

he has routed the arrogant of heart.
> *He has pulled down princes*
from their thrones
> *and raised high the lowly."* (Luke 1:51-52)

4.   *"He has filled the starving with good things,*
sent the rich away empty.
> *He has come to the help*
> *of Israel his servant,*
> *mindful of his faithful love*
—according to the promise
he made to our ancestors—
of his mercy to Abraham
and to his descendants for ever." (Luke 1:53-55)

5.   "Mary stayed with her some three months and then went home." (Luke 1:56)

6.   **R.** Jesus accepted His cross. He took up His cross. Mary did God's will to humbly serve, support & strengthen her cousin.
Jesus: I give you strength and mercy.

7.   **Jesus:** I died for your sins.

8.   **Jesus:** I give you healing.

9.   **Jesus:** I give you compassion.

10. **R.** Live to serve and love God.

Birth of Jesus

1.   "... and laid him in a manger because there was no room for them in the living–space." (Luke 2:7)

2.   " Today in the town of David a Saviour has been born to you; he is Christ the Lord." (Luke 2:11)

3.   And here is a sign for you: you will find a baby wrapped in swaddling clothes and lying in a manger.' (Luke 2: 12)

4.   "And all at once with the angel there was a great throng of the hosts of heaven, praising God with the words: Glory to God in the highest heaven, and on earth peace for those he favours." (Luke 2:13-14)

5.   "After Jesus had been born at Bethlehem in Judaea during the reign of King Herod, suddenly some wise men came to Jerusalem from the east asking, 'Where is the infant king of the Jews? We saw his star as it rose and have come to do him homage.' ... And suddenly the star they had seen rising went forward and halted over the place where the child was. The sight of the star filled them with delight, and going into the house they saw the child with his mother Mary, and falling to their knees they did him homage. Then, opening their treasures, they offered him gifts of gold and frankincense and myrrh."
(Matthew 2:1-2, 9-11)

6. **Mary:** I treasured all these things and kept them in my Heart.
7. **Jesus:** I am lovingly holding you and protecting you just as your Mother did to Me. I hold you, nourish you, and protect you.
8. **Jesus:** I love you so much.
9. **Jesus:** I died, I rose for you.
10. **Jesus:** I give you a special sharing in My life through baptism.

Presentation

1. "It had been revealed to him by the Holy Spirit that he would not see death until he had set eyes on the Christ of the Lord." (Luke 2:26)
2. "'Look, he is destined for the fall and for the rise of many in Israel, destined to be a sign that is opposed—'" (Luke 2:34)
3. "There was a prophetess, too, Anna the daughter of Phanuel, of the tribe of Asher. She was well on in years. Her days of girlhood over, she had been married for seven years before becoming a widow. She was now eighty–four years old and never left the Temple, serving God night and day with fasting and prayer. She came up just at that moment and began to praise God; and she spoke of the child to all who looked forward to the deliverance of Jerusalem." (Luke 2:36-38)
4. **R.** Jesus meets His Mother on the way to Calvary.
5. "Simeon blessed them and said to Mary his mother, ... and a sword will pierce your soul too—so that the secret thoughts of many may be laid bare.'" (Luke 2:34-35)
6. "... and when the parents brought in the child Jesus to do for him what the Law required," (Luke 2:27)
7. **R.** Look at Mary & Jesus' eyes meet on Calvary.
8. **R.** See Simeon hold the child.
9. **R.** Listen to Simeon' prophecy.
   "Simeon blessed them and said to Mary his mother, 'Look, he is destined for the fall and for the rise of many in Israel, destined to be a sign that is opposed—and a sword will pierce your soul too—so that the secret thoughts of many may be laid bare.' (Luke 2:34-35)
10. **R.** Through baptism we receive a special sharing in His life.

Finding of the Child Jesus in the Temple

1. "Simeon blessed them and said to Mary his mother, 'Look, he is destined for the fall and for the rise of many in Israel, destined to be a sign that is opposed—and a sword will pierce your soul too—so that the secret thoughts of many may be laid bare.'"(Luke 2:34-35)

2. "Every year his parents used to go to Jerusalem for the feast of the Passover. When he was twelve years old, they went up for the feast as usual." (Luke 2:41-42)

3. "When the days of the feast were over and they set off home, the boy Jesus stayed behind in Jerusalem without his parents knowing it." (Luke 2:43)

4. "It happened that, three days later, they found him in the Temple, sitting among the teachers, listening to them, and asking them questions; and all those who heard him were astounded at his intelligence and his replies." (Luke 2:46-47)

5. "They were overcome when they saw him, and his mother said to him, 'My child, why have you done this to us? See how worried your father and I have been, looking for you.'" (Luke 2:48)

6. "He replied, 'Why were you looking for me? Did you not know that I must be in my Father's house?'" (Luke 2:49)

7. "He went down with them then and came to Nazareth and lived under their authority." (Luke 2:51)

8. "Then Jesus came with them to a plot of land called Gethsemane; ... And going on a little further he fell on his face and prayed. 'My Father,' he said, 'if it is possible, let this cup pass me by. Nevertheless, let it be as you, not I, would have it.'" (Matthew 26: 36, 39)

9. **Jesus:** I obeyed My Father. I died on the cross.

10. **Mary:** My babies are suffering.

The Word became flesh, ... (John 1:14)   12/94

Letter to Jesus

Messenger: To know You is to want You, to long for You, to want You so much closer. My heart feels as if it will break to want You ever so much. It aches and longs and wants You so much. I love You so much. Words are so weak for anything I feel. There are not words to say what in my heart I feel. Such intense craving for oneness I feel as if my heart will break within my chest.

I am overwhelmed with awe that the Son of God, born in a manger is present in this room. My life finds joy in Him.

Jesus, Jesus, Jesus, this is the suffering to know Him a little and want ever so much more. My heart aches within my chest to such intense longing and wanting.

Jesus: Oh, dear little child, how your heart aches, how My Heart aches on this My birthday for the million souls who give not a thought to Me. I thirst after the love of souls. I thirst, I long, I wait, oh beloved of My Father, oh blind men on this your earth, you wonder and roam and search your barren deserts and your hearts are at such unrest. I was born a little child in the little town of Bethlehem. I am, Jesus Christ the Son of God and who pays heed. All are busy for their useless tasks and think so little of God this day. Suffer this My aching Heart for all those who reject Me and treat Me so cold.

I love, I love, I love and who comes here. Who gives a thought to God? It is My birthday and who pays heed to the King that comes as a baby.

I LONG, I THIRST, I WANT, I WAIT for your love and this My blind men is what My Heart ached for on Calvary. Heart ached. How My Divine love is available and waiting and who My beloved ones know. You tap so lightly, when My Heart is a roaring furnace of Divine LOVE waiting to fill you and set your heart on fire.

12/25/94 - 6:55 a.m. - Holy Spirit Chapel

In Front of Mary Statue

Messenger: Mary saw and felt Jesus' sufferings as He fell under the cross. How her Heart knew Jesus. She knew the baby Jesus in her Heart, she knew Him, His whole life in her Heart. It is through Mary's Heart, I will know Jesus, I will know His love.

She held Him as a baby, she watched Him take His first step, but she knew Jesus, deeply in her Heart. This is why the peering look on Calvary is so important — the oneness of Jesus and Mary in Their Hearts.

The union of the Two Hearts is the secret to our union in love with God. The Holy Spirit gives us great grace and wisdom — He imparts knowledge to us about God.

Her Heart felt this baby inside of her womb, she knew Jesus in her Heart. Seeing, watching, holding are ways They touched each other, but the union in the Hearts was so deep, oneness. The burning love in the Hearts, the aching in the Hearts, the hurts in the Hearts.

This is the depth, union in Their Hearts, oneness. I touch, I use my body, I see, I use my body. I know, I feel, I ache in my heart, these are untouchable. I cannot touch these things. It is beyond the physical. We cannot touch love, happiness. We cannot touch the spiritual things.

Mary through the Spirit leads us to this deep intimacy with your precious child, the child Jesus.

If I see my son get injured, I see his wound, but what I feel in my heart, all the knowing and loving I feel in my heart with that child is what makes it so intense. It is not the wound, it is what goes on inside, the depth to the things I do not see.

Mary knew the Christ child from the first moment of conception. To see Him now fall under the cross, the anguish was so great in her soul.

The eyes see, the heart knows and loves and aches, it expresses all the depth of the union.

She knows and loves and followed Christ more than any other person. It is through her Heart we will know Him the most.

I can most easily unite with someone who is likened to Christ. He is love, the more I love, the more I open myself up to unite to Jesus, to unite better to others, more like Jesus. The further I am from Him the more closed I am to unite. I love more deeply when I am most like Him. To unite with others in deep love, my heart must be more pure. I can more deeply unite with a person, the "purer" my heart, because I am more like Jesus, the more I am like Him, the more I can give love.

Love is giving, love is open, love exists for the sake of the other.

Jesus is love. Love gives, when we love we outpour love to others.

Loving Jesus gives us a greater capacity to love. He is the source of all love. The more I am filled up with Him, the more I have to give away.

To know Him is to love Him. He is all good, I cannot know Him, really know Him, in truth and not love Him. God is love.

God calls us to two things - love of God, love of one another, but I can love others better when I am united to God.

The whole secret is to realize His love, to receive His love, to be closely united to Him.

He is love. He is all good, it is in Him I find happiness. God is love and all good.

A Message to Fr. Carter

The Holy Spirit

Jesus: My beloved friend, tell My people to pray daily to the Holy Spirit. They are to pray for an increase in His gifts. My people must realize that the Holy Spirit comes to transform them. The Spirit desires to transform you more and more according to My image. Those who are docile to His touch become increasingly shaped in My likeness. He performs this marvel within Mary's Immaculate Heart. The more one dwells in My Mother's Heart, the more active are the workings of the Spirit. The Spirit leads Mary to place you within My own Heart. In both Our Hearts, then, your transformation continues. The more you are formed after My own Heart, the more I lead you to the bosom of My Father. Tell

My people all this. Tell them to pray daily for a greater appreciation of these wondrous gifts. I am Lord and Master. All who come to My Heart will be on fire to receive the gifts of the Spirit in ever greater measure! I love and bless My people!

Reflection: The Holy Spirit is given to us to fashion us ever more according to the likeness of Jesus. And the more we are like Jesus, the more Jesus leads us to the Father. Do we, each day, pray to the Holy Spirit to be more open to His transforming influence? Do we strive each day to grow in union with Mary? The greater our union with our Mother, the spouse of the Holy Spirit, the greater is the transforming action of the Holy Spirit within us."   *Excerpt from Tell My People*

Messenger: The more I become likened to Him the closer I get to the Father who is all good and all love.

The closer I become to Him the more joy and peace and happiness I have.

Song: *I Love You Jesus*

I see so clear that the depth of my union with Him is tied up in knowing Him ever so dearly through Mary's Heart.

I see my son, but the knowing I have is in my heart.

Every person was created in the image and likeness of God.

This is how I love my brother to see this likeness of Christ in them.

Jesus: Look into their eyes, My child and see the child created and loved by My Father.

The eyes are the windows of the soul, the doorway to the heart. Open your eyes and reflect the God that lives within. Beauty on the outside is a reflection of the heart that is within. Love, Love, Love as I have loved you.

Philippians 2:7

But he emptied himself,
taking the form of a slave,
becoming as human beings are;
and being in every way
 like a human being,
he was humbler yet,
even to accepting death,
 death on a cross.

Messenger: He came and showed us the way.

The heart is the way to Him. Let our hearts be united to God and have deeper union with Mary.

They pierced His most precious Heart and what flowed out was blood and water —

Ascension

Messenger: He never leaves us, no fear of abandonment. He is truly here this day in His Divinity and humanity in the Eucharist.

He lives in us in a special way when we are in the state of grace.

Jesus loves us so much He remains with us today in the Eucharist. He loved us so much. He came, He died, He rose, He now remains with us.

The greatest love, He loves us so much. He gives us all we need.

Descent of Holy Spirit

Messenger: Nobody can ever take away my union with Father, Son and Holy Spirit.

Such burning, longing, wanting. I cried to receive Him in the Eucharist. I feel His presence, to realize He is here and what is going on.

12/25/94 - 7:15 a.m.

This Is My Mother's House

Jesus: This is My Mother's house. I was born in a stable. Her house is in need of repairs. So, too, are the hearts of men.

Messenger: Mary and Jesus will work in their hearts to restore the peace and harmony for which they were created.

Mary: As this building, which has turned shabby, is restored, men's hearts will be restored here to the burning love of my Son.

Messenger: Take out the debris from your hearts, make them pure and restore them to vibrant life in Him.

Mary: Your building will be restored more quickly the more you help to enkindle the love of my Son in their hearts.

As the progress is slow, so, too, is the restoration slow.

Circulate these letters of my Son's love this day.　　　12/25/94

After Communion

Messenger: Every time Mary looked at her beloved Son she remembered the prophesy of Simeon. When she saw His little tender hands and feet she knew He would suffer a brutal death.

Think of the glories of that night as the angels sang, think of such glory of that night in the simplicity of the stable.

We are in union with the angels and saints praising and honoring God. We are all one, united in the Church. We are so close to the angels and saints and souls in purgatory. I saw the saints on the picture. They are united to us in praising God, they are with us even when we do not see them.   12/25/94

Glorious Mysteries

Rosaries from the Hearts of Jesus and Mary from Mary's Daily Apparitions

Resurrection

1. **R.** Jesus died for us.
2. **R.** Jesus rose.
3. **R.** Jesus gives us a special sharing in His life at baptism.
4. **R.** Think of that — Jesus rose from the tomb — Jesus rose from the dead.
5. **R.** Mary Magdalene came to the tomb and the stone had been rolled back.
6. "But Mary was standing outside near the tomb, weeping. Then, as she wept, she stooped to look inside, and saw two angels in white sitting where the body of Jesus had been, one at the head, the other at the feet. They said, 'Woman, why are you weeping?' 'They have taken my Lord away,' she replied, 'and I don't know where they have put him.'" (John 20:11-13)
7. "As she said this she turned round and saw Jesus standing there, though she did not realise that it was Jesus. Jesus said to her, 'Woman, why are you weeping? Who are you looking for?' Supposing him to be

the gardener, she said, 'Sir, if you have taken him away, tell me where you have put him, and I will go and remove him.' Jesus said, 'Mary!' She turned round then and said to him in Hebrew, 'Rabbuni!'—which means Master." (John 20:14-16)

R. Imagine how Mary Magdalene felt to see Jesus.

8. "Jesus said to her, 'Do not cling to me, because I have not yet ascended to the Father." (John 20:17)

9. "In the evening of that same day, the first day of the week, the doors were closed in the room where the disciples were, for fear of the Jews. Jesus came and stood among them. He said to them, 'Peace be with you,' and, after saying this, he showed them his hands and his side. The disciples were filled with joy at seeing the Lord, and he said to them again, 'Peace be with you. 'As the Father sent me, so am I sending you.' After saying this he breathed on them and said: Receive the Holy Spirit. If you forgive anyone's sins, they are forgiven; if you retain anyone's sins, they are retained." *(John 20:19-23)*

10. **R.** Jesus gives us a special sharing in His life at baptism.

Ascension

1. **R.** Jesus remained on the earth 40 days after His resurrection before He ascended into heaven.
2. **R.** He gave them the power to baptize and forgive sins.
3. "Then he took them out as far as the outskirts of Bethany, and raising his hands he blessed them." (Luke 24:50)
4. **R.** He ascended into heaven.
5. **R.** Think of what it would be like to see Jesus ascend into heaven.
6. **R.** They all stood by in awe and wonder at what they had seen.
7. "But our homeland is in heaven and it is from there that we are expecting a Saviour, the Lord Jesus Christ, who will transfigure the wretched body of ours into the mould of his glorious body, through the working of the power which he has, even to bring all things under his mastery." (Philippians 3:20-21)
8. **R.** Jesus has not left, He remains with us in His Divinity and humanity in the Eucharist this very day.
9. "Then he took them out as far as the outskirts of Bethany, and raising his hands he blessed them. Now as he blessed them, he withdrew from them and was carried up to heaven." (Luke 24:50-51)
10. "... I have come so that they may have life and have it to the full." (John 10:10)

Descent of the Holy Spirit

1. "John baptised with water but, not many days from now, you are going to be baptised with the Holy Spirit.'" (Acts 1:5)

2. "In my earlier work, Theophilus, I dealt with everything Jesus had done and taught from the beginning until the day he gave his instructions to the apostles he had chosen through the Holy Spirit, and was taken up to heaven. He had shown himself alive to them after his Passion by many demonstrations: for forty days he had continued to appear to them and tell them about the kingdom of God. While at table with them, he had told them not to leave Jerusalem, but to wait there for what the Father had promised. 'It is', he had said, 'what you have heard me speak about: John baptised with water but, not many days from now, you are going to be baptised with the Holy Spirit.'" (Acts 1:1-5)

3. "When Pentecost day came round, they had all met together, when suddenly there came from heaven a sound as of a violent wind which filled the entire house in which they were sitting; and there appeared to them tongues as of fire; these separated and came to rest on the head of each of them. They were all filled with the Holy Spirit and began to speak different languages as the Spirit gave them power to express themselves." (Acts 2:1-4)

4. **R.** What joy for Mary to see the fearlessness of the Apostles.

5. **R.** The Holy Spirit appeared to Mary and the Apostles.

6. **R.** The Apostles went out and preached and all understood.

7. **R.** Oh Holy Spirit fill us with Your love.

8. **R.** Oh Holy Spirit give us Your gifts.

9. **R.** Holy Spirit let our hearts burn with love for God.

10. **R.** Holy Spirit let our hearts burn with love for others.

Assumption

1. "So they hurried away and found Mary and Joseph, and the baby lying in the manger. When they saw the child they repeated what they had been told about him, and everyone who heard it was astonished at what the shepherds said to them. As for Mary, she treasured all these things and pondered them in her heart." (Luke 2:16-19)

2. "Near the cross of Jesus stood his mother and his mother's sister, Mary the wife of Clopas, and Mary of Magdala. Seeing his mother and the disciple whom he loved standing near her, Jesus said to his mother, 'Woman, this is your son.' Then to

the disciple he said, 'This is your mother.' And from that hour the disciple took her into his home." (John 19:25-27)

3. "And after this perishable nature has put on imperishability and this mortal nature has put on immortality, then will the words of scripture come true: Death is swallowed up in victory. Death, where is your victory? Death, where is your sting?" (1 Corinthians 15:54-55)

4. "The sting of death is sin, and the power of sin comes from the Law. Thank God, then, for giving us the victory through Jesus Christ our Lord." (1 Corinthians 15:56-57)

5. "And when the day came for them to be purified in keeping with the Law of Moses, they took him up to Jerusalem to present him to the Lord—observing what is written in the Law of the Lord: Every first-born male must be consecrated to the Lord—and also to offer in sacrifice, in accordance with what is prescribed in the Law of the Lord, a pair of turtledoves or two young pigeons. Now in Jerusalem there was a man named Simeon. He was an upright and devout man; he looked forward to the restoration of Israel and the Holy Spirit rested on him. It had been revealed to him by the Holy Spirit that he would not see death until he had set eyes on the Christ of the Lord. Prompted by the Spirit he came to the Temple; and when the parents brought in the child Jesus to do for him what the Law required, he took him into his arms and blessed God; and he said:" (Luke 2: 22-28)

6. "And they ran out of wine, since the wine provided for the feast had all been used, and the mother of Jesus said to him, 'They have no wine.' Jesus said, 'Woman, what do you want from me? My hour has not come yet.' His mother said to the servants, 'Do whatever he tells you.' There were six stone water jars standing there, meant for the ablutions that are customary among the Jews: each could hold twenty or thirty gallons. Jesus said to the servants, 'Fill the jars with water,' and they filled them to the brim. Then he said to them, 'Draw some out now and take it to the president of the feast.' They did this; the president tasted the water, and it had turned into wine. Having no idea where it came from —though the servants who had drawn the water knew—the president of the feast called the bridegroom and said, 'Everyone serves good wine first and the worse wine when the guests are well wined; but you have kept the best wine till now.'
(John 2:3-10)

7. **R.** Mary was Christ's perfect disciple.
8. **R.** Mary and Jesus looked into each other's eyes on the way to Calvary.
9. Song: *On this Day*
10. Song: *See the Eyes that Look at Mary*

Mary Crowned Queen of Heaven and Earth

1. Song: *See the Eyes that Look at Mary*
2. Song: *Little Baby Hands and Feet*
3. Song: *Hail Holy Queen*
4. Song: *Immaculate Mary*
5. Song: *The Rosary Song*
6. "Now a great sign appeared in heaven: a woman, robed with the sun, standing on the moon, and on her head a crown of twelve stars." (Revelation 12:1)
7. "It happened that, three days later, they found him in the Temple, sitting among the teachers, listening to them, and asking them questions; and all those who heard him were astounded at his intelligence and his replies." (Luke 2:6-47)
8. "Mary set out at that time and went as quickly as she could into the hill country to a town in Judah. She went into Zechariah's house and greeted Elizabeth. Now it happened that as soon as Elizabeth heard Mary's greeting, the child leapt in her womb and Elizabeth was filled with the Holy Spirit. She gave a loud cry and said, 'Of all women you are the most blessed, and blessed is the fruit of your womb. Why should I be honoured with a visit from the mother of my Lord? Look, the moment your greeting reached my ears, the child in my womb leapt for joy.'" (Luke 1:39-44)
9. "Near the cross of Jesus stood his mother and his mother's sister, Mary the wife of Clopas, and Mary of Magdala. Seeing his mother and the disciple whom he loved standing near her, Jesus said to his mother, 'Woman, this is your son.'" (John 19:25-26)
10. "Then to the disciple he said, 'This is your mother.' ..." (John 19:27)

12/94

Christmas Day Children's Rosary
The Joyful Mysteries

The Annunciation

1. **R.** The Angel Gabriel appeared to Mary and asked Mary to be the Mother of Jesus.
2. **R.** Mary always complied with the Will of the Father. She said "yes" to the angel.
3. **R.** She was filled with the Holy Spirit and the

Word was made flesh.
4. Song: *Come Holy Ghost...*
5. **R.** There was such intimacy between Mary and Jesus from the first moment of conception.
6. **R.** She felt the life of the child Jesus grow within her womb.
7. **R.** It was in her womb that the most Sacred Heart of Jesus was formed through the Holy Spirit.
8. **R.** It is in realizing this connection between the Hearts of Jesus and Mary that we will grow in greater union with God.
9. **R.** The Holy Spirit forever transforms us more and more into the image of Jesus.
10. **R.** The womb of the Virgin Mary is the holy dwelling place of our beloved Savior.

The Visitation

1. **R.** Mary, being pregnant herself, but hearing through the angel that Elizabeth had conceived a child in her old age, made haste to the hill country to be with her cousin Elizabeth.
2. **R.** When she arrived, the child in Elizabeth's womb leapt for joy.
3. **R.** Mary was filled with the Holy Spirit and cried out in a loud voice the Magnificat.
4. "Mary said,
    'My soul proclaims
        the greatness of the Lord
    and my spirit rejoices
    in God my Savior.'" (Luke 1:46,47)
5. "...because he has looked upon
        the humiliation of his servant.
    Yes, from now onwards
        all generations will call me blessed." (Luke 1:48)
6. "...for the Almighty
        has done great things for me.
    Holy is his name," (Luke 1:49)
7. **R.** Jesus is no less present this day in the Eucharist than He was in Mary's womb.
8. **R.** How He waits and yearns for us to come and to be with Him because He loves us so much!
9. **R.** If we realized how much He loves us, we would never fear.
10. Song: *O come, O come, Emmanuel, and ransom captive Israel, that mourns in lonely exile here, until the Son of God appears. Rejoice! Rejoice! Emmanuel shall come to you, O Israel!*

Birth of Jesus

1. **R.** Think of the glorious night when Jesus was born in a stable. The angels sang and shepherds watched.
2. **R.** The cows and the sheep were there to keep them warm.
3. **R.** This is truly Jesus Christ, the Son of God, who humbled Himself to share in our humanity.

4. Song: *Angels we have heard on high, sweetly singing o'er the plains. And the mountains in reply, echoing their joyous strains.*
5. Song: *Gloria in excelsis Deo, Gloria in excelsis Deo.*
6. Song: *Away in a manger, no crib for a bed, the little Lord Jesus lay down His sweet head. The stars in the sky looked down where He lay, the little Lord Jesus asleep on the hay.*
7. Song: *O come let us adore Him, O come let us adore Him, O come let us adore Him, Christ the Lord.*
8. Song: *What child is this who lay to rest, on Mary's lap is sleeping? Whom angels greet with anthem sweet, while shepherds watch are keeping.*
9. **R.** See Jesus, Mary and Joseph in the stable and see the tenderness in the eyes of Mary as she gazes on her newborn baby child, who is truly God!
10. **R.** The birth of Jesus is at the heart of salvation history.

The Presentation of Jesus in the Temple

1. **R.** Mary and Joseph took the child Jesus to the temple.
2. **R.** While they were there, the prophet Simeon prophesied the sufferings of Jesus and Mary to come.
3. "Simeon said to Mary, "...and a sword will pierce your soul, too..."" (Luke 2:35)
4. **R.** As he prophesied the sufferings of Jesus and Mary, he also prophesied how many souls would be saved through Jesus.
5. **R.** Mary gazes so tenderly on her precious child and, from this moment on, every time she looked at Jesus, she remembered the prophecy of Simeon.
6. **R.** She had a constant ache in her Heart since the prophecy of Simeon.
7. Song: *See the eyes that look at Mary, her tender infant Child...*
8. **R.** She looked at the baby Jesus. She held Him in her arms. All through their life together, she knew His Heart. There was such love

from the moment of conception between her and her Son! There was such intimacy between the Heart of Jesus and the Heart of Mary.

9. **R.** Dear Mary, you knew the Heart of your beloved Son Jesus. Please lead us to closer intimacy with Him. It is in loving Him through your pure and tender Heart that I too will love Him more tenderly.

10. **R.** Let us love, through your Heart, our beloved Father, Son and Holy Spirit.

The Finding of the Child Jesus in the Temple

1. **R.** How the Heart of Mary knew the Heart of Jesus! How the Heart of Mary suffered every sorrow. How she suffered when they lost the child Jesus in the temple.

2. **R.** She calls out to us today to pray for her little lost children of the world.

3. "It happened that, three days later, they found him in the Temple, sitting among the teachers, listening to them, and asking them questions; and all those who heard him were astounded at his intelligence and his replies." (Luke 2:46,47)

4. "When His parents saw Him "...his mother said to him, 'My child, why have you done this to us? See how worried your father and I have been, looking for you?'" (Luke 2:48)

5. "He went down with them then and came to Nazareth and lived under their authority. His mother stored up all these things in her heart." (Luke 2:51)

6. **R.** She was His Mother. She took care of Him. She knew Him with a deep, motherly love in her Heart.

7. **Mary:** My beloved children, pray to the child Jesus. He will answer your prayers.

8. **R.** I see Mary before me alive many times when I pray this mystery of the rosary. I see her and hear her call out. She begs us to pray for her lost children so that they will not be condemned to hell for their sinfulness and willfulness.

9. **Mary:** I am Mary, your Mother. I am urgently calling you to spread the love of my Son Jesus to the world. Make this your Christmas gift to this world: to help spread these rosaries from the Hearts of Jesus and Mary. Please spread them to the children and the adults.

10. Song: *O come, little children...*

Christmas Message after the Rosary

Mary: (She had appeared during the rosary and during this message.) I am the Immaculate Heart of Mary. It is through my Immaculate Heart that you will be joined ever so closely to my most precious Son. I know the love that my Son has for you. I saw my Son all through His life. I know His Heart. I know how His Heart beats and longs for your love. He was born an infant, He died on the cross for love of you. He rose to bring you greater life in Him. He wants to fill you with His love. This day He is here in your midst. Let me lead you ever closer to His Heart, for it is my Heart that knows Him so well. I pondered the ways of His Heart, complying always to the Father's will. With greatest love, He was born a baby for love of you. Spread His love with the purest heart. You will be united deeply to Him the more you love. Pray that your heart will be pure. Strive to have a pure heart. He loved you so much and He wants you to be the light that shines in the darkness to this world. Carry His love with you in your heart. Show the world the love of Jesus through your action. He is alive this day. Be of a pure heart. Let the world see the love of Jesus within you. Let His love radiate from within you.

Song: *See the Eyes That Look At Mary*

Mary: See through my eyes the love that my Son has for you this day. See the love He outpours to you. Spread this love to your brothers.

Song: *To Jesus Heart All Burning*
Song: *A Song From Jesus*
Song: *O Lady of Light*
Song: *Silent Night*

The Blessed Mother appeared to Rita during the entire rosary. At the end of the seven sorrows Mary gave the above message. Fr. Carter S.J. led the rosary. Rita's two children were there, Harold Kellner, his wife and some of his family and Marty.   12/25/94

The World May Hate You

Messenger: As You Jesus looked at this world through blood stained eyes, as You felt the trickle of blood run down Your temples, You knew the Father's love. Always perfect peace. Dear Spirit open me and help me not to give into any temptations of satan, cast him far from me. Let me be forever transformed into the image of Jesus, so that I may more abundantly realize the Father's love for me.

I may receive knocks from this world to make my heart bleed, but I am clearer in my vision the more I keep my eyes fixed on You.

Jesus: I am alive and in this world I live in you. You are not of this world. The world may hate you, they hated Me, but to all who listened to My teachings, they were taught My ways. Listen to Me, My beloved, I teach to you so that you may carry My teachings to others. I call out to you, you who profess the greatest love for Me. Love is giving, I call you to give your life for the sake of your brothers. Spread My words, despite your fears and persecutions. Souls are at stake, I will never abandon you.

I want you to spread the devotion to the rosary and preach about the real presence and My love. I give you these messages for the souls that are hurting. You may cry tears of blood, but I am forever with you. Never do I leave your side. Souls will be lost. They need to know Me and My ways. I call out to you to answer this call. Turn yourself over to Me. Satan wants you stopped. I am calling you, My Mother is calling you. Put the world aside, your job is to act on love. Love your brothers with My love. I am Jesus and I love you so dearly.   12/26/94

After Communion

Messenger: In the beginning of His life she holds Him in her arms,

When His life is ended she holds Him in her arms under the cross.

She holds Him when He takes His first breath in this world, she holds Him when He has not a breath left in His body.

What is in between is the lives of Jesus and Mary. The oneness between this Son and His Mother. Let her hold us and take us to the gentle loving Heart of the most Sacred Heart of Jesus.

From the beginning of His life to the end of His life, she was so closely united to Him.

It is through this union of these two Hearts I will be joined ever closer in union with God.

Mary did not question, always complying to His will. The angel appeared she said yes, always saying yes to the Father. Mary is so closely united to the Trinity. It is through her Heart we will be joined ever closer to the Father, Son and Holy Spirit.

I feel such insight into Their union meditating on her sorrows.

Jesus loves His Mother so much, if she asks Him something He will not refuse her.

Jesus will never abandon me.

Jesus: Even if a mother forsake her child, I will never abandon you.

I am God. I love you with My burning Heart on fire, I would give My life for you this day.

Now do you know how you are loved? I fill you, I give Myself to you.

I love you. My love is overflowing, let go of all pain of the past, all hurts you feel toward those who withheld love or did not know how to love.

I am LOVE and I give that love to you this day. Divine love I pour out to you. No love compares to My Divine love, it is there and in your life TODAY.

Do not search, look with the eyes of faith.   12/26/94

Personal

Messenger: I think, if I get close to someone, they won't love me and all of a sudden I am finished. From my relationships I feel this way.

Jesus will never go.   12/94

Message for Father Carter

Jesus: My beloved priest-son,

I have chosen you to spread My light and My love to this world. It is through this Newsletter to My beloved priests I will give My love to so many hurting souls.

I am Jesus Christ, the Son of God. I thank you for responding to My call to write and publish this Newsletter. I thank all who are involved in this Movement. My blessings are forever given to all who promote this endeavor, Shepherds of Christ. I am Chief Shepherd of the Flock and I give to you My greatest love. Your prayers for the priests will turn many hearts to the love of My most Sacred Heart through My Mother's Heart.

This Christmas season, I turn to you and thank you for responding to this call. I ask you to continue with greater fervor to support this Movement as it extends to every corner of this earth. My flock will return to the love of My most Sacred Heart through your prayers and support. Pray fervently everyday for all priests of this world. Pray fervently for the success of this Movement. Pray for all priests who read this letter to receive and cooperate with the grace I am giving to them through your prayers. Pray to the Holy Spirit to work in the hearts of the priests reading My Newsletter. Your prayers will help light up the dark world when My love grows ever brighter in the hearts of My priests.

I ask you to make this commitment to pray every day in your Morning Offering for the priests and the Movement, Shepherds of Christ. Pray at Mass for priests to be drawn ever closer to My Sacred Heart. Pray that they cooperate with the grace I am giving to them.

I am Jesus, Chief Shepherd of the Flock. I thank you for your prayers and give you great graces to lead you, My beloved ones, ever closer to My most Sacred Heart. Come and dwell in My Heart. I love you so much.

12/27/94

A Letter to Fr. Carter

Messenger: Dear Father,

I am learning to love from Jesus through you. You truly show Christ in your being.

Thank you for all the love you have given to me and leading me closer and closer to God.

I love others because of the love of Jesus you have given to me. You are so much like Him.

I love all priests because I love you. I see Christ in you and I see Christ in all priests from seeing Him in you.

My whole way of loving has been extended to others from seeing Christ in you.

Thank you for the deep love of Jesus that you have extended to me.

You are truly His light to this world. May the light of Jesus, light this world through the Newsletter, and the love that will grow in the priests' hearts who read it. May His grace abundantly flow in their hearts as He uses this instrument to spread His love through you.

12/27/94 - After Communion

Sorrowful Mysteries

This rosary was prayed just prior to the Shepherds of Christ Meeting and Mary appeared at the 6:30 Daily Apparition.

His Greatest Anguish Was His Sufferings to His Most Sacred Heart

Agony in the Garden

1. **R.** The agonies of the heart are the greatest of agonies. How Jesus suffered in the garden.
2. **R.** The sufferings to Jesus' most Sacred Heart were so great that we can never comprehend them; Jesus loves us so much.
3. **R.** Jesus saw before Him all the souls that would be condemned to eternal damnation despite all His suffering.
4. **R.** Put yourself in the garden and be there with Jesus. Hear the sounds of the night and realize that He is God. He saw before Him everything that He would experience in His whole Passion. He suffered willingly for us. He loves us so much.
5. **R.** Jesus saw before Him all the souls that He loved so dearly and would neglect Him and treat Him with such indifference for their whole lives.
6. **R.** Jesus saw all the souls that would receive Him in the Sacrament of His greatest love, the Eucharist, and would not even talk to Him.
7. **R.** Jesus saw all the sins of all men, before this time and after this time.
8. **R.** Jesus suffered so for the anguish that He felt to His Heart for all the souls that would not have time for Him and would not come to be with Him, and for the endless hours that He would spend in the Tabernacle in which no one was there.
9. **R.** Jesus' anguish was so great that His sweat became as great drops of blood on the ground.
10. **R.** As Jesus suffered so for our sins, He was comforted by the acts of

love that we give to Him this day.
Song between decades: *A Song From Jesus*

Scourging at the Pillar

1. **R.** Jesus suffered so because He loved Judas so much and Judas betrayed Him with a kiss.
2. "Jesus said, 'Judas, are you betraying the Son of man with a kiss?'" (Luke 22:48)
3. "His followers, seeing what was about to happen, said, 'Lord, shall we use our swords?' And one of them struck the high priest's servant and cut off his right ear."   (Luke 22:49-50)
4. "Then Jesus said to the chief priests and captains of the Temple guard and elders who had come for him, 'Am I a bandit, that you had to set out with swords and clubs? When I was among you in the Temple day after day you never made a move to lay hands on me. But this is your hour; this is the reign of darkness.'" (Luke 22: 52-53)
5. **R.** They tied Him to a pillar.
6. **R.** Be there at the pillar and hear the blows that they gave to Jesus, and Jesus did not cry out; He barely made noise as they beat Him to their own exhaustion.
7. **R.** Jesus had wounds on His body from His head to His feet.
8. **R.** Jesus loved those so much who beat Him.
9. **R.** How could I not love my brother when Jesus suffered these beatings for love of my brother?
10. **R.** Jesus would suffer for each one of us this day again because He loves us so much.

Crowning of Thorns

1. **R.** They pounded into Jesus' most Precious Head, a piercing crown of thorns.
2. **R.** They clothed Him in a dirty purple robe and gave Him a scepter to hold.
3. **R.** They hit Him.
4. **R.** They persecuted Him; they spit on Him; they treated Him with such cruelty.
5. **R.** The blood ran down Jesus' face into His eyes and blurred His vision.
6. **R.** Dear Jesus, please help us to see You more clearly, not with the blurred vision that we see You sometimes.
7. **R.** Open our eyes to see that You are truly in our midst this day in the Eucharist.
8. **R.** Open our eyes so that we can see that it is through Your blood that You paid the price for our sins.

9. Let us see that You live in us in a very special way when we are baptized and in the state of grace.

10. Song: *Crown Him With Many Crowns*

Carrying of the Cross

1. **R.** They gave to Jesus a heavy wooden cross that He carried on His shoulder, and His shoulder felt as if it would crack through to the ground.

2. **R.** Mary stood by and she saw her beloved Son as Jesus fell under the cross. Mary kept all these things in her Most precious Heart. Mary felt the pain and the anguish that her Son, Jesus, suffered, helplessly she stood by. Mary was Jesus' Mother, but Mary could not raise a hand to help Him.

3. **R.** Do we even know a little bit the anguish of Mary's most precious Heart?

4. **R.** Mary's eyes peered into the eyes of her beloved Son, and in that peering look is the deepest intimacy between Mary's Heart and Jesus' Heart, Mary saw Jesus suffer and Jesus saw Mary suffer. In that look is the knowledge, love, memories of their lives, the intense knowing of each other in Their Hearts, the intense love that They had for one another.

5. **R.** How well the Heart of Mary knows the Heart of Jesus. Mary rocked Jesus when He was a baby; she held Him; she carried Him; she was with Him all through His public life. Now on Calvary she walked every step with Him, unable to do anything.

6. **R.** Mary's Heart was pierced with an invisible sword as time and time again she walked beside Jesus. Mary heard the cross as it bumped along, her Heart in such anguish.

7. **R.** Only by the grace of God could Mary withstand what she went through during the Passion. Mary walks by our side this day. It is by the grace of God that we will be able to handle the difficulties for she is forever by our side, ever watching us, and ever there to be our most loving Mother.

8. **R.** Veronica wiped Jesus' face and on that cloth was the blood stained face of our Beloved Savior.

9. **R.** This cloth stands today with the stain as a remembrance of Jesus' greatest love, that He gave Himself on Calvary, and He gives Himself to us this day in the Eucharist.

10. **R.** Do we know how much Jesus and Mary, so closely united in their Hearts, love each one of us. They suffered so for each one of us and they call out for us to love God and to love one another. They showed us the way.

Jesus is Crucified and Dies on the Cross

1. **R.** As Mary held the little baby hands and baby feet of the child Jesus, she now stood by and watched them as they pounded into His most precious hands the nails that went through to the cross.

2. **R.** These wounds to Jesus' most precious hands and feet were so deep that they went all the way through His hands and feet.
Song: *Little Baby Hands and Feet*

3. **R.** Jesus' greatest agony was to His most precious Heart. How deep were the wounds that He suffered to His Heart for all the souls that neglect Him this day, and for all the souls that use His name in vain and do not even think of Him. He loves each soul with the most burning love and longs and thirsts for them to come and give Him their love.

4. **R.** Jesus hung on the cross for three agonizing hours while His Beloved Mother stood beneath the cross supported by her beloved John. Mary scarcely could stand, but she stood and withstood the tortures that Jesus went through. She did not leave but she stayed there as she stands with us in all of our trials that we undergo this day. She is forever by our side.

5. **R.** Mary, help us to see more through your eyes and through your Heart the love of the Sacred Heart of Jesus, so that we may more closely unite to this overabundant source of love... divine love ... Help us to be an instrument to promote love and oneness.
Song: *See the Eyes that Look at Mary*

6. **R.** See Jesus hang on the cross in total surrender, humped over in a darkened sky. Jesus shed the last drop of His blood. He gave His all for each of us, and He calls us to love. He showed us how to love and He calls us to love Him and to love one another.

7. **R.** With greatest love for each one of us, Jesus remains with us this very day, the same as the day He died on the cross, waiting for us to come and receive Him in the Eucharist and wait with Him in the Tabernacle.

8. **R.** See Mary under the cross hold the lifeless body of her beloved Son... the love that both Mary and Jesus have poured out for each one of us.

9. **R.** See Mary weep outside of His tomb as they lock Jesus in the tomb.

10. "Near the cross of Jesus stood his mother and his mother's sister, Mary the wife of Clopas, and Mary of Magdala. Seeing his mother and the disciple whom he loved standing near her, Jesus said to his mother, 'Woman, this is your son.' Then to the disciple he said, 'This is your mother.' And from that hour the disciple took her into his home." (John 19:25-27)

Rita saw Jesus appear as the Divine Mercy Jesus in tremendous light.

Marty saw the Sacred Heart picture in brilliant light.

This rosary was prayed just prior to the Shepherds of Christ Meeting. Marty led the rosary, many people in attendance.

12/27/94 - Feast of St. John the Evangelist

Joyful Mysteries

Jesus appeared during this rosary.
Tuesday, Shepherds of Christ Meeting

Annunciation

1. **R.** The angel Gabriel appeared to Mary and asked Mary to be the Mother of Jesus.
2. "Mary said, 'You see before you the Lord's servant, let it happen to me as you have said.' And the angel left her." (Luke 1:38)
3. "And Mary said: My soul proclaims the greatness of the Lord and my spirit rejoices in God my Saviour;" (Luke 1:46)
4. Song: *Come Holy Ghost*
5. "... the angel of the Lord appeared to him in a dream and said, 'Joseph son of David, do not be afraid to take Mary home as your wife, because she has conceived what is in her by the Holy Spirit." *Matthew 1:20*
6. **R.** There was such intimacy between Jesus and Mary from the first moment of conception.
7. **R.** Mary carried His life within her womb.
8. **R.** It was in Mary's womb that the most Sacred Heart of Jesus was formed.
9. **R.** Jesus wants to be alive in our hearts.
10. Song: *O Holy Mary*

Visitation

1. "Mary set out at that time and went as quickly as she could into the hill country to a town in Judah. She went into Zechariah's house and greeted Elizabeth." (Luke 1:39-40)
2. "Now it happened that as soon as Elizabeth heard Mary's greeting, the child leapt in her womb and Elizabeth was filled with the Holy Spirit." (Luke 1:41)
3. **R.** Mary was filled with the Holy Spirit and cried out in a loud voice the Magnificat.
4. Song: *My Soul Rejoices*
5. The Magnificat
        "And Mary said:
        My soul proclaims

the greatness of the Lord
and my spirit *rejoices*
    in God my Saviour;
because *he has looked upon*
    the humiliation of his servant.
Yes, from now onwards
    all generations will call me blessed,
for the Almighty
    has done great things for me.
Holy is his name,
and *his faithful love extends age after age*
    to those who fear him.
He has used the power of his arm,
he has routed the arrogant of heart.
He *has pulled down* princes
    from their thrones
        and raised high the lowly.
He has filled the starving with good things,
    sent the rich away empty.
He has come to the help
    of Israel his servant,
        mindful of his faithful love
—according to the promise
    he made to our ancestors—
of his mercy to Abraham
    and to his descendants for ever." (Luke 1:46-55)

6. **R.** Mary is sinless.
   Song: *Immaculate Mary*
7. **R.** Jesus is no less present in our hearts after Communion than He was in Mary's womb.
8. **R.** Jesus longs for our love and thirsts for our love. He wants us to come to Him in communion in such anticipation and to realize that we receive Jesus Christ, the Son of God.
9. **R.** Jesus waits in the Tabernacle for us to come. Jesus, in His Divinity and humanity, waits for us to come and He wants to shower us with His grace and His abundant Divine Love.
10. **R.** Jesus wants to outpour His abundant Divine Love to us.

Birth of Jesus

1. **R.** Jesus Christ, the Son of God, was born in a stable.
2. **R.** The cows and the sheep are there to keep Jesus warm.
3. **R.** The shepherds watch and the angels sing.
4. Song: *Angels we have Heard on High*
5. Song refrain: *Gloria in excelsis Deo*

6. Song: *Away in a Manger*
7. Song: *O Come let us Adore Him* - refrain
8. Song: *What Child is This?*
9. Song: *Oh Holy Night*
10. Song: *See the Eyes That Look at Mary*

Presentation in the Temple

1. "When the eighth day came and the child was to be circumcised, they gave him the name Jesus, the name the angel had given him before his conception. And when the day came for them to be purified in keeping with the Law of Moses, they took him up to Jerusalem to present him to the Lord—" (Luke 2:21-22)
2. **R.** Simeon prophesied the sufferings of Jesus and Mary to come.
3. **R.** A sword, too, shall pierce your Heart, O Mary.
4. **R.** Mary holds her infant child so lovingly in her arms, and His eyes look at her eyes.
5. **R.** Such intimacy between this Son and this Mother. After Simeon's prophesy, Mary forever remembered what Simeon said every time she looked at the child Jesus.
6. **R.** Mary knew how He would suffer.
7. Song: *Mary's Song*
8. **R.** How Mary's Heart knows the Heart of Jesus.
9. **R.** See through Mary's eyes all through Jesus' life, from the time He was an infant till when He ascended into heaven.
10. **R.** Ask Mary to lead you ever closer to the most tender love of the Sacred Heart of Jesus.

Finding of Jesus in the Temple

1. "Every year his parents used to go to Jerusalem for the feast of the Passover. When he was twelve years old, they went up for the feast as usual." (Luke 2:41-42)
2. "When the days of the feast were over and they set off home, the boy Jesus stayed behind in Jerusalem without his parents knowing it. They assumed he was somewhere in the party, and it was only after a day's journey that they went to look for him among their relations and acquaintances." (Luke 2:43-44)
3. "When they failed to find him they went back to Jerusalem looking for him everywhere." (Luke 2:45)
4. "It happened that, three days later, they found him in the Temple, sitting among the teachers, listening to them, and asking them questions;" (Luke 2:46)
5. "and all those who heard him were astounded at his intelligence and his replies." (Luke 2:47)
6. **R.** Mary told Jesus how Their Hearts were in such sorrowing.

7. "...Did you not know that I must be in my Father's house?'" *(Luke 2:49*
8. "He went down with them then and came to Nazareth and lived under their authority..." (Luke 2:51)
9. **R.** Mary, if we ever wander or stray or are lost from the child Jesus, please lead us back to His most Sacred Heart.
10. **R.** God, grant to us the grace to know and love the child Jesus ever closer.

Rita saw Jesus appear as the Divine Mercy very illuminated. Marty saw the Sacred Heart of Jesus picture illuminate and pulsate with light especially during the reading of the promises of the Sacred Heart.

Father Edward Carter led the rosary. All those attending, the Shepherds of Christ Meeting, that evening participated.

12/27/94 - Feast of St. John the Evangelist

Sorrowful Mysteries
Feast of the Holy Innocents
Before the tabernacle in Church

The Agony in the Garden
1. **R.** Jesus suffered such agonies to His most Sacred Heart in the Garden.
2. **R.** Jesus, the Son of God, is truly present in this room at this very moment.
3. **R.** As present as He was in the Garden that night as He felt all the agonies to His most Sacred Heart. He is with us this very moment, God, in the Tabernacle.

4. **R.** He saw before Him all the sins of all men for all time, and He felt anguish to His Heart to see men commit such vile deeds.
5. **R.** Such anguish to His Heart to love each and every person so dearly and to see them choose evil and hatred in their way of life.
6. **R.** He saw before Him all His sufferings, His entire Passion, every blow, every kick, the nails in His hands, and He saw at the same time all those souls that would be condemned to death to final damnation despite His suffering.
7. **R.** He loves us so much that He remains with us this day in His Divinity and His humanity, no less present than the day Mary held Him in her arms and the day that He walked on Calvary with a cross on His back. No less present was He there than He is in this room at this time with us.
8. **R.** See Jesus in the darkened night, and see Him and His infinite love

that He has for each one of us, in such anguish that His sweat became as great drops of blood upon the ground.

9. **R.** He cries out to us as He did to the apostles ... Can you not wait one hour with me?

10. **R.** He suffered such anguish to His Heart for all the souls that would receive Him in communion and not even talk to Him or realize that they were truly receiving the Son of God with His Heart on fire for love of them.

The Scourging at the Pillar

1. **R.** Hear the jeers and the angry sounds of the men as they seize Jesus and tie Him with such hatred to the pillar.

2. **R.** They whipped Jesus so harshly to their own exhaustion. They whipped Him and whipped Him.

3. **R.** Hear the blows as they give the blows to Jesus, the hard blows, and listen to the sounds and hear Jesus as He so softly makes silent cries.

4. **R.** His once unblemished back is now covered with wounds.

5. **R.** Jesus' Heart is open and is on fire and is all pure and is totally a Heart of pure love, and men and their hearts can be filled with such hatred and anger for one another. He calls us to love Him and to love each other.

6. **R.** What of the hearts of these men who beat Jesus so harshly? Such anger such hatred, to beat Jesus until He bled.

7. **R.** The heart is whereby we connect with Jesus. Pray to the Holy Spirit to help us be more deeply united to Jesus.

8. **R.** He asks us to make our hearts pure, to pray for the grace to help us to let go of the things that are unloving so that love can penetrate our hearts and His love can flow through us to our brothers.

9. **R.** He longs and thirsts and waits for our love. He loves us so much. He waits here, Jesus the Son of God, waiting for us to come and tell Him how we truly love Him.

10. **Jesus:** I love you, my dearly beloved ones, with a Heart that is open and filled with fire for love of you.

The Crowning of Thorns

1. **R.** They pounded into Jesus' most precious head a sharp crown of piercing thorns.

2. **R.** They clothed Him in a dirty purple robe and they mocked Him and gave Him a scepter and they said that He was a King.

3. **R.** The blood ran from His thorns down the side of His face and into His eyes.

4. **R.** His vision was blurred. He ached from His head to His feet with such pain from the deep wounds that they had inflicted on Him. But His greatest suffering was that to His Heart for He loved those men that treated Him so cruelly. He loved each and every one of those men as they beat Him and they mocked Him and they spit on Him. The agonies to His most precious Heart were what He suffered the greatest.

5. **R.** As He suffered so for the sins of men, He was comforted by the love that we give to Him this day. He suffered for our indifferences, for our neglect, for our hot and cold hearts. But He was comforted by the great acts of love, by the time that we spend with Him, by the time that we spend after communion with Him. These were the sweet tastes to His mouth when He suffered this bitterness all through His Passion.

6. **R.** The blood ran from His mouth because of the blows they gave to His most precious head.

7. Song: *Only This I Want*

8. **R.** This is the reality: that God runs this world, that Jesus Christ, the Son of God, truly came to this earth and suffered and gave His life and rose on the third day because He loves us so very much.

9. **R.** Our every breath is dependent on God.

10. **R.** Help me to see, dear Jesus, through the eyes of God all that You want me to see where I am blind, so that I may see more and more the love that You outpour to me here and the love that You have to give so that I can love more my brothers.

Jesus Carries His Cross

1. **R.** Jesus truly carried His cross. See Him with a cross on His back and at that point see all the sins of all men for all time, the heaviness of the cross, the wounds on His body, the wounds on His most precious head, and to His most precious Heart to see all the sin and the hatred and the anger. How it broke His Heart to see the souls that He had so much love for reject His love and choose this hate and this anger.

2. **R.** He walked the walk; His Mother by His side always on Calvary, walking and hearing the sounds of the crowd that poked and laughed. And she stood by helplessly, the Mother in her Heart not able to raise her hand and help Him, and watched this persecution of her beloved child.

3. **R.** And in His Heart, this Heart of love, the suffering that He went through to His Heart was so immense that we have no idea.

4. **R.** The Son of God came to earth as a little baby and He took on a human body out of greatest love for us..
5. **R.** The pressure from the cross was so hard on His shoulder, His shoulder ached so badly He felt as if it would break.
6. **R.** Look at His arms that held the cross as He walked and see these beautiful arms of Jesus, battered, splintered, and so tired from carrying this heavy cross.
7. **R.** See the wounds to Jesus' body: His back badly wounded, His shoulder, His head crowned with piercing thorns. Wounds all over tore His flesh and He carries this heavy cross with love for all those who stand by and jeer at Him.
8. **R.** He asks us to carry our cross with love for one another. He says that The Way is not always the easy way. The Way to Him is to pick up your cross and to follow Him.
9. Song: Lord, let me walk that lonesome road with You, under the weight of the wood. Lord, let me walk that last mile in Your shoes, under the weight of the wood.
10. Hail Mary

Jesus is Crucified and Dies on the Cross

1. **R.** Such intimacy between Jesus and Mary. She held Him as an infant, she was with Him all through His life. Now she walked the Passion and she stood under the cross. Her once baby, little hands and feet ... now His hands and feet were pounded into the cross with big nails.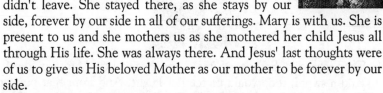
2. **R.** Mary stood under the cross without a scar on her body, but her Heart was in such anguish as she watched and she suffered. She withstood it all. She didn't leave. She stayed there, as she stays by our side, forever by our side in all of our sufferings. Mary is with us. She is present to us and she mothers us as she mothered her child Jesus all through His life. She was always there. And Jesus' last thoughts were of us to give us His beloved Mother as our mother to be forever by our side.
3. **R.** Jesus gave His all. He gave all of His blood to the last beat of His Heart. He said yes to the Father's Will to give Himself for love of us.
4. **R.** Be there and stand with Mary and hear the sounds. Hear the wind blow and see it dark as night as Jesus hangs. He doesn't hang straight as we see Him on some of the crosses, but He is hanging on a cross, holding on so close to death. Jesus loved us so much He died for us.
5. **R.** He calls out to us from the Tabernacle. He says "I gave Myself for love of you." For love of us, He gives Himself to us this day and remains with us. Just as present as the day He hung on the cross, He

is with us in this room with the greatest love and He wants us to know how He thirsts and how He longs and waits for us to come so He can shower this love upon us. And He waits for us to tell Him how we truly love Him.

6. Song: *A Song From Jesus*

7. **R.** The Heart of Mary knows the Heart of Jesus. Mary knew Jesus as a child. Mary knew Jesus in her womb. Mary knew Jesus so well in her Heart, and it is through her loving Heart and her love for Jesus that we will be in such union with Him.

8. **R.** Mary, as you held Jesus so closely to your chest, hold us so tightly close to your chest and lead us to the deepest recesses of Jesus' Heart where He wants to love us so intently.

9. **R.** Mary held Him in her arms when He took His first breath in this world and she held Him in her arms when He died, when He after His death lay under the cross. In between are the lives of Jesus and Mary, this closeness between Their two Hearts. Mary and Jesus so one. Mary and Jesus love us in such love. And it is in this love that we will be led to the closest union with God through the Spirit.

10. **R.** Mary, help us to know and to love Jesus as you loved Jesus. Help us to be saturated with His grace and be loving. Nothing here can compare to love that God has for us. He wants to give to us His love. He outpours this love in front of the tabernacle.

Song: *I Love You Jesus.*

Seven Sorrows of Mary

1. *The Prophecy of Simeon.*   Simeon prophesied how Mary would suffer. And a sword, too, would pierce her Heart. And from that point on whenever she beheld her child, she had in her Heart the sufferings that Simeon prophesied.

2. *The Flight Into Egypt.* Joseph and Mary went with the child to Egypt.

3. *The Loss of the Child Jesus in the Temple.*

4. *Jesus and Mary Meet on the Way to the Cross.*

5. *Jesus Dies on the Cross.*

6. *Jesus is Taken Down from the Cross and laid in Mary's arms.*

7. *The Burial of Jesus.*

12/28/94 - Wednesday
Feast of the Holy Innocents

What You Do to the Least of My Brethren You Do unto Me

Jesus: Oh My dear one, do you not see Me in your brother starving to death, do you not look into his eyes and see that what you do to him you are doing to Me?

When you give do you not know that you are giving to Me? Your acts of kindness given to one of these My little loved ones is given to Me.

For I am gentle and kind of Heart. I am all loving. Give freely of yourselves. I want to give My love to this world. As you give to your brothers you are giving to Me.

For I was naked and you clothed Me. I was in need and you came to My aid. It is in giving that you receive.

What do I ask, but that you share your wealth with each other. Some have more than others, if you see Me in your brother you are loving Me when you love him.

The secrets of your life is to learn My ways. Study My life. Pray for a heart that is likened to Mine. Oh dear ones do not live your lives in vain.

You are here today, you are gone from this life tomorrow. Give to your brother as you would give to Me and your joy and love will abound. For I am in your brother, I am in his smile and in his heart — look into his eyes and see the God who dwells within. I am Jesus, your Savior, come to save the world from its sin and I come to you that you might have life and have it to the full. Life is found in loving and your hearts will know peace. Love, Love, Love, be a cheerful giver, give as you would to Me and your Father in heaven will bless you for your undertakings. I love you, I am Jesus the Savior of this world. I live in you this day, be the light that shines in the darkness, be Me to those who are bowed down. I am the Alpha and the Omega, I come to you with greatest love, I come to you this day. I live in you in this world, such dignity I impart to you My beloved ones, such dignity indeed.

12/29/94 - 7:00 a.m. - Holy Spirit Chapel

I Carried this Heavy Cross
Laden with Your Sins

Messenger: Before Communion, after the Lamb of God, I saw His bare skin on the top of His body, a bare arm. I saw His head. I felt so connected to the fact that He was a man. Such a realization that Jesus said people dead in sin can be brought back to life. He rose from the dead. I wanted to touch His skin and hold His lifeless body. Two days ago after the consecration I had such a realization of Him carrying the cross so heavy with our sins. Almost as if I felt the weight of it, as if I was there - so close to Him and looking into His face. In my heart I felt Him saying, "I carried this heavy cross laden with sins and they do not remember Me."

One night and the next day, I had such an awareness of His arm. Such love for the left arm that carried the cross and hung to the cross with a nail. It's like I can see His skin. I am there with Him. It's such a visual experience, but I'm there and I'm feeling it. I would have liked to have touched His skin and held His body. It's like I'm there. I am there with Him, that's what it is. I'm not thinking about the passion during the Mass. These experiences just happen.   12/30/94

Sorrowful Mysteries

The Agony in the Garden

1. **R.** Jesus' greatest agony all through His passion, were the agonies He felt to His most Sacred Heart because He loves each one of us all so dearly.

2. **R.** Put yourself in the Garden and hear the sounds of the night. See Jesus there. Jesus sees before Him all of the sufferings that He will undergo His whole entire Passion, and with greatest love He complies to the will of the Father to go through this suffering for great love of each of us.

3. **R.** Jesus loves each soul with the most tender love; and He saw before Him all the souls that He loved so dearly that would be condemned to eternal damnation forever.

4. **R.** Jesus saw before Him all the men from all time and all the sins that

they would commit despite His grace and His great love that He outpours to them from His most Sacred Heart.

5. **R.** Jesus is Love. He has the tenderest Heart and He loves each soul so dearly. And to be neglected and treated so indifferently, how it wounded His most Sacred Heart; and He suffered this agony so greatly in the garden.

6. **R.** Jesus suffered so for the indifference shown to Him around the Sacrament of the Eucharist where He is truly present in His Divinity and humanity. Jesus gives Himself to souls and they neglect Him; some do not even talk to Him.

7. **R.** Jesus' agony was so great that His sweat became as great drops of blood.

8. **Jesus:** I sweat Blood for My Beloved souls.

9. **Jesus:** I love you so much.

10. Song: *Come unto Me all who are weary*

The Scourging at the Pillar

1. **R.** Jesus suffered so much agony to His Heart because Judas, whom He loved so dearly, Judas betrayed Jesus with a kiss.

2. **R.** They tied Jesus to the pillar.

3. **R.** Be there at the pillar with Jesus and hear the blows that He received to His most precious back. Hear the sounds as the angry men with such hatred in their hearts, such anger, beat Jesus to their own exhaustion.

4. **R.** Jesus' once unblemished back was an open wound from the anger and hatred that these men beat Him as they did.

5. **R.** From His head to His feet, Jesus was beaten so badly. Jesus, who is the Son of God, who is Love, who comes to us with the greatest love and asks us to love God and to love one another was beaten by those He loved so much.

6. **R.** Jesus' greatest agony was not His wounds to His Body or the blood that ran down His body; but His greatest agony was for the cold hearts that will not open their hearts to the love that He pours out to them this day. He calls out to us to come to the love of God.

7. **R.** Jesus remains in the Eucharist, no less present than the day they scourged Him at the pillar; and He wants us to come and to be so close to Him so He can give us such love.

8. **R.** Jesus loves us no less than the day they beat Him for our sins. Jesus would die for us this day.

9. **R.** Jesus is in the tabernacle. Jesus is waiting for us. Jesus loves us always — in joy and suffering. Jesus will never abandon us; Jesus is forever by

our side. Jesus wants us to come to Him always.

10. **Jesus:** Oh, you cold hearts! Do you not listen to My call to you to open up your heart and to let Me in? I suffered so much agony. Meditate on My passion. Open up your heart this evening. Let Me speak to you in your heart. It is there that your peace and love and your joy lies. I am Jesus, your Beloved Savior. I wait for you; I long for you. I want to share My love with you; the love that I have for you this day. Open your heart to My Love. Let Me penetrate your being with My love; and the joy that you will have is a joy that nothing on this earth can give to you. It is My Divine Love, My Divine Life that I give to you this day. Open your heart and let Me in.

The Crowning of Thorns

1. **R.** They wove for Jesus a sharp crown of piercing thorns and they pounded it into His Most Precious Head.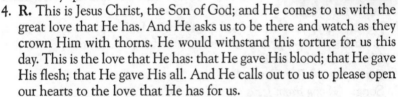

2. **R.** They clothed Him with a dirty purple robe and gave Him a scepter to hold and mocked Him as a King.

3. **R.** They spit on Him and mocked Him.

4. **R.** This is Jesus Christ, the Son of God; and He comes to us with the great love that He has. And He asks us to be there and watch as they crown Him with thorns. He would withstand this torture for us this day. This is the love that He has: that He gave His blood; that He gave His flesh; that He gave His all. And He calls out to us to please open our hearts to the love that He has for us.

5. **R.** As He suffered so for all the sins of all men, He was comforted by the acts of love that we give to Him this very day: the time that we spend with Him after the Eucharist and the time that we spend with Him in front of the Tabernacle.

6. **R.** Jesus loves us so much He withstood this beating for love of us.

7. **R.** Jesus suffered for our sins.

8. **R.** Jesus wants us to love Him today.

9. **R.** Jesus wants a personal love relationship with Him.

10. **R.** Jesus is our spouse — the bridegroom of our soul.

Jesus Carries His Cross

1. **R.** See the men as they stand around Jesus. With a lance they poke at him. See Jesus, His face always at total peace because He knew the Father's love. His hands were tied. He stood there, Jesus, who is all loving; and they condemn Him to death on the cross.

2. **R.** Jesus remained at peace through all the torture that He withstood because He knew the Father's love. The Father loves each one of us so much. The Father created each one of us uniquely special. There is not another person that is quite like us. The Father has a plan for each one of us and He wants us to be happy and to live this plan.

3. **R.** They gave to Jesus a heavy cross that they put on His shoulder; and His shoulder felt as if it would break through to the ground.

4. **R.** Jesus' eyes met the eyes of His loving Mother. Mary, who raised Jesus as a little baby, who carried Him in her womb, who stood by Him all through His life, and now walks by Jesus on Calvary and her eyes met His. There is such intimacy between Jesus and His Mother. Such love between His Heart and her Heart. And it is the love that They have in Their Hearts that They want to give to us this very day.

5. **R.** As Mary walked by Jesus' side, she walks by our side this very day. She never abandons us. She withstood all of His suffering on Calvary; and God will give us the grace to withstand our trials if we pray for it this day. And Mary walks by our side as she walked by the side of Jesus, her Son, on Calvary.

6. Song: Lord, let me walk that lonesome road with you under the weight of the wood. Lord, let me walk that last mile in your shoes, under the weight of the wood.

7. **Jesus:** Carry your crosses today and love Me. Tell the world to carry the little crosses I give them and to pray for grace for the priests, the Church and the world.

8. Song: *See the Eyes that look at Mary*

9. Song: *A Song From Jesus*

10. Song: *I Love You Jesus*

Jesus is Crucified and Dies on the Cross

1. **R.** See Mary as she held Jesus, His little baby hands and feet; and see her as she stands by as they nail His precious hands and feet to the cross.

2. Song: *Little Baby Hands and Feet*

3. **R.** Mary cries out this day; Mary has come as Our Lady of Light to tell us to turn our lives back to the love of her Son. It is there that our peace and our joy lie.

4. **R.** Jesus gave His flesh; He gave His blood; He gave the last beat of His Heart; and He asks us for two things; He asks us to love God and to love one another.

5. **R.** Jesus loved those who persecuted Him; Jesus loved those who crucified Him.

6. **R.** As Jesus gave Himself, His arms outstretched and gave His all for

love of us, He asks us today to come to the Eucharist. Jesus gives Himself to us there. Jesus gave Himself to us when He died on the cross. And He waits for us with such love that only He can give to us.

7. **R.** He hung for three agonizing hours on the cross and His last thoughts were for us; and He gave His Mother. As Mary mothered Jesus, she mothers each and everyone of us.

8. **R.** Mary, open our hearts to the love of your Precious Son. It is through your Most Immaculate Heart, your Heart that knew Him, that we will be led to closer union with Jesus who loves us so much.

9. **R.** As she held Him in her arms as a baby, she now receives His lifeless body in her arms under the cross. Battered, bruised and bloody, He has not a breath in His body. He gave His all because He loves us so much. Jesus calls us to love God and love of one another.

10. **Jesus:** I AM JESUS, THE SON OF GOD AND I LOVE YOU SO MUCH — I DIED FOR YOU AND I remain with you today, truly present in the Eucharist.

Jesus appeared in magnificent light as the Sacred Heart. Jesus illuminated brightly throughout the entire rosary and throughout the entire talk.

This rosary was prayed at the home of a friend of Rita's. There were about 20 people present. Marty led the rosary. Rita gave a witness/talk and sang some of the songs she received from Jesus.

12/30/94 - Friday - Feast of the Holy Family

How Mary's Heart Knows Jesus

Messenger: Mary felt Jesus' sufferings as He fell under the cross. She knew Him as a baby in her Heart. It is through her Heart I will know Jesus, I will feel His love.

She held Him as a baby, she watched Him as a child, she watched Him take His first step, she knew Jesus deeply in her Heart.

The peering look on Calvary signified such union in Their Hearts. Their whole life, all Their feelings for one another can be seen in that look on Calvary.

The union between the two Hearts is the secret to our union with God.   12/94

December 1994

Messenger: His body held lifeless by His loving Mother. Look upon the lifeless body of Christ. This is love that He gave Himself for love of us. To His death on the cross He loved us.

Jesus: Be the light to the world. I live within you — others see My light in you. I am He who loves this world so much, My Father gave to you His only Son.

Messenger: I see the wrapped up body of Jesus being placed in the tomb. What Jesus did for us. He came into this world wrapped in swaddling clothes and lying in a manger. He was wrapped after His death and laid in a tomb. Mary was there, with joy in her Heart at the birth of Jesus and immense sorrow in her Heart weeping as they laid Him in the tomb. How well the Heart of Mary knows the precious Heart of her Son.

He was born a baby. Wrapped and lifeless He was laid in the tomb. This is God who humbled Himself to be born a baby and lifelessly laid in the tomb.

Oh what of this lifeless body of Jesus. What of He who laid as an infant in a manger, this is, my children, the Son of God, born of Mary, in a little town of Bethlehem for our Salvation. He took the nature of a slave to be a man like us, a man like us.

Oh are we loved, dear little ones, are we love or do we wonder and complain for no one cares and loves us.

What do we want? He came as a baby, He showed us how to live. He died on the cross, He was laid lifeless in a tomb, to bring us His life. Life eternal. He rose on the third day.

Oh good God, who am I that You shed this goodness to me. You who are all good, how can I say I love You and not give good to my brothers.

Open my heart to be like Your Heart Lord.

I close my heart up and put up walls to protect me. when You are my DIVINE protector. You protect me, my job is to live in You. Oh I consecrate my heart and my life to You. I consecrate my life to You.

Song: *See the Eyes That Look At Mary*

Wake us up, let us see that You are truly Christ the Lord, we need Your grace, we consecrate ourselves to You.

See the eyes that look at Mary, she is gazing steadily upon her infant Son.

Let me gaze on You steadily Lord. You are my Savior. Help me to keep my eyes on You. You were born a little baby to show me the way. Now I must gaze on You ever steadily for You are the Savior of the World. It is through You I am raised to new life. From the tomb He came forth at the resurrection in His glorified body, that we may share in His life and have it to the full.

Song: *Now We Remain*

Jesus: Be of a pure heart. Wash away all debris in your heart. Love each child as the unique child of My Father.

Oh children how you love with such reservation. Pureness, let go, surrender to the loving arms of God.

Messenger:

Love of Mother

Love of Father

Love of Husband

Love of children

He provides love for our every need, so we are not slavishly dependent.

He and He alone feeds the hungry soul.

We have need for approval — God the Father created us, we are His creation.

He loves me. If I realize this I can give His love to others. He really loves me that He died for me.   12/94

Jesus Appearing as the Resurrected Lord

Jesus Appearing as the Resurrected Lord, All White, Sitting Next to Where Mary Appeared.

1 Corinthians 15:54 -58

So by our baptism into his death we were buried with him, so that as Christ was raised from the dead by the Father's glorious power, we too should begin living a new life.

Romans 6:4, 9

But we believe that, if we died with Christ, then we shall live with him too. We know that Christ has been raised from the dead and will never die again. Death has no power over him any more.

1 Corinthians 15: 54 -58

And after this perishable nature has put on imperishability and this mortal nature has put on immortality, then will the words of scripture come true: Death is swallowed up in victory. Death, where is your victory? Death, where is your sting? The sting of death is sin, and the power of sin comes from the Law.

Thank God, then, for giving us the victory through Jesus Christ our Lord.

Messenger: I love my son so dearly, there is such a connection in my heart to him. He is ten years old. I know him in my heart from a little baby, when I carried him in my womb. His whole life is recorded in my memory

Mary's Heart knew her Son. The anguish at losing Him in the temple, the anguish, how her Heart was in such pain, it is inexpressible in words.

As is the joy, inexpressible for me of the resurrected Lord to appear to me next to the Sorrowful Mother. It is such joy for me to meditate on this mystery to remember the vision, to see Him clothed in white, His body so beautiful. I saw Him so beautiful, sitting all in white next to where Mary appeared triumphant! Jesus rose from the dead. I cannot express this magnificent sight of Jesus in His resurrected beauty as I saw Him.

Note today December 28, 2005: (I recalled the vision of December 5th, 96 when He appeared to me at the point of death hanging on the cross.)

Death - Resurrection

Why do we worry about so many things Jesus is with us. He shows us His death and resurrection.

God took the nature of a slave, He put on a human body, He was born a baby, He died by crucifixion.

Jesus: Do not fear, there is fear in your heart, I am with you, surrender totally to the will of the Father.

Messenger: I see the risen Lord as He sits all in white in a chair, here, next to the Sorrowful Mother. When I saw Jesus in the parking lot He was wearing a white tunic looking like the resurrected Lord with His hands outstretched.

I want to get in touch with Jesus. He took on a human body, He lived, He died, He rose.

Jesus is God, He is Lord over all the earth and He took on a human form for greatest love of us. He was born a baby. He was carried in His Mother's womb. Oh Holy dwelling place of God, Mary's womb, Oh Holy Mary, Mother of God.

Song: *Oh Holy Mary*

Philippians 2:7-8

But he emptied himself,
taking the form of a slave,
becoming as human beings are;
and being in every way
    like a human being,
he was humbler yet,

even to accepting death,
death on a cross.
Song: *The Song of Jesus Christ*

Acts 1:6-11

Now having met together, they asked him, 'Lord, has the time come for you to restore the kingdom to Israel?' He replied, 'It is not for you to know times or dates that the Father has decided by his own authority, but you will receive the power of the Holy Spirit which will come on you, and then you will be my witnesses not only in Jerusalem but throughout Judaea and Samaria, and indeed to earth's remotest end.'

As he said this he was lifted up while they looked on, and a cloud took him from their sight. They were still staring into the sky as he went, when suddenly two men in white were standing beside them, and they said, 'Why are you Galileans standing here looking into the sky? This Jesus who has been taken up from you into heaven will come back in the same way as you have seen him go to heaven.'

Messenger: The Apostles' hearts were in such sorrow to see Jesus go, their eyes in awe to see Jesus go to heaven.

God the Father: I am pleased, My daughter, with the work you are doing, how I love you, My beloved one.

Do not focus on yourself, focus on the other, always the other, Jesus focused on the other.

Messenger: Think of the love of the Trinity -- it is a mystery -- the love of the Trinity.

Excerpt from Response to God's Love Chapter 1 by Father Edward Carter, S.J.

"...In reference to Christianity, God himself is the ultimate mystery. Radically, God is completely other and transcendent, hidden from man in his inner life, unless he chooses to reveal himself. Let us briefly look at this inner life of God.

The Father, in a perfect act of self-expression, in a perfect act of knowing, generates his son. The Son, the Word, is, then, the immanent expression of God's fullness, the reflection of the Father. Likewise, from all eternity, the Father and the Son bring forth the Holy Spirit in a perfect act of loving.

At the destined moment in human history, God's self-expression, the Word, immersed himself into man's world. God's inner self-expression now had also become God's outer self-expression. Consequently, the mystery of God becomes the mystery of Christ. In Christ, God tells us about himself, about his inner life, about his plan of creation and redemption. He tells us how Father, Son, and Holy Spirit desire to dwell within us in the most intimate fashion, how they wish to share with us their own life through grace. All this he has accomplished and does accomplish through Christ. St. Paul tells us: "I became a minister of this Church through the commission God gave me to preach among you his word in its fullness, that mystery hidden from ages and generations past but now revealed to his holy ones. God has willed to make known to them the glory beyond price which this mystery brings to the Gentiles—the mystery of Christ in you, your hope of glory. This is the Christ we proclaim while we admonish all men and teach them in the full measure of wisdom, hoping to make every man complete in Christ" (Col 1:25-28)."

Messenger: The more I realize the love of the Triune God, love of Mary, the love of the angels and saints -- I am in awe!!

Jesus takes care of my needs. Why should I talk about myself or anyone else when we could be talking about the mystery of God.

Why talk about incidentals when I could be talking about God.

He is Divine, He is who I love, that is it, when people are discussing the napkins, I want to talk about Jesus.

Descent of the Holy Spirit on the Apostles

Acts 2:1-4

When Pentecost day came round, they had all met together, when suddenly there came from heaven a sound as of a violent wind which filled the entire house in which they were sitting; and there appeared to them tongues as of fire; these separated and came to rest on the head of each of them. They were all filled with the Holy Spirit and began to speak different languages as the Spirit gave them power to express themselves.

Messenger: The Apostles were transformed from fear to fearlessness.

Acts 2:5-8

Now there were devout men living in Jerusalem from every nation under heaven, and at this sound they all assembled, and each one was bewildered to hear these men speaking his own language. They were amazed and astonished. 'Surely,' they said, 'all these men speaking are Galileans? How does it happen that each of us hears them in his own native language?

Mary Went Up into Heaven

Song: *Immaculate Mary*

Song: *On This Day Oh Beautiful Mother*

Luke 1:26-38

In the sixth month the angel Gabriel was sent by God to a town in Galilee called Nazareth, to a virgin betrothed to a man named Joseph, of the House of David; and the virgin's name was Mary. He went in and said to her, 'Rejoice, you who enjoy God's favour! The Lord is with you.' She was deeply disturbed by these words and asked herself what this greeting could mean, but the angel said to her, 'Mary, do not be afraid; you have won God's favour. Look! You are to conceive in your womb and bear a son, and you must name him Jesus. He will be great and will be called Son of the Most High. The Lord God will give him the throne of his ancestor David; he will rule over the House of Jacob for ever and his reign will have no end.' Mary said to the angel, 'But how can this come about, since I have no knowledge of man?' The angel answered, 'The Holy Spirit will come upon you, and the power of the Most High will cover you with its shadow. And so the child will be holy and will be called Son of God. And I tell you this too: your cousin Elizabeth also, in her old age, has conceived a son, and she whom people called barren is now in her sixth month, for nothing is impossible to God.' Mary said, 'You see before you the Lord's servant, let it happen to me as you have said.' And the angel left her.

Luke 2:1-7

Now it happened that at this time Caesar Augustus issued a decree that a census should be made of the whole inhabited world. This census—the first—took place while Quirinius was governor of Syria, and everyone went to be registered, each to his own town. So Joseph set out from the town of Nazareth in

Galilee for Judaea, to David's town called Bethlehem, since he was of David's House and line, in order to be registered together with Mary, his betrothed, who was with child. Now it happened that, while they were there, the time came for her to have her child, and she gave birth to a son, her first–born. She wrapped him in swaddling clothes and laid him in a manger because there was no room for them in the living–space.

John 19:25-27

Near the cross of Jesus stood his mother and his mother's sister, Mary the wife of Clopas, and Mary of Magdala. Seeing his mother and the disciple whom he loved standing near her, Jesus said to his mother, 'Woman, this is your son.' Then to the disciple he said, 'This is your mother.' And from that hour the disciple took her into his home.

From the Glorious Rosary Aves

3. **Messenger:** Imagine her joy to hear the choirs of angelic voices! Imagine her joy to see the angels and saints praising God!

4. **Messenger:** She-who carried the baby Jesus in her womb, who held Him in her arms, who walked by His side during the Passion, who stood under His cross, who held His lifeless body and watched Him locked in the tomb-was now crowned Queen of Heaven, forever to reign in the court of heaven with her beloved Son.

Mary is Crowned as Queen of Heaven and Earth

Revelation 12:1

Now a great sign appeared in heaven: a woman, robed with the sun, standing on the moon, and on her head a crown of twelve stars.

Song: *Hail Holy Queen*

Revelation 21:1-10

Then I saw a new heaven and a new earth; the first heaven and the first earth had disappeared now, and there was no longer any sea. I saw the holy city, the new Jerusalem, coming down out of heaven from God, prepared as a bride dressed for her husband. Then I heard a loud voice call from the throne, 'Look, here God lives among human beings. He will make his home among them; they will be his people, and he will be their God, God-with-them. He will wipe away all tears from their eyes; there will be no more death, and no more mourning or sadness or pain. The world of the past has gone.'

Then the One sitting on the throne spoke. 'Look, I am making the whole of creation new. Write this, "What I am saying is trustworthy and will come true.'" Then he said to me, 'It has already happened. I am the Alpha and the Omega, the Beginning and the End. I will give water from the well of life free to anybody who is thirsty; anyone who proves victorious will inherit these things; and I will be his God and he will be my son. But the legacy for cowards, for those who break their word, or worship obscenities, for murderers and the sexually immoral, and for sorcerers, worshippers of false gods or any other sort of liars, is the second death in the burning lake of sulphur.'

One of the seven angels that had the seven bowls full of the seven final plagues came to speak to me and said, 'Come here and I will show you the bride that the Lamb has married.' In the spirit, he carried me to the top of a very high mountain, and showed me Jerusalem, the holy city, coming down out of heaven from God.

Revelation 22:20

The one who attests these things says: I am indeed coming soon. Amen; come, Lord Jesus.

Song: A Song from Jesus

12/31/94 - Very Early Morning at Our Lady of the Holy Spirit Center

December 31, 1994

Messenger: I felt such yearning for Jesus. I felt as if my heart would break. I received Him and I went into such an ecstasy I cannot ever explain it. I longed for completeness in Him.

Started to cry went into the bathroom. I felt as if I could roll up in a ball, my heart ached so bad. It is still much later and my heart ached on the left side of my chest.

If I do not allow others to get close to me, if I put a wall around my heart, if I do not realize the love of God, if I measure God's love through imperfect harsh relationships that went before me, I may put a wall around my heart to protect myself but interfere with my union with God and others. At St. Joseph's Church, the St. Joseph's statue looked like someone who was close to me when I was a child. Jesus told me that sometimes our parents or others who should have loved us in childhood, that loved us imperfectly, being stern or hard may affect our love of The Father and Mary our Mother. Our love union with God can be affected by our relationship with parents when we were children. We must see the love the all perfect God wants to give us. Parents who loved us may have been stern, loved us in imperfect ways and may affect our love relationships today with God and others. In knowing God's love we can grow in the ways of loving more purely.

In recognizing the imperfection in our love relationship where there may have been hurts, where anger was shown, where needs were not met, it may affect us today. God has given to us these love letters to know more of His pure undying love for us. In knowing the pureness of God's love, in knowing the faithfulness of God's love, in knowing God's love we come from a place of strength being more capable of loving others more purely.

In this fifth Blue Book as God describes to us clearly what love is all about love of God, love of each other, we become strengthened in loving others as God intends us to do.

This Book will change your life if you apply the messages God has given and keep it ever by your side.

Jesus has promised great grace to those who open their hearts to His words of love here and apply the principles of loving He teaches us here to the relationships of loving Him more purely and loving others more purely as He desires.

We come from an imperfect world, from imperfect relationships, from the weaknesses of our human nature, the concupiscence of the flesh. God gives us a special sharing in His life through baptism. Our understanding of the Divine mysteries is heightened through this gift. Our love capacity grows the more we are one in Him.

God gives to us these letters of love to help to bring about the great reign of love of the Hearts of Jesus and Mary.

We are children of God, ready to be taught by the Master of love, ready to be formed more in the image and likeness of God. God is love and God teaches us in these love letters about Himself.

Jesus is a Divine Person. Mary is the highest human person, conceived without sin. In the fourth Blue Book Jesus and Mary tell us about love. Their love for us, Their love for each other, the relationship between the Divine God and the highest human person, the Virgin Mary. This is our model in the fourth Blue Book. In reading the love letters of Jesus and Mary and living by them we learn more how we as human persons created by God can love our Master, the Divine God. Mary tells us about her pure love of God. Jesus tells us of the pure love for His espoused. We are the brides of Christ. He is the Divine bridegroom.

The Blue Books are love letters from God to His people to teach us how to love intimately and love one another purely in living. By these messages we are preparing ourselves for our love relationships for eternity. These books were given as gifts from God to His beloved souls to help to bring about the great era of love, the era of the love of the Two Hearts and God's people. In the end men will make Jesus the King and Center of their hearts. Jesus is the teacher He teaches us about love.

Spread these letters from God to the souls of this earth, it is our mission to spread this good news.

Mark 16: 6

But he said to them, 'There is no need to be so amazed. You are looking for Jesus of Nazareth, who was crucified: he has risen, he is not here. See, here is the place where they laid him.

Acts 1: 11

This Jesus who has been taken up from you into heaven will come back in the same way as you have seen him go to heaven.

Messenger: Jesus loves me with the purest Heart.

Jesus: Remove the debris from your heart. I am Jesus your God. Your heart is not free. You cannot put up walls around your heart to protect yourself that block your union with Me and others. Do not operate from fear. I love you. Say always: "Most Sacred Heart of Jesus I place my trust in Thee." I never abandon you. I love you to My death on the cross.

Song: *A Song from Jesus*

Messenger: The sun shone over the dark hill, glistening light to remind us that God is light and in Him there is no darkness.   12/31/94

July 31, 1994

Words of Jesus to Members of Shepherds of Christ Associates:

"My beloved priest-companion, I intend to use the priestly newsletter, Shepherds of Christ, and the movement, Shepherds of Christ Associates, in a powerful way for the renewal of My Church and the world.

"I will use the newsletter and the chapters of Shepherds of Christ Associates as a powerful instrument for spreading devotion to My Heart and My Mother's Heart.

"I am calling many to become members of Shepherds of Christ Associates. To all of them I will give great blessings. I will use them as instruments to help bring about the triumph of the Immaculate Heart and the reign of My Sacred Heart. I will give great graces to the members of Shepherds of Christ Associates. I will call them to be deeply united to My Heart and to Mary's Heart as I lead them ever closer to My Father in the Holy Spirit."

Message from Jesus to Father Edward J. Carter, S.J.,
Founder, as given on July 31, 1994,
Feast of Saint Ignatius Loyola,
Founder of the Society of Jesus (The Jesuits)

A Priest Is a Gift from God

by Rita Ring

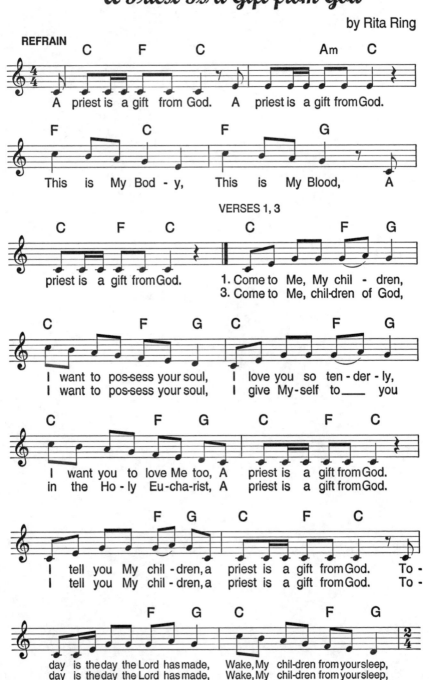

A Song from Jesus

by Rita Ring

REFRAIN

I come to you with great - est love, I
am your lov - ing Sav - ior. I am your God, I
died for you, I come to you this day.

VERSES

1. You are My pre - cious lit - tle one, I
2. Reach out to Me and do not fear, I

love you oh so dear - ly. Come close to Me, My
want to be so close to you. You are My child, My

lit - tle one, I loved you to My death.
pre - cious one, I love you ten - der - ly.

Come to My Heart

by Rita Ring

REFRAIN

C   Dm

Let go to Me, My child, I want to

C   F   Dm

be with you. Come, dear child, I

C   F   G   C

love you so much, Come and sur - ren - der to Me.

VERSES 1,2

F

1. My moth - er calls out to you, She
2. I want you to dwell in My Heart, I

Cmaj7   F

wants you to come to her Son, My Heart is
call you to come for My love, I will give you

Dm   F   G   C   D.C.

wait - ing for you. Come and be lost in My love.
all that you need. Come deep - ly in - to My Heart.

230

Glory, Glory, Glory Lord

by Rita Ring

VERSES 1,2,3

1. Glo - ry, Glo - ry, Glo - ry Lord!___
2. Ho - ly Spir - it give___ us fire!___
3. We are chil - dren of___ the Fa - ther.

You have ris - en from the tomb!
Fill us with___ Your ra - diant love!
He___ has___ a plan for us.

Give us (life Lord,) Your pre-cious life! You __ have
Fill us with the fire of God's love! Mold __ us
Come to Him as His lit - tle child. He who cre -

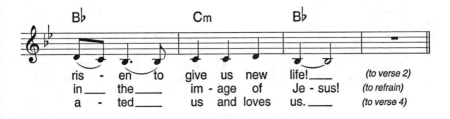

ris - en to give us new life!___ *(to verse 2)*
in ___ the___ im - age of Je - sus! *(to refrain)*
a - ted___ us and loves us. ___ *(to verse 4)*

VERSE 4

4. Fa - ther, Son, and Ho - ly Spir - it!

231

Dwell with - in _____ our fee - ble hearts!

We praise You with all _____ our hearts! How we

thank - You for giv - ing us life! *(to refrain)*

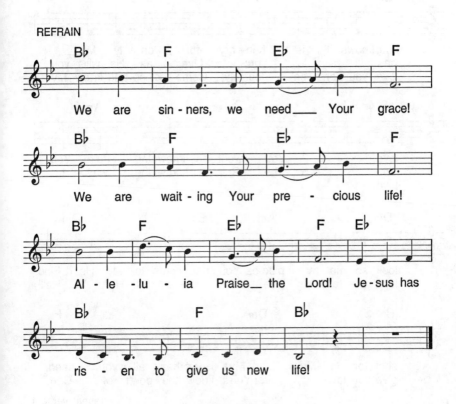

REFRAIN

We are sin - ners, we need _____ Your grace!

We are wait - ing Your pre - cious life!

Al - le - lu - ia Praise _____ the Lord! Je - sus has

ris - en to give us new life!

God's Love

by Rita Ring

1. I love you this ___ day; I am your ar-dent
3. The Fa-ther made ___ you; No one is just like
4. I want to give you love; You are My spe-cial

love; You wan - der oh so far; Your
you; You are His lit - tle child; He
love; You are My Fa - ther's child; I

soul knows it is hun - gry for on - ly My ___
has a plan for you; Live as He wills you
love you oh so dear - ly; Come close and know My

love. 2. You want to know the truth; You
to. 5. The Spir - it knows the way to
love.

look so ma - ny plac-es; You must come to My Heart; Find
lead you to God's love. Be fill - ed with His life; He'll

shel - ter in My Heart; My Heart has all you need.
give you love on fire; You'll know the pow'r of God.

(repeat verse 1
after verse 5)

I Am a Child of God

First transcribed in my notebook.
Dedicated to Fr. Carter S. J.

by Rita Ring

1. Oh I am a child of God,
2. Oh I am a child of God,
3. Oh lit - tle son of Him,

Oh I give my life to You,
I know of my love for Thee,
Oh come with hu - mil - i - ty,

I see Your Heart up - on Your
I know my life de - pends on
And ask Him now to grace your

breast and hope I can dwell__ in Thee.
You and know I will strug-gle for Thee.
soul with love that is lik-ened to God.

I Am Your Sacred Heart

by Rita Ring

REFRAIN

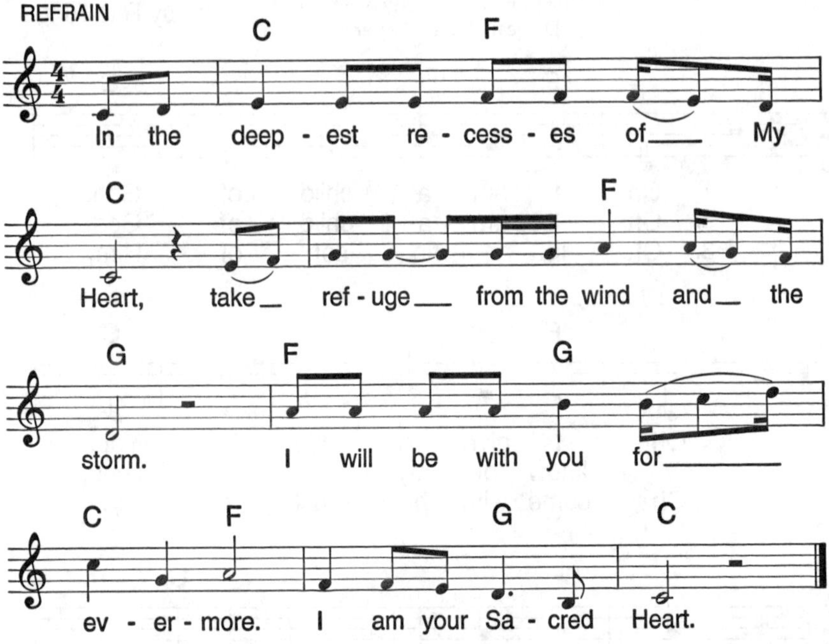

C F
In the deep - est re - cess - es of___ My
C F
Heart, take__ ref - uge___ from the wind and__ the
G F G
storm. I will be with you for________
C F G C
ev - er - more. I am your Sa - cred Heart.

VERSE 1

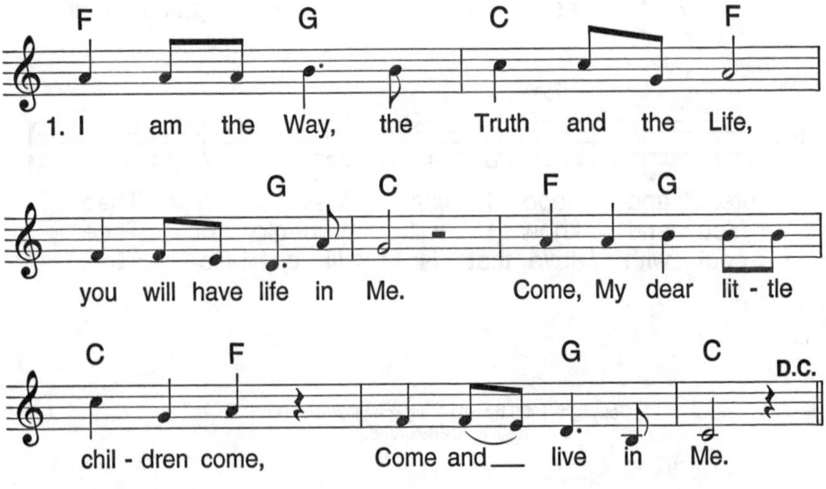

F G C F
1. I am the Way, the Truth and the Life,
G C F G
you will have life in Me. Come, My dear lit - tle
C F G C
D.C.
chil - dren come, Come and___ live in Me.

VERSE 2

2. The on-ly way to_ My Fa-ther is through_ Me.

Come to Me and know His_love, His love will give you peace.

VERSE 3

3. I will shel-ter you in_ My burn-ing Heart,

My Heart_ beats for you. Come and know I

am your_ Love, You can_ trust in Me.

I Love You Jesus

by Rita Ring

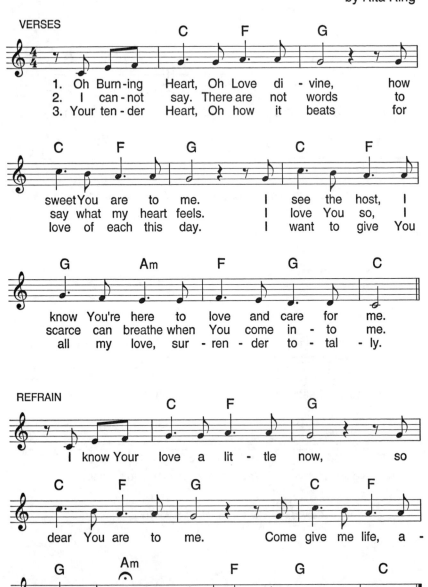

VERSES

1. Oh Burn-ing Heart, Oh Love di - vine, how
2. I can - not say. There are not words to
3. Your ten - der Heart, Oh how it beats for

sweet You are to me. I see the host, I
say what my heart feels. I love You so, I
love of each this day. I want to give You

know You're here to love and care for me.
scarce can breathe when You come in - to me.
all my love, sur - ren - der to - tal - ly.

REFRAIN

I know Your love a lit - tle now, so

dear You are to me. Come give me life, a -

bun - dant life, I thirst to be with Thee.

Little Baby Hands and Feet

by Rita Ring

REFRAIN

Lit-tle ba-by hands and feet, Loved and cared for by His Moth-er;

Sim - e-on fore - told the pain, Je-sus Lord is nailed to the cross.

VERSES 1,2,3

1. Ten-der ba - by lit - tle hands, Mar-y's heart is pierced with a sword;
2. Mar - y is our Moth-er too, She will lead us to His __ love;
3. Mar - y stood be- neath the cross, How her heart __ knows His __ Heart;

He has come to give us life, God our Fa-ther gave His Son.
He has giv - en us His life, See Him hang __ on the cross.
She watched Him her ten-der Child, Now she takes us to His Heart.

VERSE 4

4. Stand be-side Him know the joy, He has come to bring new life;

Now He ris - es from the dead, Gives us life a - bun-dant life.

no refrain

Little Child

by Rita Ring

VERSE 1

C   F   Dm

1. Lit - tle child, lit - tle child, come and rest in My

C   Dm   F

arms. Be with Me, lit - tle child, I want you with

G   F   Dm   G

Me. You are hurt-ing My lov-ed one, I'm wait - ing for

C   F   G   C

you. Come in - to My Heart now, I love you.

REFRAIN

C   F   Dm

I am Je - sus, lit - tle child, I have al - ways loved

C   F   Dm

you. From the day you were born, I've been here with

G   C   G   F

you. Do not for - sake Me, I want you to

C   F   Dm   C

know, lit - tle child, lit - tle child, I love you so!

VERSE 2

2. Let__ go, let__ go, you hold on__ so tight to the things that are near you, Come in - to My light. Your__ heart knows__ long - ing, I am what you crave. Let go to My pres-ence, I ne - ver go.

Live This Day

by Rita Ring

1. I can on-ly live this day. To-mor-row
2. Ev-'ry day is a new day, You can

is so far a-way. Yes-ter-day is in the past now.
live it and be glad. Look a-round life is so good,

The on-ly mo-ment I can live is right now.
This is the day the Lord has made for you now.

Live ev-'ry day, let each mo-ment count, If you
Look to the sky to the heav-ens a-bove, Je-sus

do it will all work out. So stop your fret-ting
cares, You can ask for His love to help you dai-ly

and live the on-ly life you have, and ask
in ev-'ry-thing you do, and He will

Je-sus to guide you from a-bove.
guide you to live your life a-new.

My Open Heart

by Rita Ring

My Heart is o - pen and on fire_____ for you.

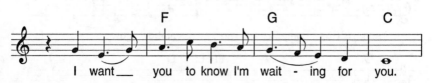

I want___ you to know I'm wait - ing for you.

Come in - to My Heart, I___ long for you.

Do you hear My beating heart? Do you know how near I am?

I am Je - sus lit - tle one, I___ wait for you.

242

Our Lady of Clearwater

Words and music
by Joseph Lee

REFRAIN

Our La-dy of Clear-wa-ter, is shin-ing like the sun, She comes to us in rain-bow gown, to lead us to her Son.

VERSES

1. The La-dy came with-in our midst, on that De-cem-ber day, To lead us to the Eu-cha-rist, and kneel us down to pray.
2. She asked that He be placed be-hind the im-age of her face, To bring us to His Sac-red Heart, where He pours out His grace.
3. So come right in and be filled up, He's wait-ing there for all, To give His love for all the world, please ans-wer now her call.
4. Our La-dy came at Fa-ti-ma, and asked we con-se-crate, To give our hearts to Their two Hearts, be-fore it is too late.
5. To lead us to her Son, she leads us to her Son, She leads us, she's Our La-dy.

See the Eyes That Look at Mary

by Rita Ring

REFRAIN

See the eyes that look at Mar - y, this ten - der in - fant Child. See this Child's Heart beat so tender - ly, the Sav - ior of the world!

VERSES 1,2

1. His__ eyes are gaz - ing stead-i - ly____ up - on His lov - ing Moth-er. She__ sees the Child__ Je - sus, the new-born ba - by here. He__ comes in His en - tire - ty, the Son of God is He.

2. He__ gives us now His bo - dy in the Ho - ly Eu - cha - rist.__ He__ comes with this in - tense_ love to be so close to us. He__ longs for us to come to Him, His Heart__ waits for us.

244

Wake us up, ____ Let us see that You are tru - ly
Fill us now, Give us Your love. ____ Let us be so

Christ the Lord! _ We are blind, we need Your grace, please
close to You! _ We are blind, we need Your grace, please

o - pen up our eyes to You!
o - pen up our eyes to You!

to refrain

VERSE 3

3. We are Yours, we give our-selves, we con - se-crate our

hearts to You. We con - se - crate our

hearts to You, we give You all our love!

no refrain

Teach Me to Love with Your Heart

by Rita Ring

The Rosary Song

by Rita Ring

REFRAIN

Oh the ro - sa - ry, __ the ro - sa - ry __ is the

love of their two hearts, Oh the ro - sa - ry, __ the

ro - sa - ry __ is the love of their two hearts.

VERSES 1-4

1. A - ve Ma - ri - a, A - ve Ma - ri - a. Oh the
2. Je - sus we love You, Ma - ry we love __ you. Oh the
3. This is her peace plan, Chil - dren must pray __ it. Oh the
4. We turn to Ma - ry, She is the Queen of Peace. Oh the

VERSE 5

No left hand

5. Oh Sa - cred Heart di - vine, Oh heart of Ma - ry pure,

A - ve Ma - ri - a, We love to pray it! Oh the

Why Do We Hurt the Ones We Love?

by Rita Ring

248

Your Presence Pervades My Soul

by Rita Ring

REFRAIN

C ... **G** ... **C**

Your pres-ence per - vades my soul, __ Your burn-ing

G ... **Dm** ... **Am** ... **G**

love in my heart. __ My heart knows You dear-ly, my

Am ... **C** ... **F** ... **G** ... **C**

soul knows Your pres-ence. Oh Je-sus, I long for Your love.

VERSE 1

Am ... **G** ... **F** ... **G**

1. You are my way, my truth and my life, I for-

Am ... **G** ... **F** ... **G** D.C.

ev - er want Your pres - ence with - in me.

VERSE 2

Am ... **G** ... **F** ... **G**

2. To You, Oh Lord, I lift up my soul. I

Am ... **G** ... **F** ... **G** D.C.

give You my life to use as You will.

250

VERSE 3

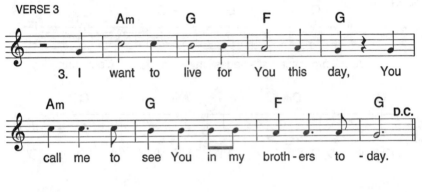

3. I want to live for You this day, You
call me to see You in my broth-ers to-day.

VERSE 4

4. I am in your broth-er, I call you to
love___ them. Do not turn Me a-way.

Introduction to the
Shepherds of Christ Prayers

Here are the prayers that so many pray every day at 6:30, especially for the priests. Prayer chapters have helped many priests in parishes and people in these parishes to grow in greater holiness.

Will you form a prayer chapter in your parish and pray with us at 6:30?

One priest praying the prayers can tremendously boost the prayer power.

These are the prayers Father Carter gave us to pray in the Shepherds of Christ Prayer Manual.

Shepherds of Christ

Prayers

Written by Fr. Edward Carter, S.J.

Father Carter requested
that these be prayed in prayer chapters
all over the world.

These prayers are available on tapes
and discs as prayed by Fr. Carter.
Fr. Carter prayed them every day at 6:20, the Holy
Spirit Novena, Prayer Manual and Rosary

Shepherds of Christ Associates

PRAYER MANUAL

Shepherds of Christ Publications
China, Indiana

Imprimi Potest: Rev. Bradley M. Schaeffer, S.J.
            Provincial
            Chicago Province, The Society of Jesus
  Imprimatur: Most Rev. Carl K. Moeddel
            Auxiliary Bishop
            Archdiocese of Cincinnati

The Shepherds of Christ Associates Prayer Manual is published by Shepherds of Christ Publications, an arm of Shepherds of Christ Ministries, P.O. Box 627 Madison, Indiana 47250 USA.

Founder, Shepherds of Christ Ministries:
Father Edward J. Carter, S.J.

For more information contact:
Shepherds of Christ Associates
P.O. Box 193
Morrow, OH 45152-0193 USA
Tel. 513-932-4451
Toll Free: 1-888-211-3041
Fax 513-932-6791

Chapter Meeting
Prayer Format

The prayer format below should be followed at chapter meetings of Shepherds of Christ Associates. All prayers, not just those said specifically for priests, should include the intention of praying for all the needs of priests the world over.

1. **Hymns.** Hymns may be sung at any point of the prayer part of the meeting.

2. **Holy Spirit Prayer.** Come, Holy Spirit, almighty Sanctifier, God of love, who filled the Virgin Mary with grace, who wonderfully changed the hearts of the apostles, who endowed all Your martyrs with miraculous courage, come and sanctify us. Enlighten our minds, strengthen our wills, purify our consciences, rectify our judgment, set our hearts on fire, and preserve us from the misfortunes of resisting Your inspirations. Amen.

3. **The Rosary.**

4. **Salve Regina.** "Hail Holy Queen, Mother of mercy, our life, our sweetness, and our hope. To you do we cry, poor banished children of Eve. To you do we send up our sighs, our mourning, our weeping in this vale of tears. Turn, then, most gracious advocate, your eyes of mercy toward us and after this, our exile, show unto us the blessed fruit of your womb, Jesus, O clement, O loving, O sweet Virgin Mary. Amen."

5. **The Memorare.** "Remember, O most gracious Virgin Mary, that never was it known that anyone who fled to your protection, implored your help, or sought your intercession was left unaided. Inspired by this confidence, I fly unto you, O Virgin of virgins, my Mother. To you I come, before you I stand, sinful and sorrowful. O Mother of the Word Incarnate, despise not my petitions, but, in your mercy, hear and answer me. Amen."

6. **Seven Hail Marys in honor of the Seven Sorrows of Mary.** Mary has promised very special graces to those who do this on a daily basis. Included in the promises of Our Lady for those who practice this devotion is her pledge to give special assistance at the hour of death, including the sight of her face. The seven sorrows are:

(1) The first sorrow: the prophecy of Simeon (Hail Mary).
(2) The second sorrow: the flight into Egypt (Hail Mary).
(3) The third sorrow: the loss of the Child Jesus in the temple (Hail Mary).

(4) The fourth sorrow: Jesus and Mary meet on the way to the cross (Hail Mary).

(5) The fifth sorrow: Jesus dies on the cross (Hail Mary).

(6) The sixth sorrow: Jesus is taken down from the cross and laid in Mary's arms (Hail Mary).

(7) The seventh sorrow: the burial of Jesus (Hail Mary).

7. **Litany of the Blessed Virgin Mary.**

Lord, have mercy on us.

Christ, have mercy on us.

Lord, have mercy on us. Christ, hear us.

Christ, graciously hear us.

God, the Father of heaven, have mercy on us.

God, the Son, Redeemer of the world,

have mercy on us.

God, the Holy Spirit, have mercy on us.

Holy Trinity, one God, have mercy on us.

Holy Mary, pray for us (repeat after each invocation).

Holy Mother of God,

Holy Virgin of virgins,

Mother of Christ,

Mother of the Church,

Mother of divine grace,

Mother most pure,

Mother most chaste,

Mother inviolate,

Mother undefiled,

Mother most amiable,

Mother most admirable,

Mother of good counsel,

Mother of our Creator,

Mother of our Savior,

Virgin most prudent,

Virgin most venerable,

Virgin most renowned,

Virgin most powerful,

Virgin most merciful,

Virgin most faithful,

Mirror of justice,

Seat of wisdom,

Cause of our joy,

Spiritual vessel,

Vessel of honor,

Singular vessel of devotion,
Mystical rose,
Tower of David,
Tower of ivory,
House of gold,
Ark of the Covenant,
Gate of heaven,
Morning star,
Health of the sick,
Refuge of sinners,
Comforter of the afflicted,
Help of Christians,
Queen of angels,
Queen of patriarchs,
Queen of prophets,
Queen of apostles,
Queen of martyrs,
Queen of confessors,
Queen of virgins,
Queen of all saints,
Queen conceived without original sin,
Queen assumed into heaven,
Queen of the most holy rosary,
Queen of families,
Queen of peace,
Lamb of God, who take away the sins of the world,
     spare us, O Lord.
Lamb of God, who take away the sins of the world,
     graciously hear us, O Lord.
Lamb of God, who take away the sins of the world,
     have mercy on us.
Pray for us, O holy Mother of God,
     that we may be made worthy of the promises of Christ.

Let us pray: Grant, we beseech You, O Lord God, that we Your servants may enjoy perpetual health of mind and body and, by the glorious intercession of the blessed Mary, ever virgin, be delivered from present sorrow, and obtain eternal joy. Through Christ our Lord. Amen.

We fly to your patronage, O holy Mother of God. Despise not our petitions in our necessities, but deliver us always from all dangers, O glorious and blessed Virgin. Amen.

8. **Prayer to St. Joseph.** St. Joseph, guardian of Jesus and chaste spouse of Mary, you passed your life in perfect fulfillment of duty. You sup-

ported the Holy Family of Nazareth with the work of your hands. Kindly protect those who trustingly turn to you. You know their aspirations, their hardships, their hopes; and they turn to you because they know you will understand and protect them. You too have known trial, labor, and weariness. But, even amid the worries of material life, your soul was filled with deep peace and sang out in true joy through intimacy with the Son of God entrusted to you, and with Mary, His tender Mother. Amen. —(Pope John XXIII)

9. **Litany of the Sacred Heart, promises of the Sacred Heart.**
Lord, have mercy on us.
> Christ, have mercy on us.

Lord, have mercy on us. Christ, hear us.
> Christ, graciously hear us.

God the Father of heaven,
> have mercy on us (repeat after each invocation).

God the Son, Redeemer of the world,
God the Holy Spirit,
Holy Trinity, one God,
Heart of Jesus, Son of the eternal Father,
Heart of Jesus, formed by the Holy Spirit in the womb of the Virgin
> Mother,

Heart of Jesus, substantially united to the Word of God,
Heart of Jesus, of infinite majesty,
Heart of Jesus, sacred temple of God,
Heart of Jesus, tabernacle of the Most High,
Heart of Jesus, house of God and gate of heaven,
Heart of Jesus, burning furnace of charity,
Heart of Jesus, abode of justice and love,
Heart of Jesus, full of goodness and love,
Heart of Jesus, abyss of all virtues,
Heart of Jesus, most worthy of all praise,
Heart of Jesus, king and center of all hearts,
Heart of Jesus, in whom are all the treasures of wisdom and knowl-
> edge,

Heart of Jesus, in whom dwells the fullness of divinity,
Heart of Jesus, in whom the Father is well pleased,
Heart of Jesus, of whose fullness we have all received,
Heart of Jesus, desire of the everlasting hills,
Heart of Jesus, patient and most merciful,
Heart of Jesus, enriching all who invoke You,
Heart of Jesus, fountain of life and holiness,
Heart of Jesus, propitiation for our sins,
Heart of Jesus, loaded down with opprobrium,

Heart of Jesus, bruised for our offenses,
Heart of Jesus, obedient even to death,
Heart of Jesus, pierced with a lance,
Heart of Jesus, source of all consolation,
Heart of Jesus, our life and reconciliation,
Heart of Jesus, victim of sin,
Heart of Jesus, salvation of those who hope in You,
Heart of Jesus, hope of those who die in You,
Heart of Jesus, delight of all the saints,
Lamb of God, Who take away the sins of the world,
    spare us, O Lord.
Lamb of God, Who take away the sins of the world,
    graciously hear us, O Lord.
Lamb of God, Who take away the sins of the world,
    have mercy on us.
Jesus, meek and humble of heart,
    make our hearts like unto Yours.

Let us pray: O almighty and eternal God, look upon the Heart of Your dearly beloved Son and upon the praise and satisfaction He offers You in behalf of sinners and, being appeased, grant pardon to those who seek Your mercy, in the name of the same Jesus Christ, Your Son, Who lives and reigns with You, in the unity of the Holy Spirit, world without end. Amen.

Promises of Our Lord to those devoted to His Sacred Heart (these should be read by the prayer leader):

(1) I will give them all the graces necessary in their state of life.
(2) I will establish peace in their homes.
(3) I will comfort them in all their afflictions.
(4) I will be their refuge during life and above all in death.
(5) I will bestow a large blessing on all their undertakings.
(6) Sinners shall find in My Heart the source and the infinite ocean of mercy.
(7) Tepid souls shall grow fervent.
(8) Fervent souls shall quickly mount to high perfection.
(9) I will bless every place where a picture of My Heart shall be set up and honored.
(10) I will give to priests the gift of touching the most hardened hearts.
(11) Those who promote this devotion shall have their names written in My Heart, never to be blotted out.
(12) I promise you in the excessive mercy of My Heart that My all-powerful love will grant to all those who communicate on the first Friday in nine consecutive months the grace of final penitence;

they shall not die in My disgrace nor without receiving their sacraments; My divine Heart shall be their safe refuge in this last
moment.

10. **Prayer for Priests.** "Lord Jesus, Chief Shepherd of the Flock, we
pray that in the great love and mercy of Your Sacred Heart You
attend to all the needs of Your priest-shepherds throughout the
world. We ask that You draw back to Your Heart all those priests
who have seriously strayed from Your path, that You rekindle the
desire for holiness in the hearts of those priests who have become
lukewarm, and that You continue to give Your fervent priests the
desire for the highest holiness. United with Your Heart and Mary's
Heart, we ask that You take this petition to Your heavenly Father in
the unity of the Holy Spirit. Amen."

11. **Prayer for all members of the Shepherds of Christ Associates.**
"Dear Jesus, we ask Your special blessings on all members of
Shepherds of Christ Associates. Continue to enlighten them regarding the very special privilege and responsibility you have given them
as members of Your movement, Shepherds of Christ Associates.
Draw them ever closer to Your Heart and to Your Mother's Heart.
Allow them to more and more realize the great and special love of
Your Hearts for each of them as unique individuals. Give them the
grace to respond to Your love and Mary's love with an increased love
of their own. As they dwell in Your Heart and Mary's Heart, abundantly care for all their needs and those of their loved ones. We
make our prayer through You to the Father, in the Holy Spirit, with
Mary our Mother at our side. Amen."

12. **Prayer for the spiritual and financial success of the priestly
newsletter.** "Father, we ask Your special blessings upon the priestly
newsletter, Shepherds of Christ. We ask that You open the priest-
readers to the graces You wish to give them through this chosen
instrument of Your Son. We also ask that You provide for the financial needs of the newsletter and the Shepherds of Christ Associates.
We make our prayer through Jesus, in the Holy Spirit, with Mary at
our side. Amen."

13. **Prayer for all members of the human family.** "Heavenly Father, we
ask Your blessings on all Your children the world over. Attend to all
their needs. We ask Your special assistance for all those marginalized
people, all those who are so neglected and forgotten. United with
our Mother Mary, we make this petition to You through Jesus and in
the Holy Spirit. Amen."

14. **Prayer to St. Michael and our Guardian Angels:** "St. Michael the

Archangel, defend us in battle. Be our safeguard against the wickedness and snares of the devil. May God rebuke him, we humbly pray, and do thou, O prince of the heavenly hosts, by the power of God, cast into hell Satan and all the other evil spirits who prowl about the world seeking the ruin of souls. Amen."

"Angel of God, my guardian dear, to whom God's love commits me here, ever this day be at my side, to light and guard, to rule and guide. Amen."

15. **Pause for silent, personal prayer.** This should last at least five minutes.

16. **Act of consecration to the Sacred Heart of Jesus and the Immaculate Heart of Mary.**

"Lord Jesus, Chief Shepherd of the flock, I consecrate myself to Your most Sacred Heart. From Your pierced Heart the Church was born, the Church You have called me, as a member of Shepherds of Christ Associates, to serve in a most special way. You reveal Your Heart as a symbol of Your love in all its aspects, including Your most special love for me, whom You have chosen as Your companion in this most important work. Help me to always love You in return. Help me to give myself entirely to You. Help me always to pour out my life in love of God and neighbor! Heart of Jesus, I place my trust in You!

"Dear Blessed Virgin Mary, I consecrate myself to your maternal and Immaculate Heart, this Heart which is symbol of your life of love. You are the Mother of my Savior. You are also my Mother. You love me with a most special love as a member of Shepherds of Christ Associates, a movement created by your Son as a powerful instrument for the renewal of the Church and the world. In a return of love, I give myself entirely to your motherly love and protection. You followed Jesus perfectly. You are His first and perfect disciple. Teach me to imitate you in the putting on of Christ. Be my motherly intercessor so that, through your Immaculate Heart, I may be guided to an ever closer union with the pierced Heart of Jesus, Chief Shepherd of the flock."

17. **Daily Prayers.** All members should say the Holy Spirit prayer daily and make the act of consecration daily. They should also pray the rosary each day. They are encouraged to use the other above prayers as time allows.

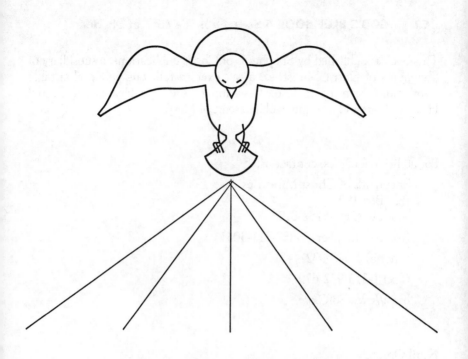

HOLY SPIRIT NOVENA

Shepherds of Christ Publications
Madison, Indiana
El Paso, Texas

This book is published by Shepherds of Christ Publications, a subsidiary of Shepherds of Christ Ministries, a tax exempt religious public charitable association organized to foster devotion to the Two Hearts, the Sacred Heart of Jesus and the Immaculate Heart of Mary.

For additional copies, contact us:

Shepherds of Christ Ministries
P.O. Box 193
Morrow, OH 45152-0193
(toll free number) 1-888-211-3041
(phone) 1-513-932-4451
(fax) 1-513-932-6791
http://www.SofC.org

Nihil Obstat:
Rev. Daniel J. Mahan, S.T.L.
Censor Librorum
Archdiocese of Indianapolis

Imprimatur:
Archbishop Daniel M. Buechlein, O.S.B.
Archbishop of Indianapolis
Archdiocese of Indianapolis

First Printing: March, 1999
Second Printing: April, 2000

DAILY NOVENA PRAYERS

Opening Prayer

In the name of the Father and of the Son and of the Holy Spirit. Amen.

Dear Father, we come to You in the name of Jesus, in union with Him in the Holy Sacrifice of the Mass, in the Holy Spirit. We come to You united to the Child Jesus of Good Health and the Infant of Prague. We come to You in the perfect, sinless heart of Our Mother Mary, asking her powerful intercession, uniting ourselves to her holy tears. We come to You united to all the angels and saints, and the souls in purgatory.

Prayer for Holy Spirit

We pray for an outpouring of the Holy Spirit on us, to be baptized by the Holy Spirit, that He will descend mightily on us as He did on the Apostles at Pentecost. That the Holy Spirit will transform us from fear to fearlessness and that He will give us courage to do all the Father is asking of us to help bring about the Reign of the Sacred Heart and the triumph of Mary's Immaculate Heart. We pray for the Holy Spirit to descend mightily on the Jesuits and the Poor Clares on the Shepherds of Christ leaders and members and on the whole Body of Christ and the world.

Protection by the Blood of Jesus

We pray that the Blood of Jesus will be spread on us, everyone in our families, and the Shepherds of Christ Movement, that we will be able to move steadfastly ahead and be protected from the evil one.

Healing

We pray for healing in body, mind, and soul and generational healing in ourselves, in all members in our families, and in all members of the Shepherds of Christ Movement, the Jesuit Community, the Poor Clares, the Body of Christ, and the world.

Prayer for Strength and Light

We adore You, oh Holy Spirit. Give us strength, give us light, console us. We give ourselves entirely to You. Oh Spirit of light and grace, we want to only do the will of the Father. Enlighten us that we may live always in the Father's will.

Eternal Spirit fill us with Your Divine Wisdom that we may comprehend more fully insight into Your Divine Mysteries.

Give us lights, Oh Holy Spirit that we may know God. Work within the heart, the spiritual womb of the Virgin Mary, to form us more and more into the image of Jesus.

Prayer to Be One with God, Father, Son and Holy Spirit

We long for You, Oh Spirit of Light, we long to know God, we want to be one with Him, our Divine God. We want to be one with the Father, know Him as a Person most intimately. We want to know the beloved One, the Sacred Heart of Jesus, and live and dwell in Him at all times, every moment of our lives. We want to be one with You, Oh Spirit of Light, that You move in us in our every breath.

Prayer to Be One in Jesus

Let us experience life in the Sacred Heart of Jesus, so we can say as Saint Paul, "I have been crucified with Christ and yet I am alive; yet it is no longer I, but Christ living in me...." Let us live, united to the Mass, all through the day being one in Him. Let us be able to love and know in this elevated state of oneness with our God. We long for Thee, oh beauteous God, we love You, we love You, we love You. We praise You, worship You, honor You, adore You, and thank You, our beloved God, Father, Son, and Holy Spirit.

Prayer to Dwell in the Hearts of Jesus and Mary

We seek to be one in God, to live and dwell in the Hearts of Jesus and Mary, our little heaven on earth, to experience life in the all perfect, pure, sinless heart of our Mother. We want the Holy Spirit to move in us and to be united to Jesus as the Bridegroom of our souls and be a most perfect sacrifice offered to the Father at every moment as we unite in the Holy Sacrifice of the Mass around the world to help in the salvation of souls.

Prayer for the Holy Spirit and His Gifts

Come Holy Spirit, come, come into our hearts, inflame all people with the fire of Your love.

Leader: Send forth Your Spirit and all will be reborn.

All: And You will renew the face of the earth.

We pray for the seven gifts of the Holy Spirit, we ask for perfection in our souls to make us holy, holy souls likened to God.

Dear Holy Spirit, we give ourselves to You soul and body. We ask You to give us the Spirit of Wisdom, Understanding, Counsel, Fortitude, Knowledge, Piety, and Fear of the Lord.

Prayer for the Word Alive in Our Hearts

We know, dear Holy Spirit, the Word in His human nature was brought forth within the womb of the woman. We pray that His word will be brought forth in our hearts as He lives and dwells in us. We want the incarnation to go on in our lives. Dear Holy Spirit, work in us.

Little Prayers to the Holy Spirit

Dear Holy Spirit, help us not to be ignorant or indifferent or weak, help us to be strong with the love of God.

Dear Holy Spirit, please pray for our needs for us.

Dear Holy Spirit, help us to respect God and to avoid sin. Help us to live in the Father's will.

Dear Holy Spirit, help us to keep Your commandments and to respect authority. Help us to love all things as You will us to love them. Help us to want to pray and always serve God with the greatest love. Help us to know the truth. Help us to have the gift of faith, hope, and love. Help us to know what is right and what is wrong.

A Prayer for Intimacy with the
Lamb, the Bridegroom of the Soul

Oh Lamb of God, Who take away the sins of the world, come and act on my soul most intimately. I surrender myself, as I ask for the grace to let go, to just be as I exist in You and You act most intimately on my soul. You are the Initiator. I am the soul waiting Your favors as You act in me. I love You. I adore You. I worship You. Come and possess my soul with Your Divine Grace, as I experience You most intimately.

FIRST WEEK
MEDITATIONS NINE DAYS

1. **Romans 8:14-17**

   All who are guided by the Spirit of God are sons of God; for what you received was not the spirit of slavery to bring you back into fear; you received the Spirit of adoption, enabling us to cry out, 'Abba, Father!' The Spirit himself joins with our spirit to bear witness that we are children of God. And if we are children, then we are heirs, heirs of God and joint-heirs with Christ, provided that we share his suffering, so as to share his glory.

2. **Romans 8:5-9**

   Those who are living by their natural inclinations have their minds on the things human nature desires; those who live in the

Spirit have their minds on spiritual things. And human nature has nothing to look forward to but death, while the Spirit looks forward to life and peace, because the outlook of disordered human nature is opposed to God, since it does not submit to God's Law, and indeed it cannot, and those who live by their natural inclinations can never be pleasing to God. You, however, live not by your natural inclinations, but by the Spirit, since the Spirit of God has made a home in you. Indeed, anyone who does not have the Spirit of Christ does not belong to him.

3.   1 John 4:12-16

No one has ever seen God, but as long as we love one another God remains in us and his love comes to its perfection in us. This is the proof that we remain in him and he in us, that he has given us a share in his Spirit. We ourselves have seen and testify that the Father sent his Son as Saviour of the world. Anyone who acknowledges that Jesus is the Son of God, God remains in him and he in God. We have recognised for ourselves, and put our faith in, the love God has for us. God is love, and whoever remains in love remains in God and God in him.

4.   1 John 4:17-21

Love comes to its perfection in us when we can face the Day of Judgement fearlessly, because even in this world we have become as he is. In love there is no room for fear, but perfect love drives out fear, because fear implies punishment and no one who is afraid has come to perfection in love. Let us love, then, because he first loved us. Anyone who says 'I love God' and hates his brother, is a liar, since whoever does not love the brother whom he can see cannot love God whom he has not seen. Indeed this is the commandment we have received from him, that whoever loves God, must also love his brother.

5.   1 John 4:7-11

My dear friends, let us love one another, since love is from God and everyone who loves is a child of God and knows God. Whoever fails to love does not know God, because God is love. This is the revelation of God's love for us, that God sent his only Son into the world that we might have life through him. Love consists in this: it is not we who loved God, but God loved us and sent his Son to expiate our sins. My dear friends, if God loved us so much, we too should love one another.

6.   Acts of the Apostles 1:1-5
In my earlier work, Theophilus, I dealt with everything Jesus had done and taught from the beginning until the day he gave his instructions to the apostles he had chosen through the Holy Spirit, and was taken up to heaven. He had shown himself alive to them after his Passion by many demonstrations: for forty days he had continued to appear to them and tell them about the kingdom of God. While at table with them, he had told them not to leave Jerusalem, but to wait there for what the Father had promised. 'It is', he had said, 'what you have heard me speak about: John baptised with water but, not many days from now, you are going to be baptised with the Holy Spirit.'

7.   Acts of the Apostles 1:6-9
Now having met together, they asked him, 'Lord, has the time come for you to restore the kingdom to Israel?' He replied, 'It is not for you to know times or dates that the Father has decided by his own authority, but you will receive the power of the Holy Spirit which will come on you, and then you will be my witnesses not only in Jerusalem but throughout Judaea and Samaria, and indeed to earth's remotest end.'
As he said this he was lifted up while they looked on, and a cloud took him from their sight.

8.   Acts of the Apostles 1:12-14
So from the Mount of Olives, as it is called, they went back to Jerusalem, a short distance away, no more than a Sabbath walk; and when they reached the city they went to the upper room where they were staying; there were Peter and John, James and Andrew, Philip and Thomas, Bartholomew and Matthew, James son of Alphaeus and Simon the Zealot, and Jude son of James. With one heart all these joined constantly in prayer, together with some women, including Mary the mother of Jesus, and with his brothers.

9.   Acts of the Apostles 2:1-4
When Pentecost day came round, they had all met together, when suddenly there came from heaven a sound as of a violent wind which filled the entire house in which they were sitting; and there appeared to them tongues as of fire; these separated and came to rest on the head of each of them. They were all filled with the Holy Spirit and began to speak different languages as the Spirit gave them power to express themselves.

SECOND WEEK
MEDITATIONS NINE DAYS

1.   **John 14:21-31**

Whoever holds to my commandments and keeps them is the one who loves me; and whoever loves me will be loved by my Father, and I shall love him and reveal myself to him.'

Judas—not Judas Iscariot—said to him, 'Lord, what has happened, that you intend to show yourself to us and not to the world?' Jesus replied:

'Anyone who loves me will keep my word, and my Father will love him, and we shall come to him and make a home in him. Anyone who does not love me does not keep my words. And the word that you hear is not my own: it is the word of the Father who sent me. I have said these things to you while still with you; but the Paraclete, the Holy Spirit, whom the Father will send in my name, will teach you everything and remind you of all I have said to you. Peace I bequeath to you, my own peace I give you, a peace which the world cannot give, this is my gift to you. Do not let your hearts be troubled or afraid. You heard me say: I am going away and shall return. If you loved me you would be glad that I am going to the Father, for the Father is greater than I. I have told you this now, before it happens, so that when it does happen you may believe.

'I shall not talk to you much longer, because the prince of this world is on his way. He has no power over me, but the world must recognise that I love the Father and that I act just as the Father commanded. Come now, let us go.

2.   **John 17:11-26**

I am no longer in the world, but they are in the world, and I am coming to you. Holy Father, keep those you have given me true to your name, so that they may be one like us. While I was with them, I kept those you had given me true to your name. I have watched over them and not one is lost except one who was destined to be lost, and this was to fulfil the scriptures. But now I am coming to you and I say these things in the world to share my joy with them to the full. I passed your word on to them, and the world hated them, because they belong to the world no more than I belong to the world. I am not asking you to remove them from the world, but to protect them from the Evil One. They do not belong to the world any more than I belong to the world. Consecrate them in the truth; your word is truth. As you sent me into the world, I have sent them into the world, and for their sake I consecrate myself so that they too may be consecrated in truth. I pray not only for these but also for those who through their teaching will come to believe in me. May they all be one, just as, Father, you are in me and I am in you, so that they also may be in us, so that the world may believe it was you who sent me. I have given them the glory you gave to me, that they may be one as we are one. With me in them and you in me, may they be so perfected in unity that the world will recognise that it was you who sent me and that you have loved them as you have loved me.

Father, I want those you have given me to be with me where I am, so that they may always see my glory which you have given me because you loved me before the foundation of the world. Father, Upright One, the world has not known you, but I have known you, and these have known that you have sent me. I have made your name known to them and will continue to make it known, so that the love with which you loved me may be in them, and so that I may be in them.

3. I Corinthians 15:20-28

In fact, however, Christ has been raised from the dead, as the first-fruits of all who have fallen asleep. As it was by one man that death came, so through one man has come the resurrection of the dead. Just as all die in Adam, so in Christ all will be brought to life; but all of them in their proper order: Christ the first-fruits, and next, at his coming, those who belong to him. After that will come the end, when he will hand over the kingdom to God the Father, having abolished every principality, every ruling force and power. For he is to be king until he has made his enemies his footstool, and the last of the enemies to be done away with is death, for he has put all things under his feet. But when it is said everything is subjected, this obviously cannot include the One who subjected everything to him. When everything has been subjected to him, then the Son himself will be subjected to the One who has subjected everything to him, so that God may be all in all.

4. Revelation 3:1-3,12,16-19

'Write to the angel of the church in Sardis and say, "Here is the message of the one who holds the seven spirits of God and the seven stars: I know about your behaviour: how you are reputed to be alive and yet are dead. Wake up; put some resolve into what little vigour you have left: it is dying fast. So far I have failed to notice anything in your behaviour that my God could possibly call perfect; remember how you first heard the message. Hold on to that. Repent! If you do not wake up, I shall come to you like a thief, and you will have no idea at what hour I shall come upon you.

Anyone who proves victorious I will make into a pillar in the sanctuary of my God, and it will stay there for ever; I will inscribe on it the name of my God and the name of the city of my God, the new Jerusalem which is coming down from my God in heaven, and my own new name as well.

'…but since you are neither hot nor cold, but only lukewarm, I will spit you out of my mouth. You say to yourself: I am rich, I have made a fortune and have everything I want, never realising that you are wretchedly and pitiably poor, and blind and naked too. I warn you, buy from me the gold that has been tested in the fire to make you truly rich, and white robes to clothe you and hide your shameful nakedness, and ointment to put on your eyes to enable you to see. I reprove and train those whom I love: so repent in real earnest.'

5.   Revelation 5:9-14

They sang a new hymn: You are worthy to take the scroll and to break its seals, because you were sacrificed, and with your blood you bought people for God of every race, language, people and nation and made them a line of kings and priests for God, to rule the world.

In my vision, I heard the sound of an immense number of angels gathered round the throne and the living creatures and the elders; there were ten thousand times ten thousand of them and thousands upon thousands, loudly chanting:

Worthy is the Lamb that was sacrificed to receive power, riches, wisdom, strength, honour, glory and blessing. Then I heard all the living things in creation—everything that lives in heaven, and on earth, and under the earth, and in the sea, crying:

To the One seated on the throne and to the Lamb, be all praise, honour, glory and power, for ever and ever.

And the four living creatures said, 'Amen'; and the elders prostrated themselves to worship.

6.   Revelation 7:14-17

I answered him, 'You can tell me, sir.' Then he said, 'These are the people who have been through the great trial; they have washed their robes white again in the blood of the Lamb. That is why they are standing in front of God's throne and serving him day and night in his sanctuary; and the One who sits on the throne will spread his tent over them. They will never hunger or thirst again; sun and scorching wind will never plague them, because the Lamb who is at the heart of the throne will be their shepherd and will guide them to springs of living water; and God will wipe away all tears from their eyes.'

7.   **Revelation 12:1-8**
Now a great sign appeared in heaven: a woman, robed with the sun, standing on the moon, and on her head a crown of twelve stars. She was pregnant, and in labour, crying aloud in the pangs of childbirth. Then a second sign appeared in the sky: there was a huge red dragon with seven heads and ten horns, and each of the seven heads crowned with a coronet. Its tail swept a third of the stars from the sky and hurled them to the ground, and the dragon stopped in front of the woman as she was at the point of giving birth, so that it could eat the child as soon as it was born. The woman was delivered of a boy, the son who was to rule all the nations with an iron sceptre, and the child was taken straight up to God and to his throne, while the woman escaped into the desert, where God had prepared a place for her to be looked after for twelve hundred and sixty days.

And now war broke out in heaven, when Michael with his angels attacked the dragon. The dragon fought back with his angels, but they were defeated and driven out of heaven.

8.   **Revelation 14:1-7**
Next in my vision I saw Mount Zion, and standing on it the Lamb who had with him a hundred and forty-four thousand people, all with his name and his Father's name written on their foreheads. I heard a sound coming out of heaven like the sound of the ocean or the roar of thunder; it was like the sound of harpists playing their harps. There before the throne they were singing a new hymn in the presence of the four living creatures and the elders, a hymn that could be learnt only by the hundred and forty-four thousand who had been redeemed from the world. These are the sons who have kept their virginity and not been defiled with women; they follow the Lamb wherever he goes; they, out of all people, have been redeemed to be the first-fruits for God and for the Lamb. No lie was found in their mouths and no fault can be found in them.

Then I saw another angel, flying high overhead, sent to announce the gospel of eternity to all who live on the earth, every nation, race, language and tribe. He was calling, 'Fear God and glorify him, because the time has come for him to sit in judgement; worship the maker of heaven and earth and sea and the springs of water.'

Revelation 19: 7-8

let us be glad and joyful and give glory to God, because this is the time for the marriage of the Lamb. His bride is ready, and she has been able to dress herself in dazzling white linen, because her linen is made of the good deeds of the saints.'

9.   **Revelation 21:1-10**

Then I saw a new heaven and a new earth; the first heaven and the first earth had disappeared now, and there was no longer any sea. I saw the holy city, the new Jerusalem, coming down out of heaven from God, prepared as a bride dressed for her husband. Then I heard a loud voice call from the throne, 'Look, here God lives among human beings. He will make his home among them; they will be his people, and he will be their God, God-with-them. He will wipe away all tears from their eyes; there will be no more death, and no more mourning or sadness or pain. The world of the past has gone.'

Then the One sitting on the throne spoke. 'Look, I am making the whole of creation new. Write this, "What I am saying is trust-worthy and will come true." ' Then he said to me, 'It has already happened. I am the Alpha and the Omega, the Beginning and the End. I will give water from the well of life free to anybody who is thirsty; anyone who proves victorious will inherit these things; and I will be his God and he will be my son. But the legacy for cowards, for those who break their word, or worship obscenities, for murder-ers and the sexually immoral, and for sorcerers, worshippers of false gods or any other sort of liars, is the second death in the burning lake of sulphur.'

One of the seven angels that had the seven bowls full of the seven final plagues came to speak to me and said, 'Come here and I will show you the bride that the Lamb has married.' In the spirit, he carried me to the top of a very high mountain, and showed me Jerusalem, the holy city, coming down out of heaven from God.

Revelation 22:20

The one who attests these things says: I am indeed coming soon.

Amen; come, Lord Jesus.

Scriptural quotations are taken from
The New Jerusalem Bible, Doubleday & Co.
Imprimatur granted by Cardinal Hume.

Shepherds of Christ
Prayer Cards

Contact us to obtain
these for your parish,
friends, or loved ones.

PRAYER FOR PRIESTS

"Lord Jesus, Chief Shepherd of the Flock, we pray that in the great love and mercy of Your Sacred Heart You attend to all the needs of Your priest-shepherds throughout the world. We ask that You draw back to Your Heart all those priests who have seriously strayed from Your path, that You rekindle the desire for holiness in the hearts of those priests who have become lukewarm, and that You continue to give Your fervent priests the desire for the highest holiness. United with Your Heart and Mary's Heart, we ask that You take this petition to Your heavenly Father in the unity of the Holy Spirit. Amen."

Published by Shepherds of Christ Ministries, P.O. Box 193, Morrow, OH 45152-0193   Phone (toll free): 1-888-211-3041 Fax: (513) 932-6791
Imprimatur: Most Rev. Carl K. Moeddel, Vicar General and Auxiliary Bishop Archdiocese of Cincinnati

PRAYER FOR UNION WITH JESUS

Come to me, Lord, and possess my sou Come into my heart and permeate my sou Help me to sit in silence with You and let Yo work in my heart.

I am Yours to possess. I am Yours to use. I war to be selfless and only exist in You. Help me t spoon out all that is me and be an empty vesse ready to be filled by You. Help me to die to myse and live only for You. Use me as You will. Let m never draw my attention back to myself. I onl want to operate as You do, dwelling within me.

I am Yours, Lord. I want to have my life i You. I want to do the will of the Father. Give m the strength to put aside the world and let Yo operate my very being. Help me to act as Yo desire. Strengthen me against the distractions o the devil to take me from Your work.

When I worry, I have taken my focus off o You and placed it on myself. Help me not to giv in to the promptings of others to change what i my heart You are making very clear to me. I wo ship You, I adore You and I love You. Come ar dwell in me now.

Imprimatur: Most Rev. Carl K. Moeddel, Vicar General ar Auxiliary Bishop Archdiocese of Cincinnati

Shepherds of Christ Ministries
P.O. Box 193, Morrow, OH 45152-0193
Toll Free (888) 211-3041
Phone: (513) 932-4451   Fax: (513) 932-6791

PRAYER BEFORE THE
HOLY SACRIFICE OF THE MASS

Let me be a holy sacrifice and unite with God in the sacrament of His greatest love.

I want to be one in Him in this act of love, where He gives Himself to me and I give myself as a sacrifice to Him. Let me be a holy sacrifice as I become one with Him in this my act of greatest love to Him.

Let me unite with Him more, that I may more deeply love Him. May I help make reparation to His adorable Heart and the heart of His Mother, Mary. With greatest love, I offer myself to You and pray that You will accept my sacrifice of greatest love. I give myself to You and unite in Your gift of Yourself to me. Come and possess my soul.

Cleanse me, strengthen me, heal me. Dear Holy Spirit act in the heart of Mary to make me more and more like Jesus.

Father, I offer this my sacrifice, myself united to Jesus in the Holy Spirit to You. Help me to love God more deeply in this act of my greatest love.

Give me the grace to grow in my knowledge, love and service of You and for this to be my greatest participation in the Mass. Give me the greatest graces to love You so deeply in this Mass, You who are so worthy of my love.

Imprimatur: Most Rev. Carl Moeddel Vicar General and Auxiliary Bishop
Archdiocese of Cincinnati

To order more copies contact: Shepherds of Christ Ministries, P.O. Box 193, Morrow, OH 45152   (toll free) 888-211-3041   www.Shepherds-of-Christ.org

A Prayer for Intimacy with the Lamb, the Bridegroom of the Soul

Oh Lamb of God, Who take away the sins of the world, come and act on my soul most intimately. I surrender myself, as I ask for the grace to let go, to just be as I exist in You and You act most intimately on my soul. You are the Initiator. I am the soul waiting Your favors as You act in me. I love You. I adore You. I worship You. Come and possess my soul with Your Divine Grace as I experience You most intimately.

Imprimatur:

Archbishop Daniel M. Buechlein, O.S.B.
Archdiocese of Indianapolis

Shepherds of Christ Ministries
P.O. Box 193 Morrow, Ohio 45152-0193 USA
(toll free number) 1-888-211-3041
(phone) 513-932-4451   (fax) 513-932-6791
http://www.SofC.org

These cards are available in large print for nursing homes. Please circulate to all.

Front

SAY DAILY

GOD, I GIVE YOU MY LIFE IN UNION WITH THE MASS AS AN OFFERING FOR THE SOULS, THE CHURCH AND THE PRIESTS.

HELP US!

Back

Your life is so important for souls,
you can help bring down great grace.

Shepherds of Christ Ministries
P.O. Box 193   Morrow, OH 45152-0193
Tel: (513) 932-4451 Fax: (513) 932-6791
Toll Free: (888) 211-3041 Internet: www.SofC.org

Front

I Give My Heart to Jesus and Mary With You in Love.

Back

We Pray for Priests and
Renewal of the Church
and World.
Holy Spirit Fill Me.

Shepherds of Christ Ministries
P.O. Box 193 Morrow, OH 45152-0193
Toll Free (888) 211-3041
Tel: (513) 932-4451   Fax: (513) 932-6791
www.SofC.org

Shepherds of Christ Associates
Prayer Chapters

Here are the steps for forming a Shepherds of Christ Associates Prayer Chapter:

Bring together family, friends, or parish members to answer this call of the Lord. Follow the format in the Shepherds of Christ Associates Prayer Manual. The steps are simple:

1. Designate a coordinator for the chapter.
2. Have everyone fill out the membership form and return it to our Morrow Center.
3. Give everyone a Shepherds of Christ Prayer Manual.
4. Choose a regular time and place to meet (at church or in the home).
5. You may meet daily, once a week or at least monthly.
6. It only takes two people to form a prayer chapter.

Please call our Morrow, Ohio Center. We would be happy to answer any questions. We can also send you a prayer chapter information packet, Shepherds of Christ Spirituality Handbooks, or Shepherds of Christ Prayer Manuals. We may be reached by electronic mail at info@SofC.org or by postal mail.

Shepherds of Christ Ministries
P.O. Box 193
Morrow, OH 45152-0193

telephone   (toll free in USA) 1-888-211-3041
         or International (513) 932-4451
fax: (513) 932-6791

Shepherds of Christ Associates

Chapter title (name of place held): _____

Chapter Coordinator(s):_____

Address: _____

Telephone: _____

City, State, Zip code: _____

Members of this chapter: **Please Print.**

Name	Address	City	State	Zip	Telephone

Please return a copy of this form to:
**Shepherds of Christ, P.O. Box 193, Morrow, OH 45152-0193 USA.
Or fax us at: (513) 932-6791**

Apostles of the Eucharistic Heart of Jesus

We are asking for volunteers who are willing to pray before the Blessed Sacrament for one hour, twice-weekly. Members of the Shepherds of Christ prayer chapters, as well as others, are invited to join this movement.

These apostles are to pray for the intentions given. For part of the hour they are to use the prayers of the Shepherds of Christ Associates Prayer Manual. They may spend the rest of the hour as they so choose.

This new prayer movement within the Shepherds of Christ Ministries is a powerful way to help in the renewal of the Church and the world.

This is indeed a special calling for us to unite in one heart with His Eucharistic Heart and pray for the following intentions:

1. For the spread of the devotion to the Hearts of Jesus and Mary culminating in the reign of the Sacred Heart and the triumph of the Immaculate Heart.

2. For the Pope.

3. For all bishops of the world.

4. For all priests.

5. For all sisters and brothers in the religious life.

6. For all members of the Shepherds of Christ Movement, and for the spread of this movement to the world.

7. For all members of the Catholic Church.

8. For all members of the human family.

9. For all souls in purgatory.

Apostles of the Eucharistic Heart of Jesus

Membership Form

Name	Address	City	State	Zip	Telephone

Please return a copy of this form to **Shepherds of Christ Ministries, Apostles of the Eucharistic Heart of Jesus, P.O. Box 193, Morrow, OH 45152-0193.**

Prayer Apostles

Prayer Apostles are often shut-ins, some are able to go to church and pray. They spend much of their lives praying for the Movement. Prayer apostles are invited to do the following as time allows:

1) Pray the Morning Offering
2) Pray the Hourly Prayers
3) Spend at least one hour in prayer
4) Pray Rosaries
5) Pray the Shepherds of Christ Prayers
6) Pray the Holy Spirit Novena

OUR FOCUS in the Shepherds of Christ is to be intercessors praying fervently for the priests, the Church and the world.

Shepherds of Christ Ministries

For Helping in the Renewal of the
Church and the World

WE PRAY FOR PRIESTS, THE RENEWAL OF THE CHURCH, AND THE WORLD.

We join as a body united to the Holy Sacrifice of the Mass offering our lives to the Father as intercessors praying for our priests, the Church, and the world.

WILL YOU PRAY WITH US?

Your prayers united to ours will help the priests, the Church, and the world.

Our Focus

WE HAVE PRAYER CHAPTERS PRAYING ALL OVER THE WORLD for the priests, the Church, and the world.

OUR PRIMARY FOCUS is the circulation of a newsletter.

WE CIRCULATE A SPIRITUALITY NEWSLETTER written by Fr. Edward Carter, S.J., a Jesuit Theologian with a Doctor's degree in Theology and author of 18 books, to about 75,000 priests in the world in both English and Spanish. Father Carter was a professor of Theology for over 30 years.

Besides being sent to about 75,000 priests and bishops in the U.S.A., the newsletter is sent internationally to about 245 bishops, including 4 cardinals, who distribute copies to all of their priests, and also, in some cases, to their deacons and seminarians.

The newsletter is centered in consecration to the Hearts of Jesus and Mary. It features writings regarding our union with Jesus and the Father and the Holy Sprit and Mary. The newsletter also stresses the Eucharist, the Church, prayer, and one's responsibility regarding the social order. The newsletter stresses sound doctrine as found in Scripture, the writings of the Popes and other Church documents. It also presents selected writings from the saints and competent priest-theologians and others.

The newsletter can be used by all for development in the spiritual life centered in consecration.

About Shepherds of Christ Ministries

MINISTRIES

1. **PRIMARY MINISTRY** - CIRCULATING PRIESTLY NEWSLETTERS TO PRIESTS ALL OVER THE WORLD IN ENGLISH AND SPANISH to promote priestly holiness.
2. **PRAYER CHAPTERS** praying for the priests and the renewal of the Church and the world.
3. School Rosary Program and Junior Shepherds of Christ Ministry.
4. Nursing Home Ministry.
5. Special retreats and adoration before the Blessed Sacrament.
6. Apostles of the Eucharistic Heart of Jesus.

7. Promoting the rosary to all, rosary meditations.
8. Prison Ministry to promote prayer and spiritual renewal.
9. Handmaids and Servants of the Good Shepherd.
10. Audio/Video Departments (priestly newsletters on tape).
11. Prayer books, newsletters, newsletter books, and other spiritual aids.

We want to be intercessors promoting unity in prayer with all people of the world, praying for the priests, the Church and the world.

We have described above the primary ministry of the Movement, the spirituality newsletter for priests, Shepherds of Christ. The 2nd most important ministry is the prayer chapters, whose members pray for the needs of priests and for the needs of all others also. Other ministries include promoting the act of consecration to the Hearts of Jesus and Mary as widely as possible. Promoting this act of consecration permeates all of our ministries. We also promote the praying of the rosary, and we have a special program regarding the rosary and the act of consecration for school children. We have programs for prisons and nursing homes to encourage the residents to pray for priests, the Church, and the world. We also publish various books, cassette tapes, and other materials to help in the ongoing work of spiritual renewal.

The mission of the Shepherds of Christ Movement is closely connected to Our Lady of Fatima's mission. We hope to play a major role in helping to bring fulfillment of the Peace Plan of Our Lady of Fatima. This plan includes:

1. Consecration to the Hearts of Jesus and Mary -- until a sufficient number of people make and live the consecration, we will not have peace in the world.
2. Praying the rosary.
3. Observing the First Saturday Devotion.
4. Making reparation to the Hearts of Jesus and Mary.

In helping to bring the Fatima message to completion, the Shepherds of Christ Movement is helping to bring about the Reign of the Sacred Heart and the triumph of the Immaculate Heart. This is a great privilege and a great responsibility! We ask for your prayers and help in other ways also. May God bless you abundantly!

LEVELS OF COMMITMENT

There are seven levels of commitment in the Shepherds of Christ Movement.

1. There are **Associates** who gather and pray at least once monthly as a group and also help with donations to support the Shepherds of Christ

priestly newsletter. They can be tremendously involved. They give as they feel they are able.

2. **Apostles** are members who have restricted their apostolic activity to the Shepherds of Christ. They literally act as a body of lay people who have given their lives in their present living situation to do all that they can to bring about the Reign of the Sacred Heart and the triumph of Mary's Immaculate Heart.

3. **Prayer Apostles** are often shut-ins, some are able to go to church and pray. They spend much of their lives praying for the Movement.

4. **Apostles of the Eucharistic Heart of Jesus** are those who spend at least two separate hours weekly before the Blessed Sacrament praying for the following:
   1. For the spread of the devotion to the Hearts of Jesus and Mary culminating in the reign of the Sacred Heart and the triumph of the Immaculate Heart.
   2. For the Pope.
   3. For all bishops of the world.
   4. For all priests.
   5. For all sisters and brothers in the religious life.
   6. For all members of the Shepherds of Christ Movement, and for the spread of this Movement to the world.
   7. For all members of the Catholic Church.
   8. For all members of the human family.
   9. For all souls in purgatory.

5. **Handmaids of the Good Shepherd** are young and older women who have given their lives in community primarily to pray for the Shepherds of Christ Movement and intentions and to be special spouses of Jesus. Some have more duties than others. All have the primary duty of prayer and the desire to be a special spouse of our Lord. One of the functions of the handmaids is the involvement in praying for and helping to circulate the priestly newsletter. The handmaids are not members of a religious order.

6. **Servants of the Good Shepherd** are men who live in community with a lifestyle and purpose similar to that of the handmaids. The servants are not members of a religious order.

7. We wish to form a special congregation of priests who will realize their great oneness with Christ. They will be consecrated deeply to the Hearts of Jesus and Mary and support the Shepherds of Christ Movement as holy priests.

Whatever one's level of commitment in the Shepherds of Christ Movement, all share in promoting the overall goal of the Movement. This goal is to help in the spiritual renewal of the Church and the world. All varied ministries of the Movement are directed toward this purpose. The spirituality which the Shepherds of Christ Movement presents to its members and to those outside the Movement through its various ministries is very basic. This spirituality is explicitly Trinitarian and Christocentric. Our spirituality helps others, especially priests, to develop a very deep union with Jesus, this Jesus Who leads us to the Father in the Holy Spirit with Mary at our side. Our spirituality is deeply Eucharistic. We stress very much participation in the Mass and prayer before the Blessed Sacrament. We also emphasize the extremely important role of prayer in the spiritual life. Devotion to the Hearts of Jesus and Mary, especially consecration to Their Hearts, is also a most important and central element. We are very much interested in helping to bring the Fatima message to completion, a message which has consecration to the Hearts of Jesus and Mary at its very core.

Father Edward J. Carter, S.J.

Father Edward Carter, S.J. was a native of Cincinnati, Ohio. A graduate of St. Xavier High School and Xavier University, both in Cincinnati, he was ordained a priest in 1962 and received his doctorate in theology from Catholic University of America four years later. He was a professor of theology at Xavier University in Cincinnati for over 30 years. He has authored 18 books in the area of Catholic spirituality. His two latest books are the priestly newsletter books, which include the newsletters from almost six years. He was devoted to the Sacred Heart of Jesus, and the Immaculate Heart of Mary.

Be Part Of It!

PLEASE HELP US THROUGH YOUR PRAYERS UNITED TO OURS.

PRIESTS PRAYING WITH US WILL INCREASE THE PRAYER POWER; THEY ARE ANOINTED BY CHRIST AS HOLY PRIESTS.

PEOPLE ALL OVER THE WORLD offering up their lives in the Morning Offering for the priests, the Church, the world, and for the work of the Shepherds of Christ will help so much.

LITTLE PRAYER BOOKS OF SHORT PRAYERS CALLED THE SHEPHERDS OF CHRIST PRAYER MANUAL ARE AVAILABLE. Praying these short prayers together with us as a body united to the Holy Sacrifice of the Mass being celebrated around the world can help great grace be released on the souls of the earth.

PLEASE UNITE WITH US.

Rosary Making Clubs

We supply rosaries to schools, prisons, and others.

Making rosaries out of sparkling, colorful plastic beads is a fun year-round activity for all ages. Even five-year-olds can create beautiful ones easily without getting frustrated!

This is wonderful as an in-school, after-school, or at-home project to be coordinated by an adult. When organized as a "club," children spend time at their meetings making rosaries, saying the Rosary, sharing a snack, and enjoying each other socially. Completed rosaries can be donated to fellow students, their families, nursing home residents, and many other individuals. Rosary-making kits (include plastic beads in your choice of colors) are available FREE from the School Rosary Program. In October 2000, we supplied over 80,000 rosaries to schools; in May 2001, we supplied over 100,000 rosaries.

Rosaries are given free of charge to schools and churches and people requesting them from Shepherds of Christ Ministries.

Books

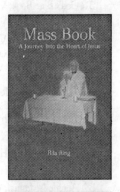

B8. *Mass Book*, by Rita Ring: Many of the entries in
the Priestly Newsletter Volume II from a spiritual journal came from this book. These entries
are to help people to be more deeply united to
God in the Mass. This book has the
Imprimatur. $12

B7. *Rosary Meditations for Parents and Children*, by
Rita Ring, Short Meditations for both parents
and children to be used when praying the rosary.
These meditations will help all to know the lives
of Jesus and Mary alive in their Hearts. This
book has the Imprimatur. $10

BN1. *Shepherds of Christ - Selected Writings on
Spirituality for all People as Published in Shepherds
of Christ Newsletter for Priests*. Contains 12 issues
of the newsletter from July/August 1994 to
May/June 1996. $15

BN2. *Shepherds of Christ - Volume 2*: Contains issues
13-29 of the newsletter (September/October
1996 - Issue 5, 1999) $15

Books (from Shepherds of Christ Publications)

B1. *God's Blue Book*, Volume 1, Teachings to Lift You Up, Rita Ring. $10

B2. *God's Blue Book*, Volume 2, The Fire of His Love, Rita Ring. $10

B3. *God's Blue Book*, Volume 3, Love God, Love One Another, Rita Ring. $10

B4. *God's Blue Book*, Volume 4, The Love of the Hearts of Jesus and Mary, Rita Ring. $10

B18. *God's Blue Book*, Volume 5, So Deep Is the Love of His Heart, Rita Ring. $10

B5. *Tell My People.* Messages given to Father Edward J. Carter, S.J. from Jesus and Mary. Messages, reflections and prayers for growing in holiness through devotion to the Immaculate Heart of Mary and the Sacred Heart of Jesus. $10

B6. *The Spirituality of Fatima,* by Father Edward J. Carter, S.J. $7

B7. *Rosaries from the Hearts of Jesus and Mary,* Red Rosary Book by Rita Ring. $10

B8. *Rosaries from the Hearts of Jesus and Mary,* Blue Rosary Book by Rita Ring. $12

B9. *Apostles' Manual,* (440 pages) A manual for Apostles in the Shepherds of Christ Movement. $20

B10. *Daily Messages from Heaven from the Florida Apparition Site* - Book 1 (Messages from July 8 1998 to August 31, 1998) $10

B11. *Daily Messages from Heaven from the Florida Apparition Site* - Book 2 (Messages from September 1, 1998 to October 31, 1998) $25

B12. *Daily Messages from Heaven from the Florida Apparition Site* - Book 3 (Messages from November 1, 1998 to January 5, 1999) $25

B13. *Daily Messages from Heaven from the Florida Apparition Site* - Book 4 (Messages from January 5, 1999 to March 5, 1999) $25

B14. *Daily Messages from Heaven from the Florida Apparition Site* - Book 5 (Messages from March 5, 1999 to April 5, 1999) $25

B15. *Mass Book II* and Other Aspects of the Spiritual Life: Selected writings about the Mass and the Spiritual life. Journal entries from the same period as the Newsletter Book II and selected writings of Father Carter on the Mass, Grace, and other aspects of the spiritual life, writings by Edward Carter, S.J. and Rita Ring. $15

B16. *Rosaries Meditations for Little People and Elderly,* by Rita Ring. $7

B17. *Mary Book,* selected writings about Mary, by Fr. Carter and Rita Ring $20

DVDs ($12) and Video Tapes ($10)

V2. *Messages from Jesus* (an interview with Rita Ring, 4/17/94)
Rita sings songs and reads messages from God's Blue Book, Volume 1. These are messages about Jesus' love for us, messages about visiting Jesus in the tabernacle. Rita tells how she started receiving messages.

V3. *A Mist Around Mary* (September 5, 1995)
Mary appeared to Rita almost every day from July 5, 1994 until September 5, 1995 at Our Lady of the Holy Spirit Center in Norwood, Ohio. A video taken at the September 5 rosary revealed a pink mist over the statue during key meditations of the rosary. This video is part of a "live" rosary (a "live" rosary is one recorded as Rita Ring receives messages from Jesus and Mary). They are taped and these meditations and messages are then transcribed from tape. Mary has requested that we circulate this video of the mist and the messages given on that date, messages Jesus and Mary want you to hear.

V4. *Mary's Message and Witnesses given in Clearwater, Florida*

V5. *Joyful Rosary Aves* - Meditations on the Joyful Mysteries of the Rosary - great for use in schools - the meditations have the Imprimatur.

V6. *Sorrowful Rosary Aves* - Meditations on the Sorrowful Mysteries of the Rosary - great for schools - the meditations have the Imprimatur.

V7. *Glorious Rosary Aves* - Meditations on the Glorious Mysteries of the Rosary - great for schools - the meditations have the Imprimatur.

V8. *Mass Video* - great for Nursing Homes and the Homebound

V9. *Nursing Home Video #1*

V10. *Nursing Home Video #2*

V11. *Nursing Home Video #3*

V12. *Nursing Home Video #4*

V13. *Nursing Home Video #6*

V14. *Nursing Home Video #7*

V15. *Nursing Home Video #8*

V16. *Nursing Home Video #9*

V17. *Nursing Home Video #10*

V18. *Nursing Home Video #15* - January 5, 2002

V19. *Nursing Home Video* - Epiphany January 5, 2003

V20. *Nursing Home Video* - Epiphany January 4, 2004

V21. *Nursing Home Video* - Epiphany January 2, 2005

V22. *An Afternoon with Mary* - September 7, 2003 from the site in Clearwater, Florida

CDs ($10) and Audio Tapes ($8)

AAA001. *Love Songs and Messages from the Hearts of Jesus and Mary*, October 1, 1995

AAA009. *Songs and Messages from the Hearts of Jesus and Mary*, October 24, 1995

AAA013. *Choose Life*, Songs and Messages, November 21, 1995.

AAA020. *Mary's Message*, December 12, 1996, Feast of Our Lady of Guadalupe

AAA025. *Songs from Jesus*

AAA026. *Daily Prayers*

AAA028. *15 Decade Rosary*, August 20, 1998. Mysteries of the rosary recited without any meditations.

AAA046. *Holy Spirit Novena*, 6:30 Prayers, and the Rosary

AAA047. *St. Michael Chaplet*

AAA060. *Consecration*, July 31, 1999, St. Ignatius Feast Day

Rosary CDs ($10) and Audio Tapes ($8)

For Children

CRA012. Children's Joyful Mysteries and the Prayer Manual Prayers, Rosary Meditations given on December 25, 1994. Rosary and prayers recited by children.

CRA040. Children's Joyful Mysteries, March 20, 1997 and Glorious Mysteries, April 15, 1995, from Florida.

CRA043. Joyful and Sorrowful Rosary Aves, short rosary meditations for school kids. These meditations contain no messages and have received the Imprimatur.

CRA062 Sorrowful Mysteries, November 2, 1995. These rosary meditations have received the Imprimatur.

Joyful Mysteries

JRA027. The Joyful Mysteries, Rosary meditations given on March 30, 1995.

Sorrowful Mysteries

SRA006. The Sorrowful Mysteries, Rosary received during a Shepherds of Christ prayer meeting on July 11, 1995.

SRA010. The Sorrowful Mysteries, Rosary meditations given on July 28, 1995.

SRA038. The Sorrowful Mysteries, March 21, 1995, From Florida.

Glorious Mysteries

GRA011. The Glorious Mysteries, Rosary meditations concerning the children of the world, July 15, 1995.

GRA039. The Glorious Mysteries, April 16, 1995, From Florida.

Live Recordings of the Rosary

JLA021. The Joyful Mysteries, Rosary meditations given on December 13, 1996.

JLA022. The Joyful Mysteries, Rosary meditations given on January 13, 1997.

SLA017. The Sorrowful Mysteries, Rosary meditations given on September 10, 1996.

SLA019. The Sorrowful Mysteries, Rosary meditations given on November 13, 1996.

SLA023. The Sorrowful Mysteries, Rosary meditations given on February 13, 1997.

SLA024. The Sorrowful Mysteries, Rosary meditations without messages recited on August 20, 1996.

GLA018. The Glorious Mysteries, Rosary meditations given on October 13, 1996.

RMA059. June 5, 1999 Rosary and June 4, 1999 Daily Message. Rosary meditations for Joyful, Sorrowful, and Glorious Mysteries

Book and Booklet CDs ($10) and Audio Tapes ($8)

Fr. Edward J. Carter S.J.

BCA002. Shepherds of Christ Associates Spirituality Handbook and Prayer Manual, Read by Fr. Edward Carter, S.J.

BCA008. Tell My People, Messages from Jesus and Mary for the world: Messages received and read by Fr. Carter.

BCA014. Shepherds of Christ Associates Prayer Manual, Read by Fr. Edward Carter, S.J.

BCA063. The Spirituality of Fatima, read by Fr. Carter.

Rita Ring

BRA043. Joyful and Sorrowful Rosary Aves, short rosary meditations for school kids.

BRA030. Messages from God's Blue Book, Volume II.

BRA046. God's Blue Book, Volume I, Messages from 5/13/93 - 10/9/93.

BRA047. God's Blue Book, Volume I, Messages from 10/10/93 - 10/29/93.
BRA048. God's Blue Book, Volume I, Messages from 10/30/93 - 11/10/93.
BRA049. God's Blue Book, Volume I, Messages from 11/10/93 - 11/20/93.
BRA050. God's Blue Book, Volume I, Messages from 11/20/93 - 11/29/93.
BRA051. God's Blue Book, Volume I, Messages from 11/30/93 - 12/11/93.

Priestly Newsletter CDs ($10) and Audio Tapes ($8)

PNA032. Shepherds of Christ Priestly Newsletter, Issue 2, 1998 - The Life of Prayer
PNA034. Shepherds of Christ Priestly Newsletter, Issue 4, 1998 - The Peace of the Lord
PNA052. Shepherds of Christ Priestly Newsletter, Issue 5, 1998 - Mother at Our Side
PNA053. Shepherds of Christ Priestly Newsletter, Issue 1, 1999 - Priesthood
PNA054. Shepherds of Christ Priestly Newsletter, Issue 2, 1999 - His Body, the Church
PNA055. Shepherds of Christ Priestly Newsletter, Issue 3, 1999 - Personal Uniqueness
PNA064. Shepherds of Christ Priestly Newsletter, Issue 4, 1999 - God with Us
PNA065. Shepherds of Christ Priestly Newsletter, Issue 5, 1999 - Priestly Ministry & Priestly Holiness
PNA066. Shepherds of Christ Priestly Newsletter, Issue 1, 2000 - Christ Is Our Strength
PNA066. Shepherds of Christ Priestly Newsletter, Issue 2, 2000 - Suffering: A Source of Life
PNA066. Shepherds of Christ Priestly Newsletter, Issue 3, 2000 - Overview of the Spiritual Life
PNA066. Shepherds of Christ Priestly Newsletter, Issue 1, 2001 - Grace
PNA066. Shepherds of Christ Priestly Newsletter, Issue 2, 2001 - The Sacraments & the Mass
PNA066. Shepherds of Christ Priestly Newsletter, Issue 1, 2004 - The Pope
PNA066. Shepherds of Christ Priestly Newsletter, Issue 1, 2005 - Mary & the Eucharist

Daily Message CDs ($10) and Audio Tapes ($8)

DMA035. Daily Messages from Heaven from the Florida Apparition Site, July 8-27, 1998
DMA036. Daily Messages from Heaven from the Florida Apparition Site, July 28 - August 10, 1998
DMA037. Daily Messages from Heaven from the Florida Apparition Site, August 11-18,1998
DMA056. Daily Messages from Heaven from the Florida Apparition Site, August 19-27, 1998
DMA057. Daily Messages from Heaven from the Florida Apparition Site, December 6-11, 1998

Prayer Cards and Booklets

The following Prayer Cards and Booklets have received the Imprimatur.
Las siguientes oraciones han recibido el Imprimátur
Les prières suivantes ont reçu l'Imprimatur
As orações abaixo receberam o Imprimatur

ENGLISH

BK001E. Shepherds of Christ Associates Prayer Manual. $.50

BK002E. Holy Spirit Novena. $1

PR001E. Daily Prayers for Shepherds of Christ Associates (donation)

PR002E. Rosary Aves short rosary meditations on the Joyful, Sorrowful, and Glorious Mysteries.

PR003E. Consecration Prayer Cards for Children

PR004E. Consecration Prayer Cards for Young Adults

PR005E. Prayer Before the Holy Sacrifice of the Mass

PR006E. Prayer for Union with Jesus

PR007E. Prayer for Priests

PR008E. Prayer for Intimacy with the Lamb

PR009E. Consecration of an Unborn Child to the Hearts of Jesus and Mary

SPANISH (ESPAÑOL)

BK001S. Manual de Oraciónes (Prayer Manual)

BK002S. Novena al Espíritu Santo (Holy Spirit Novena)

PR001S. Oraciónes Diarias (Daily Prayers for Associates)

PR003S. Oraciónes Diarias para Niños (Daily Prayers for Children)

PR004S. Oraciónes Diarias para Jóvenes (Daily Prayers for Young Adults)

PR005S. Oración para antes del Santo Sacrificio de la Misa (Prayer Before the Holy Sacrifice)

PR006S. Oración Para Union con Jesús (Prayer for Union with Jesus)

PR007S. Oración por los Sacerdotes (Prayer for Priests)

PR008S. Oración para Intimidad con el Cordero, el Esposo del Alma (Prayer for Intimacy)

PR009S. Consagración de Un Niño Aún no nacido a Jesús y María (Consecration of Unborn Child)

FRENCH (FRANÇAIS)

BK001F. Livret de Prières (Prayer Manual)

BK002F. Neuvaine au Saint-Esprit (Holy Spirit Novena)

PR001F. Prières Quotidiennes (Daily Prayers for Associates)

PR002F. Méditations pour chaque Ave du Rosaire (Rosary Aves)

PR003F. Consécrations pour les enfants (Consecrations for Children)

PR004F. Consécrations pour les jeunes (Consecrations for Young Adults)

PR005F. Prière à réciter avant la Messe (Prayer Before the Holy Sacrifice of the Mass)

PR006F. Prière pour demander l'union à Jésus (Prayer for Union with Jesus)
PR007F. Prière pour les prêtres (Prayer for Priests)
PR008F. Une Prière pour demander l'intimité avec l'Agneau (Prayer for Intimacy)
PR009F. Consécration à Jésus et Marie d'un enfant à naître (Consecration of Unborn Child)

PORTUGUESE (PORTUGUÊS)
BK001P. Manual de Orações (Prayer Manual)
BK002P. Novena do Espírito Santo (Holy Spirit Novena.)
PR001P. Orações Diárias (Daily Prayers)
PR002P. Meditando nas contas do Rosário (Rosary Aves)
PR003P. Oração Diárias para Crianças (Consecration Prayer Cards for Children)
PR004P. Oração Diárias para Crianças (Consecration Prayer Cards for Young Adults)
PR005P. Oração antes do Santo Sacrifício da Missa (Prayer Before the Holy Sacrifice)
PR006P. Oração para União com Jesus (Prayer for Union with Jesus)
PR007P. Oração pelos Sacerdotes (Prayer for Priests)
PR008P. Oração para conseguir intimadade com o cordeirom o esposo da Alma (Prayer for Intimacy with the Lamb)
PR009P. Consagração de um nascituro a Jesus e Maria (Consecration of an Unborn Child to the Hearts of Jesus and Mary)
PR010P. Diga Diariamente (Say Daily)
PR011P. Palavras de Entrega de uma alma Palavras de Consagração a Deus (Prayer of Surrender)
PR012P. Como rezar o Terço do Rosário (How to Pray the Rosary)

Order Form (BB5)

In the space provided, write in the quantity of the desired item(s) to be shipped. Please print clearly your own name and address to assure shipping accuracy.

Books :

Quantity   Item Number   Total $

____   _____   ____

____   _____   ____

____   _____   ____

____   _____   ____

DVDs and Video Tapes:

Quantity   Item Number   (T)ape or (DVD)

____   _____   _____   ____

____   _____   _____   ____

____   _____   _____   ____

____   _____   _____   ____

CDs and Audio Tapes:

Quantity   Item Number   (T)ape or (CD)

____   _____   _____   ____

____   _____   _____   ____

____   _____   _____   ____

____   _____   _____   ____

Priestly Newsletters

Quantity   Item Number

____   _____   ____

____   _____   ____

Prayer Cards and Booklets:

Quantity   Item Number   Total $

____   _____   ____

____   _____   ____

____   _____   ____

                                        SubTotal   ____
                                        Shipping   ____
                                        Total   ____

Name: _____

Address: _____

_____

_____

_____

(Please include city, state, zip code, country)

Phone: _____

SEND THIS FORM TO: **Shepherds of Christ Ministries**
P.O. Box 193
Morrow, OH 45152-0193   U.S.A.
1-888-211-3041

This movement is a nonprofit organization that relies on your financial support to function. We appreciate any donations that you give and are very grateful for your prayer support. God bless you and thank you!

Order Form (BB5)

In the space provided, write in the quantity of the desired item(s) to be shipped. Please print clearly your own name and address to assure shipping accuracy.

Books :

Quantity   Item Number   Total $

___   _____   ___

___   _____   ___

___   _____   ___

___   _____   ___

DVDs and Video Tapes:

Quantity   Item Number   (T)ape or (DVD)

___   _____   _____   ___

___   _____   _____   ___

___   _____   _____   ___

___   _____   _____   ___

CDs and Audio Tapes:

Quantity   Item Number   (T)ape or (CD)

___   _____   _____   ___

___   _____   _____   ___

___   _____   _____   ___

___   _____   _____   ___

Priestly Newsletters

Quantity   Item Number

___   _____   ___

___   _____   ___

F12   GOD'S BLUE BOOK 5 So Deep Is the Love of His Heart

Prayer Cards and Booklets:

Quantity	Item Number	Total $
____	_____	____
____	_____	____
____	_____	____

SubTotal ____

Shipping ____

Total ____

Name: _____

Address: _____

_____

_____

_____

(Please include city, state, zip code, country)

Phone: _____

SEND THIS FORM TO: **Shepherds of Christ Ministries**
P.O. Box 193
Morrow, OH 45152-0193   U.S.A.

1-888-211-3041

This movement is a nonprofit organization that relies on your financial support to function. We appreciate any donations that you give and are very grateful for your prayer support. God bless you and thank you!

Jesus' Face

Our Lady of Clearwater